The Bureaucratization
of Socialism

Donald C. Hodges

The University of Massachusetts Press

Copyright © 1981 by
The University of Massachusetts Press
All rights reserved
Printed in the United States of America
LC 80–23253
ISBN 0–87023–138–3

Library of Congress Cataloging in Publication Data
Hodges, Donald Clark, 1923–
The bureaucratization of socialism.
Bibliography:
1.Communism and society. 2. Communist state.
3. Bureaucracy. I. Title.
HX542.H59   321.9′2   80–23253
ISBN 0–87023–138–3

The scheme of a proletarian State outlined by Lenin in *The State and Revolution* has not been realized anywhere, and least of all in the country which has been presented to us and still is being presented to us today as the ideal model. . . . That type of State which has arisen in the Soviet Union, which is not a capitalist State, since it does not uphold private property, but which is not the State which Lenin imagined either—with the workers exercising power directly—how is it to be fitted in with the Marxist conception of the State?

Santiago Carrillo, *Eurocommunism and the State* (1977)

Contents

Acknowledgments

During the fall of 1966 and spring of 1967 I made two trips to the Soviet Union and Eastern Europe for the purpose of doing research on the new socialist formation. Acknowledgments are due to the College of Arts and Sciences and the Research Council of Florida State University for underwriting these trips, and to the Peace Council of the German Democratic Republic for defraying my expenses in that country. I am also grateful for invitations to lecture on aspects of my research to colleagues at the Faculty of Philosophy at Humboldt University in East Berlin, the Institute of Philosophy in Moscow, the Faculty of Law at Charles University and the Institute of Sociology in Prague, the Faculty of Philosophy at the University of Belgrade, the Faculty of Political Science at the University of Zagreb, and the Workers' University in Zrenjanin, Serbia. Through colleagues, interviews were arranged with trade union and government officials, with specialists at the Institutes of Economics in Moscow, Warsaw, Budapest, Belgrade, and Bucharest, the Institute of History in Bucharest, and the Institute of Sociology in Prague, specialists who provided valuable data on the wage and salary spread in their countries. I owe a similar debt to the Department of Sociology at the University of Havana and to the Institute of Economics in Havana for their help in my research there during 1968.

Several of my former graduate students read the original manuscript and offered valuable criticism. Special thanks are due to Mary Dickey, Susan Williams, Dr. Paul Shang, and Professor Jeff Burkhardt. I am also indebted for advice and editorial assistance to Dr. Ross Gandy and Deborah Hepburn, and to the Centro de Investigadores para el Pueblo (CIP) in Cuernavaca, Mexico. Finally, I wish to thank Professor Bruce McFarlane for the opportunity to discuss the central theses of this book in lectures and seminars arranged by the Department of Politics at the University of Adelaide, during the fall semester of 1979.

Preface

The most complete explanation of the decomposition of the capitalist world is to be found in Marx's *Capital* and in the works of political economists who applied his conceptual framework to the conditions of twentieth-century capitalism. Their efforts to explain contemporary revolutions and the emergence of a new social formation, however, adopt Marx's framework as fundamental instead of his method, a framework that has ceased to be a reliable guide to understanding advanced capitalist societies and is even less helpful to understanding socialism.

Although the new social formation departs radically from Marx's and Engels's anticipations, it can be analyzed following the same guidelines Marx applied in his study of capitalist society. Those guidelines may be found in the prefaces to his major works on political economy.

The present work based on those guidelines is an effort to analyze the new postcapitalist order. The application of Marx's method of political economy to socialist societies leads to the conclusion that organization is a factor of production independent of both labor and capital, that corresponding to this factor are new social relations of production and a new mode of extracting the economic surplus from the direct producers, and that corresponding to these are a new working class, a new ruling class, and a new type of state. This conclusion is basic to explaining the bureaucratization of socialism both as a political movement and as a new social formation. It is basic to understanding the nature of the Soviet system, the repression of revolutionary intellectuals, the conflicts between party bureaucrats and technocrats, and the emerging antagonisms and wars among socialist countries.

What distinguishes this book from other recent works on the same subject is its concept of organization as a fourth factor of production and the corresponding concept of a bureaucratic class used to analyze both the economic structure and the political superstructure of socialist societies. The result is a Marxist theory of bureaucratic exploitation and a critique of neo-Marxist and conventional Marxist theories. These are put through the same critical tests to which Marx subjected classical political economy and classical theories of the state.

This theory of bureaucratic exploitation is predicated on a reinterpretation of Marx's labor theory of value. Its elements were first sketched just over two decades ago in my articles, "The Anatomy of Exploitation," published during the summer of 1960, and "La controverse sur la reduction du travail," published in January 1961. What was sociologically implicit in these essays—the existence of a separate bureaucratic class under capitalism as well as socialism—was spelled out shortly afterward in my "Elements of a Theory of Salary" and "The New Class in Marxian Sociology" in March and April 1963.

The present book is a revised and abridged version of a larger work entitled *Marxism and Revolution in the Twentieth Century*, originally published in Spanish by Ediciones El Caballito (Mexico D.F., 1978). In the Mexican edition the conceptual framework presented here is also used to explain the bureaucratization of capitalism, to explain contemporary class struggles and abortive political revolutions in the West where the proletariat has also failed to live up to Marxist expectations. This model of classes and class struggle has also been applied to an understanding of Latin American revolutions. See, for instance, my earlier works, *Argentina 1943–1976: The National Revolution and Resistance* (Albuquerque: University of New Mexico Press, 1976) and, with Ross Gandy, *Mexico 1910–1976: Reform or Revolution?* (London: Zed Press, 1979).

Cuernavaca, Mexico
May 1980

Introduction

The intellectual legacy of Karl Marx and Friedrich Engels includes the body of knowledge loosely referred to as Marxist theory. On analysis this breaks down into the following basic components: first, a rudimentary theory of precapitalist societies and of simple commodity production in particular; second, a highly refined theory of capitalist society; third, a rudimentary theory of postcapitalist society and the transition from capitalism to socialism. Unlike the first two theories, the third contains mostly forecasts rather than explanations. Its foundations were laid by Marx in *Capital.*

Marx made his most important contribution in analyzing the tendencies toward capitalist breakdown. His contribution to an understanding of socialism is considerably less significant, for he failed, first, to forecast accurately the bureaucratic features of the new political regimes and, second, to describe faithfully the corresponding social and economic system. For that, the Marxist model of social classes is noticeably deficient. A major intellectual task today is to describe the basic features of the new social order and to anticipate its future development. This demands an end to the confusion of socialism with the lower stage of communism in an effort to understand the independent character of the new mode of production.

Lenin never lived to witness socialism but accepted Marx's and Engels's interpretation of it. Stalin was the first to adapt Marxism to the new world ushered in by the Bolshevik Revolution of October 1917. Contrary to the detractors of Stalin, to his credit little now remains of the original Marxist conception that doctrinaire Marxists transformed into a credo. These Marxists—some influenced by Lenin, others by Luxemburg, Trotsky, and Mao—have beaten a retreat from scientific to utopian socialism on the basis of a literal interpretation of Marx's and Engels's writings. Stalin replaced the traditional Marxist forecasts of a postcapitalist order with a description of the new social reality, whereas his critics on the left stuck to the original forecasts and to a socialist ideal that has little substance in fact. They seemed to have forgotten that for Marx and Engels the foundation of socialism is to be discovered in the actual tendencies of contemporary society, not in the society of Marx's time. Stalin's contribution was to bring Marxism down from heaven to earth. He preserved it by degrading it. If he had not done so, Marxism would have evaporated into a cult of ideas at the antipode of his own cult of personality.

Stalin's revision did not go far enough. His interpretation of socialism was more realistic than Lenin's, but it misrepresented the actual conditions of labor in the new society. Marx and Engels were only mistaken about those conditions, whereas Stalin distorted the Marxist texts in an effort to improve upon them and to justify his new course. In place of an accurate description of bureaucratic social relations in the USSR he and his successors offered a characterization that served their own political interests. Stalin did not guess wrong; he lied. ·

After disentangling and cutting away the self-serving elements in the Stalinist description of the new social order, we are left with only a tiny residue of Marx's and Engels's original conception. What materialized of their forecasts of a postcapitalist society was the abolition of private property in the means of production. Stalin argued that serious social antagonisms survived in the USSR but did not qualify as class antagonisms. His claim that class antagonisms had disappeared was apologetic, but not because he distorted Marx's and Engels's concept of class. To the end, he remained faithful to it.

In rethinking Marxism my purpose is to offer a further refinement of Marx's conceptual apparatus capable of describing and explaining the unique features of twentieth-century bureaucratic revolutions. Marx identified bureaucracy with the state apparatus, a social stratum or caste independent of the social classes defined by their position in the economic structure. His concept of social class excludes government functionaries from membership in any class but includes functionaries with similar skills in business and industry in an upper stratum of the working class. These he indiscriminately includes in the same class with skilled manual workers constituting the "labor aristocracy." As we shall see, the gravest defect of this concept is the presumption that class membership depends exclusively on ownership of the classical factors of production—land, labor, and instruments.

It is this defect that permits the Chinese Communists to question the socialist character of the Soviet Union. Lacking a model of social classes that includes bureaucrats and petty bureaucrats as separate classes, they include them as members of a new bourgeoisie. Claiming that bourgeois property has not been abolished in the Soviet Union, they identify the Soviet regime with a form of state capitalism rather than with socialism. This conclusion is based on their confusion of a state bureaucracy with a state bourgeoisie whose principal source of income is the presumed collective ownership of "state capital."

The perspective of twentieth-century revolutions developed in this study accepts the Soviet Union as a socialist country no less than China —but it is a socialism interpreted in terms of new bureaucratic relations of production. The thesis of the bureaucratic transformation of social relations leads to the conclusion that the bureaucracy is a new ruling class. This conclusion is interpreted not as a critique of contemporary revolutions but as an argument for them.

The recognition of the class character of the new social regimes in Eastern Europe, China, and Cuba allows for two opposing interpretations within a Marxist conceptual framework. First, we have the denial that the new order is a socialist one or even a transition to socialism as understood by Marx and Lenin. This leads to a criticism of these regimes for having betrayed the revolution. Second, there is the claim that the new order is socialist in the fundamental sense of having abolished bourgeois property, even though it fails to conform to Marx's other anticipations of postcapitalist societies. The advantage of this interpretation is that it gives precedence to the social realities over the ideal possibilities of a transition to communism. It favors a conception of socialism based not on Marx's or Lenin's theory of a new social order but on Communist practice and the actual class character of revolutions in the twentieth century.

Ironically, it is necessary to recast Marx's and Lenin's interpretation of socialism in order to explain the fundamental rupture with capitalism that began in the Soviet Union. The first step will be to examine the basic features of the new society envisioned by Marx and Engels. After going to the root of their errors, I lay the basis for a theory of the new social formation. Two fundamental classes until now alien to Marx's conceptual apparatus will be examined: the bureaucratic and petty-bureaucratic classes. Defined by the ownership of expertise, the personification of science and organizational power, these two classes are shown to be indispensable not only to understanding the revolution of our times but also to discovering its inner "contradictions" and their possible consequences for the twenty-first century.

1

Forecasts of a New Society

Communism may be regarded as both a political movement and a social formation. Though Marx's communist predecessors were mostly visionaries and would-be universal reformers, he sought to establish communism on scientific foundations, to overcome its status as a sect, and to make it an expression of actual social relations springing from existing class struggles. Was Marx successful in this endeavor to provide a realistic basis for the communist movement? We are warranted in saying so only if the new socialist order in the Soviet Union, Eastern Europe, China, and elsewhere corresponds in fact to the postcapitalist society Marx predicted.

Consider the forecasts of the new social order sketched in part 2 of the *Communist Manifesto* and reaffirmed in his later works. Marx and Engels begin by focusing on its distinguishing feature, the abolition of bourgeois property. What is bourgeois property? It is not the hard-won, self-earned property of the petty artisan and small peasant that historically antedated the emergence of the bourgeoisie. There is no need to abolish private property in general but only that which "creates capital, i.e., that kind of property which exploits wage-labor." This property consists of the means of production that provide their owners with "the power to appropriate the products of society . . . the power to subjugate the labor of others by means of such appropriation." It can be overcome, Marx says, only by raising the proletariat to the position of ruling class. The political supremacy of the proletariat is necessary for it "to wrest by degrees all capital from the bourgeoisie, to centralize all instruments of production in the hands of the state." In fact, public ownership of the means of production by the state or by other collective bodies is a distinguishing feature of all societies belonging to the socialist camp.

Let us see what this process of abolishing bourgeois property implies for Marx and Engels. In part 2 of the *Communist Manifesto* its abolition is associated with six corollaries.

First, "modern bourgeois property is the final and most complete expression of the system of producing and appropriating products that is based on class antagonisms." Marx would later repeat this forecast in his 1859 preface to *A Contribution to the Critique of Political Economy:* "The bourgeois relations of production are the last antagonistic form of the social process of production."Antagonistic in what respects? The antagonism, Marx tells us, is not only between owners and nonowners but also between the expanding forces of production and the forms of ownership operating as fetters on economic development.

Second, in the event of a revolution by which the proletariat makes itself the ruling class and sweeps away by force the former conditions of production, "it will, along with these conditions, have swept away the conditions for the existence of . . . classes generally." The result will be a classless society. This prediction includes the proletariat that will have abolished its own supremacy as a class.

Third, modern bourgeois property is the final expression of productive relations based not only on the existence of classes and class antagonisms but also "on the exploitation of the many by the few." The progressive abolition of bourgeois property implies the elimination of exploitation in all its forms.

Fourth, commodity production is brought to a halt and replaced by direct production for use. This implies the "abolition of . . . bourgeois freedom." By bourgeois freedom Marx means, in the context of bourgeois conditions of production, free trade: free selling and buying. "But if selling and buying disappear, free selling and buying disappear also."

Fifth, national antagonisms and wars between nations will cease: "In proportion as the exploitation of one individual by another is overcome, the exploitation of one nation by another will also be put to an end . . . [and] as the antagonism between classes within the nation vanishes, the hostility of one nation to another will disappear." The converse is also true: "United action of the leading civilized countries . . . is one of the first conditions for the emancipation of the proletariat." Proletarian internationalism is not only a consequence, it is also a condition of abolishing class antagonisms.

Sixth, when "class distinctions have disappeared and all production has been concentrated in the hands of a vast association of the entire nation, the public power will lose its political character." Political power, the state, is the organized power of one class for oppressing another. Marx and Engels anticipated the abolition of class antagonisms and of classes generally; they took this to imply that political power would also be overcome. The oppressive state apparatus, Engels later argued, would simply "wither away."

The full significance of this sixth corollary was not spelled out until Marx's *Civil War in France* (1871). Part 3 notes that the workers cannot simply take hold of the ready-made machinery of the state and wield this power for their own purposes. As the self-government of the producers, democracy requires a totally different apparatus without any trace of bureaucratic domination or privilege. That same year Marx wrote to Ludwig Kugelmann (12 April 1871) concerning the lessons of the Paris Commune: "If you look at the last chapter of my *Eighteenth Brumaire*, you will find that I say that the next attempt of the French Revolution will be no longer, as before, to transfer the bureaucratic-military machine from one hand to the other, but to *smash* it; this is essential for every real people's revolution on the Continent." In 1852 this was a mere forecast. In 1871 it had become a historic reality.

Although these six forecasts were made prior to Marx's extensive economic research during the 1850s and prior to the publication of *Capital*, they were never repudiated by him. On the contrary, some were reaffirmed in chapter 32 of volume 1, others in his *Critique of the Gotha Programme* published almost a decade after the first volume. They were also reaffirmed by Engels in *Anti-Dühring* (1878). Thus, it is a mistake to dismiss these forecasts as extraneous to Marx's major work, as sporadic theses rather than the systematic outcome of basic theoretical precepts.

These forecasts of a new society apply to what Marx called, in his *Critique of the Gotha Programme*, the lower stage of communist society. In the lower stage we have a society that has not yet developed on its own foundations but is still in the course of emerging from capitalist society following a "political transition period in which the state can be nothing but *the revolutionary dictatorship of the proletariat*." Although still stamped with the birthmarks of the old society, this lower stage excludes classes and therefore class antagonisms and exploitation. It excludes national antagonisms and the state because of the absence of any classes to oppress. And it excludes commodity production. Although income differentials remain, they result not from exploitation but from unequal outlays of human labor measured by its duration and intensity. "Accordingly the individual producer . . . receives a certificate from society that he has furnished such and such an amount of labor (after deducting his labor for the common fund), and with this certificate he draws from the social stock of means of consumption as much as costs the same amount of labor." There is an exchange but no buying and selling, for the certificate does not circulate as a universal equivalent, as money. In this lower stage of communist society, "the producers do not exchange their products; just as little does the labor employed on the products appear *as the value* of these products." Not only is labor power no longer a commodity; products no longer take the form of commodities.

For the higher stage of communist society Marx outlines a new set of economic and political corollaries absent from the *Communist Manifesto*. First, there is the abolition of "the enslaving subordination of individuals under the division of labor, and therewith also the antithesis between mental and physical labor." Second, there is the victory over what Marx, in his *Economic and Philosophical Manuscripts of 1844*, called the "alienation of the laborer," remedied only after "labor has become not merely a means to live but has become itself the primary necessity of life." Third, there is the overcoming of the laborer's fragmented and impoverished personality because of the growth of the productive forces and "the all-round development of the individual." And, once all these conditions have been met, there is the most important feature of the higher phase of communism, the abolition of social inequality in all its forms: "only then can the narrow horizon of bourgeois right be fully left behind and society inscribe on its banners: from each according to his ability, to each according to his needs." This highest stage of communism would do away with distribution based on the amount of each individual's labor and, by implication, with the system of labor certificates as well.

Marx's distinction between a lower and a higher stage of communist society was part of the legacy of the utopian socialists and of Robert Owen in particular. Engels himself suggested such a derivation in part 3, chapter 4, of *Anti-Dühring*: "With Owen the labor-notes are only a transitional form to complete community and free utilization of the resources of society. . . . If therefore any form of misuse should compel Owen's society to do away with labor-notes, the society would take a step forward toward its goal, entering upon a more complete stage of its development." This distinction goes beyond the limits of modern scientific socialism. Superficially, it seems that the lower stage of communism is painted in realistic colors whereas the higher stage borders on the fantastic; in fact, both stages diverge from a realistic analysis of social tendencies. Only if there are degrees of utopianism can one reasonably say that Marx's lower stage of communism comes closer to resembling conditions in the real world.

Although Marx explicitly rejected idealistic schemes of reform in favor of what Engels called scientific socialism, his passion for realism in dealing with the present was not always matched when it came to predicting the future. Most of Marx's mistakes are tied to his polarization thesis—the polarization of capitalist society into bourgeois and proletarians. This thesis together with his analysis of the capitalist mode of production led to the expectation that communism would follow capitalism. Marx's methodology was scientific, but weaknesses in his conceptual apparatus led him to make projections that grossly exaggerated the potential for human liberation. These mistakes were the result not so much of traces of utopianism in his thinking as of the influence of British political economy, its conception of social classes, and its analysis of the factors of production. If Marx believed that a system of labor notes might replace money in the future, it was because of the conceptual framework he derived from classical political economy.

The element of realism in Marx's and Engels's projections comes from their sketch of a future new order in preeminently negative terms. This is because they endeavored to base their forecasts on the operation of social forces tending to undermine the status quo. "Active social forces work exactly like natural forces," Engels wrote in the concluding section of *Socialism: Utopian and Scientific*, "blindly, forcibly, destructively, so long as we do not understand and reckon with them." These social forces will bring about a postcapitalist new order, not the pious hopes and blueprints of social reformers. To quote from Marx's *Civil War in France:* "The workers did not expect miracles from the Commune. They have no ready-made utopias to introduce *par décret du peuple.* . . . They have no ideals to realize, but to set free the elements of the new society with which old collapsing bourgeois society is pregnant." It is enough to cut away a cancer or to liberate the organism from its pathological condition to assure that it will function more effectively in the future. Similarly, it is not always necessary to replace old institutions with new ones to improve the functioning of society; it is enough to abolish oppressive property relations along with class antagonisms and classes generally.

Marx's forecasts of a new society were popularized by Engels and later by Lenin virtually in their original form as sketched in the *Communist Manifesto* and the *Critique of the Gotha Programme*. The last section of Engels's pamphlet, *Socialism: Utopian and Scientific*, is mainly a summary and restatement of the principal corollaries of the lower phase of communist society as conceived by Marx. Whatever his differences with Marx, Engels agreed that socialism would overcome both the anarchy existing in production and the class antagonisms between capitalists and wage earners. Overcoming the anarchy in production appears at first sight to be a novel feature, but on analysis it resolves into the abolition of commodity production and its replacement by a

planned economy: "With the seizing of the means of production by society, production of commodities is done away with, and, simultaneously, the mastery of the product over the producer. Anarchy in social
production is replaced by systematic definite organization. . . . In proportion as anarchy in social production vanishes, the political authority
of the state dies out." Engels also spells out what it means to abolish private capital and capitalism: "The proletariat seizes the public power,
and by means of this transforms the . . . means of production, slipping
from the hands of the bourgeoisie, into public property."

Does this mean that the predominance of public ownership is tantamount to socialism? Not at all. Public ownership does not itself do
away with capitalist relations. Initially, "production upon a definite
plan of the invading socialistic society . . . is so far still to the benefit and
advantage of the capitalists." The capitalists do not need to own the instruments of production in order to continue pocketing the lion's share
of the economic surplus; they may still pocket it as interest on state
bonds in compensation for their former property. In this way the modern state becomes the personification of the total national capital, the
national exploiter on behalf of the owners of state securities, a form of
state capitalism rather than socialism. For socialism to exist, public as
well as private capital must be abolished through complete rather than
partial expropriation of the capitalists. The capitalist relation is not
eliminated until a further condition is satisfied: the wresting of political power from the bourgeoisie. This is necessary to cancel the tribute
paid to the former owners of the means of production and to eliminate
the capitalists as a class.

As for Lenin's *The State and Revolution*, it contains a commentary
on Marx's distinction between the lower and higher stages of communist society and gives flesh to Marx's abstract notion concerning the
abolition of political power. To establish communism one must do
more than smash the republican bourgeois state machine, the standing
army, and the police. It is also necessary to abolish the monopoly of decision making by a bureaucracy of professional administrators. Lenin
notes in chapter 5 that effective administration during the first phase of
communist society depends on popular accounting and control: "From
the moment all members of society, or even only the vast majority,
have learned to administer the state *themselves* . . . the need for government of any kind begins to disappear altogether." In chapter 6 Lenin
adds to this provision the need to extend still further the scope of democracy: "Under capitalism democracy is restricted, cramped, cur-
tailed, mutilated. . . . Under socialism much of the 'primitive democracy' will inevitably be revived since, for the first time in the history of

civilized society, the *mass* of the population will rise to the level of taking an *independent* part not only in voting and elections, *but also in the everyday administration of affairs.*"

Lenin distinguished two different phases of the process of abolishing the oppressive state: the "smashing" of its bourgeois form and the "withering away" of its proletarian successor. Thus, he postponed the final advent of a stateless society to the highest or most advanced stage of communism. Chapter 4 closes with a somewhat different prediction than Marx's. The state begins to wither away when there are no longer any capitalists, any classes, and there is no class that can be suppressed. But the state does not completely wither away as long as "bourgeois right" survives, as long as inequality is sanctioned by the principle, "to each according to his work." "For the state to wither away entirely, complete communism is necessary."

This passage strikes a note of realism in an otherwise fanciful journey into the future. The fancifulness of that journey was not fully realized until after Lenin died. Only after the adoption of the Stalin Constitution in 1936 did it become evident that real socialism had hardly anything in common with the lower stage of communist society predicted by Marx.

Contrary to Marx's forecasts, the abolition of bourgeois property was achieved without any of the six corollaries that were supposed to follow from it. Class antagonisms were abolished only if we suppose—what we subsequently dispute—that Soviet bureaucrats make up a social stratum and not a class. Even according to Soviet accounts, two other classes survived: a new working class formally owning the means of production that were acquired by the state; and a new peasantry defined by the ownership of collective-farm property. Exploitation survived even if it was no longer capitalist exploitation. This is evident from the gross disparities of income between the bureaucratic and professional intelligentsia, on the one hand, and workers and peasants, on the other. Commodity production survived, although its scope was considerably diminished and limited initially to goods destined for final consumption. National antagonisms did not disappear even within the socialist camp; the military power of the Soviet Union was used to trample on the rights of dependent socialist countries. Nor did the bureaucratic apparatus of the state begin to wither away; on the contrary, it was strengthened beyond any previous anticipation.

Because the principal objective of Communist practice is still nominally the abolition of exploitation in all its forms, it would be ridiculous to call the new order a communist one. Nor should we call it socialist in the sense used by Lenin to designate the lower phase of communism. Lenin's usage preserved the utopian heritage of Marxism; it failed to correspond to the economic and political realities of postcapitalist societies.

There is, however, another well-established usage perpetuated by Communist practice without itself being Marxist. Most of the traditional Communist parties identify as socialist those countries where bourgeois private property and the corresponding class of capitalists have been either eliminated or reduced to marginal status and privilege. This interpretation of socialism is now the prevailing international one. I propose to use this term not as Lenin used it but as a label for the countries that are commonly called socialist.

This eliminates some of the confusion associated with its use, but we cannot eliminate all the confusion. The term "socialist" applies not only to a particular social formation but also to a political party or movement and to its current policies and practices. The self-styled Socialist parties also have a claim to this term even though they oppose socialism as it exists today. A similar confusion arises concerning the use of the term "communist." International usage ordinarily labels as communist the current practices of Communist parties as well as the classless social formation expected by Marx and Engels. Although these different uses are frequently contradictory, the doctrinaire effort to achieve consistency by insisting on Marx's, Engels's, or Lenin's usage gives precedence to a set of ideal meanings over the historical adaptation of language to changing circumstances.

From the vantage of hindsight we must conclude that Marx and Lenin were mistaken in all their forecasts of postcapitalist society with one exception: the abolition of bourgeois property. The question is whether their conception of the transitional period fared any better. Here we have to distinguish between the dictatorship of the proletariat in theory and in fact. Theoretically, the dictatorship covers the transition period between capitalist and communist society. In fact, it was a passing phase in the transition to a noncommunist society. The original theoretical usage no longer applies either to existing or to foreseeable reality.

Because Marx spoke only in passing of the transition to communism, we turn to Lenin for an elucidation of this concept. Lenin's view of the dictatorship of the proletariat differs from Marx's conception in three important respects. First, the revolution begins under conditions of imperialism—the stage of monopoly capitalism that Marx barely touched upon—during which the national antagonism between capital and labor is compounded by interimperialist antagonisms and struggles for national liberation by dependent countries. Second, a political rather than an economic crisis becomes the catalyst of a proletarian revolution, a governmental crisis that discredits the ruling class and prevents it from ruling in the old way, as in the case of military defeat. Third, Lenin anticipated that the revolution would break out initially where the link in the imperialist chain of oppression is weakest—where the various national and international antagonisms reinforce one another —rather than in countries with a developed capitalist economy and a strong and well-organized proletariat.

Otherwise, he agrees with Marx's view of the dictatorship of the proletariat. In chapter 5 of *State and Revolution,* in the section headed "The Transition from Capitalism to Communism," he says this dictatorship is a transitional regime between capitalism and communism, between the old mode of production and the new, during which capitalist and communist elements battle it out for supremacy. The dictatorship of the proletariat has no economic system of its own; there are no proletarian relations of production. Under this dictatorship, which is purely political, the mode of production continues to be capitalist until replaced by a new socialist economic system corresponding to Marx's lower stage of communism. At that point classes cease to exist; the proletariat ceases to exist; therefore, the dictatorship of the proletariat ceases to exist.

Lenin is unequivocal. In the next section, "The First Phase of Communist Society," the transition period has been replaced by the new communist mode of production called socialism. During its first phase this new mode of production is still tainted with bourgeois elements. "Marx also takes into account the fact that the mere conversion of the means of production into the common property of the whole of society ('socialism' in the generally accepted sense of the word) *does not remove* the defects of distribution and the inequality of 'bourgeois right' which *continue to rule* as long as the products are divided 'according to work performed.' And so in the first phase of communist society (generally called socialism) 'bourgeois right' is *not* abolished in its entirety, but . . . only in respect to the means of production." What this means is that socialism has relations of production of its own that, despite the survival of "bourgeois right" in matters of distribution, mark the end of capitalist exploitation and the division of society into classes.

The fundamental question is whether Marx's and Lenin's forecasts of a dictatorship of the proletariat and of the ensuing lower stage of communism were realistic. Did Communist practice, for example, confirm the prediction of a transitional proletarian regime leading from capitalism to communism?

It did not. The transitional regime in the classic case of the Soviet Union turned out to be much more complex than either Marx or Lenin imagined. Although it went through a proletarian phase, from the dictatorship of the proletariat emerged the dictatorship of a new class that was neither bourgeois nor proletarian. The outcome was not socialism as Marxists understood it but an altogether unexpected bureaucratic mode of production.

2

The Root of the Problem

Theory, my friend, is grey;
green is the tree of life.
Faust

In his "Letters on Tactics" (April 1917), Lenin says that "a Marxist must take cognizance of actual events, of the precise facts of *reality*, and must not cling to a theory of yesterday which, like all theories, at best only outlines the main and general, and only *approximates* to an inclusive grasp of the complexities of life." It is in this sense that Marxism is not a dogma but a guide to action. As the 1939 *History of the Communist Party of the Soviet Union (Short Course)* concludes: "To master the Marxist-Leninist theory we must first of all learn to distinguish between its letter and substance." Mastering the theory "means being able to *develop it and advance it* without hesitating to replace—in accordance with the substance of the theory—such of its propositions and conclusions as have become antiquated by new ones corresponding to the new historical situation." Marx and Engels were neither prophets nor visionaries. If they were wrong about their forecasts of a postcapitalist society, if the new social order that emerged from the Bolshevik Revolution did not turn out to be the communist society they had anticipated, then their conceptual framework was at fault. This revolution of the twentieth century was supposed to fit their particular theory; but when it failed to fit, its apologists were confronted with a dilemma. Either Marxist theory was mistaken or Communist practice had to be.

An alternative to the admission that Marx's predictions were false is to deny that a new social order ever emerged from the Russian, Chinese, and Cuban revolutions. In this way his forecasts have yet to be confirmed or disconfirmed. A foundation for this claim is sought in Marxist theory. Although the *Communist Manifesto* is unambiguous in identifying the meaning of bourgeois property with capital, and capital with the private ownership of the instruments of production applied to the exploitation of wage laborers, it is far from being the fundamental source of Marxist theory. That theory is to be found in *Capital*—and there we discover at least one usage of the term "capital" that supports the view that either an anticapitalist revolution has yet to occur anywhere in the world or, if one did occur, it was betrayed in short order.

Let us examine this usage and its rationale. In volume 1, chapter 4, capital is initially defined as "self-expanding value," a phenomenon absent from simple commodity production but crucial to understanding capitalist production. The expansion of value is the aim of every capitalist, "and it is only insofar as the appropriation of ever more and more wealth in the abstract becomes the sole motive of his operations that he functions as a capitalist, i.e., as capital personified." In precapitalist market economies, self-expanding value takes the form exclusively of "profit on alienation," that is, commercial capital. The *production* of surplus value is a much later development. Only when capital has penetrated the sphere of production does the economic system become capitalist. With or without capitalism, however, capital is "essentially the command over . . . [or] the disposal of a definite quantity of other people's unpaid labor."

This second definition in chapter 18 is no more inclusive than the preceding one. It is possible to "command" or "dispose" of other people's unpaid labor without owning the means of production and without producing surplus value—it is enough to "realize" it on the market. The form surplus value takes is also irrelevant, whether in profits, interest, dividends, capitalist rents, or salaries of the nominal directors of corporations. The high salaries of managers, state officials, and some professional workers also constitute an argument for classifying these persons as capitalists, although in fact Marx never classified them in this way. In any case, the public ownership of the means of production is no guarantee that the production and appropriation of surplus value has somehow ceased.

Suppose that the traditional capitalists are expropriated but that the production and appropriation of surplus value continue in the form of commodity production and the payment of high salaries to bureaucrats. Even with the corresponding abolition of private profit, interest, dividends, and rents, at least four possibilities present themselves. First, instead of socialism we may have state capitalism under the hegemony of so-called bureaucrat capitalists. These bureaucrats may be defined as capitalists simply because they manage the production of surplus value and appropriate the lion's share. Second, we may have state capitalism without the capitalist class. In this case the bureaucrats who manage the process of self-expanding value are not defined as capitalists because they do not juridically own the means of production, even though they collectively possess and dispose of them. Besides, they are no more

capitalists for appropriating surplus value in the form of salaries than
are landowners for pocketing it in the form of ground rent. Third, we
may have a transitional regime between capitalism and communism
—a hypothesis we have already excluded as unrealistic. Capitalism and
capitalists may have disappeared, while bourgeois forms of distribution
survive in the form of collective-farm profits and bureaucratic salaries.
Fourth, we may have a new social formation that is neither capitalist
nor communist. In that case bureaucrats who are not capitalists will
have become the new ruling class and the principal economic beneficiaries of the system. Whether this new society is called socialist or by
some other name is immaterial to the actual features it exhibits.

Is there any way of deciding this question on the basis of a careful
reading of *Capital*? Not if we limit ourselves to the first volume, where
analysis remains on a comparatively abstract level until part 8, "The So-
Called Primitive Accumulation." In the abstract sense of "capital" we
have considered, state capitalism is conceivable with or without a capitalist class; the state bureaucracy is conceivable either as a new state
bourgeoisie, as a new, nonbourgeois ruling class, or as a caste or stratum
independent of all classes. To limit ourselves to the first volume, however, would be a travesty of the structure and intent of the total work,
which must be taken as a trilogy that advances volume by volume from
the abstract to the concrete. The general or abstract skeleton of "capital" in volume 1 is given flesh only in volume 3.

How, then, is "capital" defined in the third volume? The substance of
Marx's conception is given in chapter 48: "capital is not a thing, but
rather a definite social production relation . . . which is manifested in a
thing and lends this thing a specific social character. . . . It is the means
of production monopolized by a certain section of society." Rather than
being a value-generating value in the abstract, *capital is the monopoly
of self-expanding value by a particular social class*. It takes two principal forms: money and commodities. Money capital, the paper one
holds, can buy the real capital in machines and things. Securities are
nothing more than paper duplicates of the real capital, which does not
change hands with the transfer of these duplicates from one person to
another. Such titles to real capital, guaranteeing a share in self-expanding value in the form of dividends, are a form of fictitious capital—a
point elaborated by Marx in chapter 30.

The basis for Marx's fully elaborated definition of capital may be
found in section 2 of chapter 47: "The specific form in which unpaid
surplus labor is pumped out of the direct producers determines the relationship of rulers and ruled [capitalists and wage laborers], as it grows
out of production itself and, in turn, reacts upon it as a determining ele-

ment." Furthermore, "the direct relationship of the *owners of the conditions of production* to the direct producers . . . reveals the innermost secret, the hidden basis of the entire social structure" (italics mine). For there to be capital there must be capitalists, and conversely. It is not necessary to own all the conditions of production to be a capitalist, but it is necessary to own money or commodities and to be able to purchase labor power on the market, whether for the purpose of producing or for the purpose of simply pocketing surplus value—presumably in large enough quantities to draw income principally from this rather than from some other source.

The form of ownership and the mode of appropriating surplus value are crucial in determining who is and who is not a capitalist. As Marx defines the capitalist in volume 3, chapter 2: "he is a capitalist and can undertake the process of exploiting labor only because, being the owner of the conditions of labor, he confronts the laborers as the owners only of labor-power." Marx then concludes that "it is precisely the fact that nonworkers own the means of production which turns laborers into wage-workers and nonworkers into capitalists."

Were state bureaucrats and the managers of joint-stock companies included by Marx within the class of capitalists? They were not. In chapter 4, section 4, of *Theories of Surplus Value,* Marx includes state functionaries and the bulk of so-called higher-grade workers in what he loosely termed the "ideological professions," that is, workers dissociated from the process of the production and circulation of commodities. The managers of industrial and commercial capital he includes in the upper stratum of the proletariat. Marx distinguishes in volume 3, chapter 23, of *Capital* between the functionary of the capitalist and the functioning capitalist. Like the capitalist, the functionary exploits the workers, but unlike the capitalist, he is not the legal owner of money or commodities used to produce or pocket surplus value; he is paid "wages of superintendence" corresponding roughly to the value of his labor power. The exception occurs only in the case of members of the board whose "wages of superintendence were, as a rule, inversely proportional to the actual supervision performed by these nominal directors." In their case, the prerogatives of management "serve only as a pretext to plunder the stockholders and to amass wealth."

In view of Marx's completed definition of capital and the capitalist, there is no place within his theory for the notion of state capitalism without a capitalist class, no place for the hegemony of bureaucrat capitalists or a state bourgeoisie. The term "state capitalism" is suspect. For some it signifies the state as the principal exploiter of labor power and the direct appropriator of the lion's share of surplus value. For others, and this is the traditional Marxist view, it refers to a state in which the principal economic beneficiaries are the former capitalists transformed into *rentiers*, who have been compensated for their holdings through the issue of state bonds at a guaranteed rate of interest for *x* number of years. But there are no capitalists in Marx's full sense, whether functioning or absentee, in the new, self-styled socialist societies; or, if there are, they represent only an insignificant fraction of those pocketing surplus value. Hence, there is no state capitalism in those societies. It is not Marx's theory but its misinterpretations that are at fault in characterizing in these terms the social order that issued from the Bolshevik Revolution.

Marx did go astray, but in other respects. Although right in anticipating the abolition of bourgeois property as capital, he was wrong in believing that the new social order would eliminate classes and class antagonisms. He was mistaken in believing that exploitation would be entirely abolished. Contrary to the forecasts in the *Communist Manifesto*, the new society has not overcome the commodity form of production, nor has the repressive state apparatus even begun to wither away. Nor does Marx's theory help in determining whether capitalism was displaced by a transitional society sharing features of both capitalism and communism or by an entirely new social formation distinct from both. If there is a fundamental defect in Marxist theory, it is to be traced to the premises from which his forecasts were made.

What were those premises? They included Marx's conception of social class as the touchstone for his interpretation of a social revolution and of the new mode of production to follow. What, then, is a social class? It is noteworthy that *Capital* leaves us guessing about the possible content of its unfinished chapter on classes. There Marx claims that the answer to the question, "What constitutes a class?" derives from the reply to another question, "What makes wage-laborers, capitalists, and landlords constitute the three great social classes?" Actually, his answer to this question had already been given in the penultimate chapter of volume 3.

This is what Marx says in that chapter. "In the study of distribution relations, the initial point of departure is the alleged fact that the annual product is apportioned among wages, profit and rent. But if so expressed, it is a misstatement. The product is apportioned on one side to capital, on the other to revenue [income]. One of these revenues, wages, never itself assumes the form of revenue, revenue of the laborer, until after it has first confronted this laborer in the *form of capital*." The confrontation of the direct producers with capital, with the products of past labor and the conditions of hire, presupposes a definite social character of production. It presupposes the expropriation of the direct producers from the land, implying a monopoly of landed property; it presupposes the separation of the direct producers from their tools, indicating a monopoly of the instruments of labor.

In the unfinished chapter of *Capital*, wage earners are defined by the ownership of the commodity labor power, thus only indirectly in terms of labor as a factor of production. In contrast, capitalists and landlords are defined directly in terms of the ownership, respectively, of instruments and land. To each of these forms of ownership corresponds a different type of income that also enters into the definition of each class. "The owners merely of labor-power, owners of capital, and landowners, whose respective sources of income are wages, profit and ground-rent, in other words, wage-laborers, capitalists and landowners, constitute then three great classes of modern society based upon the capitalist mode of production."

Ownership is a function of specific relations of exploitation. This is evident in chapter 51, in which the "principal agents" of the capitalist mode of production—capitalists and wage laborers—are said to be "merely embodiments, personifications of capital and wage-labor." What precise features of capitalist relations of production are fundamental? First, the production of commodities by means of wage labor under the command of a capitalist; second, "the production of surplus value as the direct aim and determining motive of production." The "principal agents" or essential classes under capitalism are determined by the mode of producing and appropriating the surplus product, by the peculiar form of domination and exploitation summarized in the relationship between wage laborers and capitalists.

Because both the capitalists and the landowners are expropriated in postcapitalist societies, however, Marx's structure of classes is unequipped to explain class antagonisms under socialism. Even should the proletariat survive as a class, there will no longer be another class to oppress it. Although functionaries of various kinds enjoy special privileges, Marx's schema includes state functionaries in a classless stratum, and it includes the corresponding functionaries in industry, commerce, and transportation in a higher stratum of the working class. There is simply no basis for future class conflicts within this framework; built into it is the impossibility of class antagonisms in postcapitalist societies. Most Marxists who acknowledge that such antagonisms exist conclude that these societies must still be capitalist. But this conclusion also flies in the face of the facts. Besides denying that class antagonisms can exist in postcapitalist societies, it denies that a social revolution took place in the Soviet Union and Eastern Europe.

The way out of this dilemma is to add a fourth great class defined by the ownership of expertise—the specialized administrative, professional, and scientific skills common to functionaries in all walks of life. Expertise is the power of a fourth factor of production that I call organization and Marx called cooperation, although he regarded it as a derivative of labor rather than as an independent factor of production. The owners of expertise, we shall see, appropriate surplus value in the form of salaries rather than profits or ground rent. The failure to distinguish a fourth factor of production as the basis of this fourth great class lies at the root of Marx's other failures. For a Marxist understanding of class antagonisms under socialism, his model has to be recast.

3

Organization: A Fourth Factor of Production

A reformulation of the basic factors of production in Marxist terms must explain the high salaries of professional workers under socialism. The general disparity between the salaries of intellectual workers and the wages of manual workers is not as gross as it is under capitalism, but we know that extensive privileges survive disguised in the form of salaries. It is naive to believe that intellectual and manual workers are paid according to the same socialist principle, "to each according to his work"—at least as Marx interpreted it. Workers do not receive back from society the equivalent of what they give to it, after deductions for the common social funds. It is necessary to be brutally frank. Intellectual workers are self-serving like everybody else. The source of their privileges is the exploitation of manual workers under both capitalism and socialism. The problem is to explain this distinctive mode of exploitation that has thus far eluded Marx's conceptual framework.

Within the framework of Marx's labor theory of value there is no explanation for this phenomenon. That is because intellectual labor is considered to be an aspect of the same factor of production as manual labor. At most Marx shows how intellectual workers perform the work *of* the capitalist by pumping out surplus value *for* the capitalists. Intellectual workers are not the beneficiaries of this process; they do not share, or do so only minimally, in the fruits of this exploitation. For Marx, they too are exploited by the capitalist. The question is how they exploit manual workers through a noncapitalist mechanism of exploitation that makes them, not the capitalists, the beneficiaries. It is this mechanism that survives the nationalization of the means of production and the abolition of capital under socialism.

In this perspective it was a mistake for Marx to include the owners of scientific and organizational skills—decisive for an understanding of postcapitalist societies—in a higher stratum of the proletariat. And it is no less a mistake today for Marxists to swing to the other extreme by including them in a "new bourgeoisie." As we shall see, they are not proletarians because their labor power is not exploited; and they are not bourgeois because they do not own the means of production required as capital. Nor do they belong to the petty bourgeoisie for reasons that will become clear in the next chapter.

Most important of all, intellectual work is valued not for the labor exerted but for the application of scientific and organizational skills. The products of intellectual work include both science and organization. Do scientific and organizational skills constitute then a fourth factor of production defining intellectual work and the intellectual worker? And do they contribute to the production of commodity values in a way distinct from both labor and capital?

The Productive Power of Organization

Although Marx expressly recognized only three *basic* factors of production in *Capital*, these are not the only productive forces. In his chapter on cooperation in volume 1 he also acknowledges that cooperation is a distinct productive force. And in the following chapter we find that the application of science in the form of technology—a result of cooperation based on the division of labor—is also a distinct factor of production.

When several laborers work together, whether in a single process or in different but connected processes, Marx writes in *Capital* 1.13, they are said to cooperate "even when the numerous workmen assembled do not assist one another, but merely work side by side." Besides simple cooperation based on economies of scale in which workers merely labor side by side, there is combined cooperation based on the division of labor in which workers assist each other. In the second case, the effect "could either not be produced at all by isolated individual labor, or it could only be produced by a great expenditure of time, or on a very dwarfed scale." Simple cooperation makes possible an increase in the productive power of each of the assembled workers; combined cooperation results in "the creation of a new power, namely, the collective power of the masses." A dozen workers assisting one another will in their collective working day complete a building in far less time than if each worked separately: "For instance, if a dozen masons place themselves in a row, so as to pass stones from the foot of the ladder to its summit, each of them does the same thing; nevertheless, their separate acts form connected parts of one total operation . . . and the stones are thus carried up quicker by the 24 hands of the row of men than they could be if each man went separately up and down the ladder with his burden."

This collective working organism, this organization of the labor of society, increases the productive powers of labor in a variety of ways. It concentrates the mechanical forces of labor; it extends the sphere of action of labor over a greater space; it sets in motion large masses of workers; it stimulates competition among them; it makes possible simultaneously different operations; it economizes the means of production by use in common. But whichever of these may be the cause of the increase, Marx says, "the special productive power of the combined working day is, under all circumstances, the social productive power of labor, or the productive power of social labor," that is, the productive power of organized labor.

Combined labor on a large scale, Marx continues in the same chapter, requires a directing and superintending authority to organize the activities of individual workers and "to perform the general functions that have their origin in the action of the combined organism, distinguished from the action of its separate organs." Originally, the work of organization was performed by the capitalists themselves; later they handed over the work of direct and continuing supervision to a special kind of worker. The capitalist was originally his own organizer; later, his entrepreneurial and organizational skills passed into the hands of specialized workers who supervised the industrial army of labor while also performing the business of the capitalist for him. "An industrial army of workers under the command of a capitalist requires, like a real army," wrote Marx, "officers (managers) and sergeants (foremen, overlookers) who, while the work is being done, command in the name of the capitalist." In time the work of organization became their exclusive function.

The productive power of organized labor is an additional source of surplus value. The capitalist pays for the value of a hundred independent labor powers, "but he does not pay for the combined labor power of the hundred." Organization enables him to increase the surplus product from the exploitation of these hundred workers by raising the productive powers of each worker above the social average. In this way an eight-hour combined workday may be the equivalent of a ten-hour day of as many independent workers.

Only if the capitalist no longer organizes his workers will he have to pay another to do this job, will he have to pay for the productive power of organized labor. In *Capital* 3.23, wages of superintendence are said to represent payment for a special kind of productive labor; the work of organization that has to be performed wherever the process of production takes the form of large-scale cooperation. This labor is characterized by Marx as "labor of exploiting" other workers, but only as long as capital survives. With the abolition of capitalism, the work of organization continues in a purely cooperative form. As Marx notes, "inasmuch as it does not confine itself solely to the function of exploiting the labor of others, inasmuch as it therefore originates from the social form of the labor process, . . . it is just as independent of capital as that form itself as soon as it has burst its capitalistic shell."

Science is a particular form of organized labor. According to Marx, it is the product of a cooperative division of labor but has its own form of organization. In section 5 of *Capital* 1.14, he describes how modern technology and machinofacture have transformed science into a distinct factor of production. At one time intelligence in production was the property of the independent artisan, but in modern industry it is lost by the detail laborer and concentrated in machinery and in the expertise of engineers, technicians, and managers. These make up what Marx called, in section 4 of *Capital* 1.15, "a superior class of workmen, some of them scientifically educated."

Yet Marx stopped short of associating science with a separate class of intellectual workers. At most he acknowledged an emerging antagonism between "hand labor" and "head labor." He agreed with the passage from William Thompson's *Inquiry into the Principles of the Distribution of Wealth*, included as a footnote to section 5 of *Capital* 1.14: "The man of knowledge and the productive laborer come to be widely divided from each other, and knowledge, instead of remaining the handmaid of labor . . . has almost everywhere arrayed itself against labor." Intellectual workers, not just the capitalists, are responsible for making the laborer's muscular powers completely mechanical and subservient to the machine and to their own barracks discipline.

Science and Organization

Both science and organization are recognized by Marx as distinct productive forces, but both are pressed into the service of the capitalist and therefore appear as capital. In *Capital* 1.13 Marx writes: "the social productive power of labor that is developed by cooperation appears to be the productive power of capital, so cooperation itself . . . appears to be a specific form of the capitalist process of production." But it is really something else. In section 2 of *Capital* 1.15 he says that "the productive forces resulting from cooperation and division of labor cost capital nothing; they are natural forces of social labor." The division of labor is also the basis of science as a distinct productive force. In section 5 of *Capital* 1.14 Marx notes that the division between manual and intellectual labor that "begins in simple cooperation . . . is completed in modern industry, which makes science a productive force distinct from labor and presses it into the service of capital."

The sequence Marx cites is the following: first, division of manual labors is a condition of simple cooperation, which is itself a definite organization of labor; second, organization in the form of simple cooperation is a condition of the more complex division between manual and intellectual labor; third, the division between manual and intellectual labor is a condition of the development of science as a productive force distinct from labor. Organization is thus a condition of science.

Science, however, reacts upon the conditions of production that generated it by generating higher forms of the organization of labor. An example of this is the scientific and technical revolution of the twentieth century, the invention of the computer, the computerization of industry, and its effects on the organization of cooperative labor. Although initially science was the product of organization, today organization is the product of science. Science is both organized knowledge and the knowledge of organization.

Science got its start, Marx says, as a product of intellectual work but afterward became its guide. Behind the intelligence materialized in machinery and the organization of labor lies the productive factor of science. Organization, whether in the form of machinery or cooperative labor, is applied science. Engineers who design the factory's machinery and managers who orchestrate the productive powers of combined labor are the personifications of this applied science. Science itself is the theoretical expression of organization in the form of human knowledge. It is not a mere aspect or subordinate function of labor; it is a distinct factor of production.

Is science a productive force distinct and separate from organization? Are there five factors of production instead of the classical three? Or is science the power of organization, and organization the embodiment of science?

Let us begin by deciphering Marx's view of the connection between science and organization. Marx made an important breakthrough in distinguishing between the factor of labor as a direct productive force that is not the personal property of the wage laborer and the labor power that is his personal property but only indirectly a productive force. Certainly, he did not argue that labor power made up another force of production alongside laboring activity.

We may make a similar distinction between the factor of organization as a direct productive force that is not the personal property of the intellectual worker and the power of science that becomes his personal property in the form of expertise but is only indirectly a productive force. Despite recent efforts to interpret science as a separate factor of production, it is the power that makes modern organization possible.

Just as nerves, muscles, sinews in operation result in laboring activity or simply labor, so the expenditure of brains and the recall of stored-up knowledge or science results in organizing activity or simply organization. Labor power lies behind labor; the organizing power of science lies behind organization. Labor is the fruit of labor power; organization is the product of science. Energy is expended in laboring, whereas science is applied in organizing this activity in the most economical way. Human energy moves; science organizes.

The laborer has skills that shape his energy in making a particular product. The organizer has expertise that is the form scientific knowledge takes in his work of organizing. Behind production we find laboring activity, and behind it the laboring power of brute energy. Behind organization we find organizing activity, and behind it the organizing power of science. Muscle power is at the root of labor; brain power is at the root of organization.

The term "labor" in Marx's writings is ambiguous. Sometimes it refers to the activity of laboring, sometimes to the product of that activity, to what Marx called "materialized labor." The term "organization" is also used in different senses. It can refer both to the activity of organizing and to the product of that activity, to what Marx called "materialized intelligence."

Although Marx showed how organization and science are productive forces distinct from labor and capital, he did not pursue this line of thought to its conclusion. To have done so would have led to the unequivocal recognition of organization as an independent factor of production. Instead, Marx treated it as a derivative and dependent factor of the labor process. On the one hand, the organization of the labor of society was explicitly defined as cooperative and combined labor; science was conceived as a form of "intelligence in production" materialized in machinery and in the expertise of intellectual workers. On the other hand, the productive force of cooperative labor was interpreted as the property of the capitalist for which he pays nothing; science was said to be purchased and pressed into the service of the capitalist. As material conditions of production, science and organization are aspects of human labor; as social relations of production and property of the enterprise, they function as capital.

How seriously should we take Marx's treatment of science and organization as productive factors? Because he did not develop this idea or include scientific and supervisory workers in a class other than the proletariat, evidently these factors are not on a par with the classical factors of production. Marx considered them to be derivative "production factors." They were distinct from labor in the sense that he could not reduce them to the simple expenditure of human energy; he saw them as functions not only of labor but also of a particular historical development in the division of labor. The science and organization incorporated in machinery, he tells us, emerged historically only with the capitalist mode of production.

Are science and organization peculiar only to these advanced forms of the division of labor? In *Capital* 3.23, Marx claims that "supervisory work necessarily arises in all modes of production based on the antithesis between the laborer, as the direct producer, and the owner of the means of production . . . [thus] the greater this antagonism, the greater the role played by supervision." Organized labor was basic to Asiatic, slave, feudal, and capitalist societies, and it is also basic to communist society characterized, in chapter 1 of volume 1, as "production by freely associated men . . . consciously regulated by them in accordance with a settled plan." In Marxist theory the elementary factors of production—land, labor, instruments—are common to all social formations based on class antagonisms; they are thus distinct from the special form taken within each successive mode of domination and exploitation. If science and organization are derivative factors of production, they are also aspects of these elementary factors.

The elementary factors of production common to every labor process are distinguished by Marx from these same factors "amalgamated with and represented by a definite social form" (*Capital* 3.48). Capital is not itself an instrument of production but "a definite social production relation, belonging to a definite historical formation of society, which . . . lends this thing a specific social character." An instrument of production is capital only if it is an instrument of wage laborers, not laborers in general. Unlike capital, land and labor are "elements of the real labor process, which in this material form are common to all modes of production . . . and have nothing to do with its social form."

The factors of production, according to Marx, are misconceived in the textbooks on economics. What the economists present in their "trinitarian formula" unites the material aspect of two of the productive forces—land and labor—with the social form taken by the third, the transformation of instruments of production into "capital." "The first striking thing about this formula is that side by side with capital . . . , side by side with an element of production amalgamated with and represented by a definite social form are indiscriminately placed: the land on the one hand and labor on the other." The material factors of production described by Marx in *Capital* 1.7 are land, labor, and instruments of production. The social forms assumed by these same factors under the capitalist mode of production are landed property, wage labor, and capital.

We may presume that science-organization also assumes distinct social forms under the capitalist and socialist modes of production. As personal property in scientific and organizing skills, expertise is pressed into the service of the capitalist as capital; but it does not take the form of variable capital or self-expanding value for the capitalist and, in this respect, it is unlike wage labor. Under socialism expertise loses the character of capital altogether but, as we shall see, it functions as self-expanding value for its owner. From the definition of capital as self-expanding value, we cannot conclude that all self-expanding value is capital.

Simple and Compound Labor

We have seen how the organization of labor increases the productive power of workers in combination. The next question is how organized skills increase the productive power of individual workers. It is common knowledge that the expenditure of simple labor power devalues the manual worker, whereas the exercise of scientific and organizing skills increases the value of the intellectual worker. The mode in which expertise contributes value is distinct from that of both simple labor and the stored-up labor in machinery.

This was not Marx's view. For Marx expertise is a compound of simple labor plus scientific and organizing skills. The mode in which expertise produces value is reducible to the way in which simple labor creates value and the stored-up labor in machinery transfers value to its products. Marx's explanation of the difference between simple and compound labor is in purely quantitative terms. Let us explore the qualitative differences.

Marx envisaged the differences between simple and compound labor in the opening chapter of volume 1: "Skilled labor counts only as simple labor intensified, or rather, as multiplied simple labor, a given quantity of skilled being considered equal to a greater quantity of simple labor." Skilled labor "counts . . . as," which is not to say that it is intensified simple labor. It cannot consist of "labor intensified" because in chapter 15 of volume 1, in a section entitled "Intensification of Labor," Marx defines intensified labor as "increased expenditure of labor in a given time, heightened tension of labor-power, and closer filling up of the pores of the working day." Here the condensation of a greater mass of labor into a given period "counts for what it really is, a greater quantity of labor." Example: "The denser hour of the ten hours' working-day contains more labor, that is, expended labor, than the more porous hour of the twelve hours' working-day."

When the exercise of skilled labor power counts as a work hour of superior density solely because it is skilled, it counts for what it really is not. Perhaps this explains Marx's afterthought, prompting him to correct his original characterization of skilled labor as "simple labor intensified" by adding, "or, rather, as multiplied simple labor."

Why does skilled labor count as multiplied simple labor? Marx's answer, in chapter 7 of volume 1, is based on the following consideration: "All labor of a higher or more complicated character . . . is expenditure of labor-power of a more costly kind, labor-power whose production has cost more time and labor, and which therefore has a higher value, than unskilled or simple labor-power." The conclusion: "This power being of higher value, its consumption is labor of a higher class, labor that produces in equal times proportionately higher values than unskilled labor does."

Marx does not explain satisfactorily how compound labor produces more value than simple labor. He never reached a decision on this crucial issue. At most, he offers suggestions that point in opposite directions. The first is in chapter 6 of volume 1, where he notes that the special education or training of the skilled worker costs more than what is necessary to provide simple labor power. The more complicated the skills, the greater the cost that in turn determines their value: "The expenses of this education (excessively small in the case of ordinary labor-power) enter *pro tanto* into the total value spent in its production." In the same context he tells us that, unlike the case of other commodities, "there enters into the determination of the value of labor-power a historical and moral element." Marx is speaking of the social costs of specialized skills, not their technical costs. Presumably, a higher standard of living, a higher level of civilization, adds to the value of labor power in much the same way as the special costs of education.

The second remark appears in chapter 8 of volume 3 where, referring to Adam Smith, Marx contends that differences in the wage scale have nothing to do with the intensity of exploitation in the different spheres of production. On the contrary, under conditions of free competition and free mobility of labor from one branch to another, the different wage scales do not imply unequal rates of exploitation. Example: "if the labor of a goldsmith is better paid than that of a day-laborer, the former's surplus labor produces proportionately more surplus value than the latter's." Marx correctly assumes that the only way the rates of surplus value can be equalized for different degrees of skilled manpower is for the higher skills to produce proportionately more values. Must these values, however, take the form of surplus value? Not at all. To return to Marx's "historical and moral element" and to the different costs of specialized skills in volume 1, these factors contribute to differences in wages without implying unequal rates of exploitation. Supposedly, the higher costs of skilled manpower can be passed on to the product and later retrieved in the form of higher wages, without the skilled worker's having to create more surplus value than the unskilled.

On this score, Engels was more fastidious than Marx. In *Anti-Dühring*, in his chapter entitled "Simple and Compound Labor," he frankly acknowledged that the superior value-producing capacity of skilled workers was still largely a mystery. Commenting on the passage already cited from chapter 7 of volume 1, Engels says: "The product of one hour of compound labor is a commodity of a higher value—perhaps double or treble—in comparison with the product of one hour of simple labor. The values of the products of compound labor are expressed by this comparison in definite quantities of simple labor; but this reduction of compound labor is established by a social process which goes on behind the backs of the producers, by a process which at this point, in the development of the theory of value, *can only be stated but not as yet explained*" (italics mine). Except for the consideration that more simple labor is involved, Marx had no explanation of the unique process by which compound labor contributes comparatively more value to its products than simple labor. In short, the mechanism was missing.

Hilferding's Accumulator

Is there any explanation for this phenomenon? Marx's successors sparred with one another in the struggle to provide one. Historically, two different and contradictory types of explanation have been advanced: first, that based on the analogy of specialized skills to a number of storage batteries used to charge a single accumulator; second, that based on the analogy of a complex skill to a machine in the head that depreciates over time.

In the effort to explain how human skills under capitalism add to the value of their products, Marxists have had only two models to follow. Both are based on *Capital*. Either human skills resemble variable capital in creating new value, or they are more like constant capital in transferring old values. Hilferding opted for the first solution; Sweezy for the second. Neither solution, as we shall see, describes this process as it really is.

In the opening chapter of his book, *Böhm-Bawerk's Criticism of Marx* (1904), Rudolf Hilferding explicates Marx's passage from chapter 1 of *Capital* on the basis of the following interpretation of multiplied simple labor: "Thus in this single act of the expenditure of skilled labor a sum of unskilled labors is expended, and in this way there is created a sum of value and surplus value corresponding to the total value which would have been created by the expenditure of all the unskilled labors which were required to produce the skilled labor-power and its function, skilled labor." In effect, the skilled laborer is several unskilled laborers compressed into one. The exercise of a specialized skill is tantamount to the simultaneous employment of several or more unskilled laborers collaborating on a single product.

To clarify his point, Hilferding uses the example of a storage battery or accumulator. Suppose a man owns ten storage batteries for driving ten different machines, but for the manufacture of a new product he needs a single machine with the power of those ten machines. In Hilferding's example this man employs the ten batteries to charge a single accumulator capable of driving the new machine: "The powers of the individual batteries thereupon manifest themselves as a unified force in the new battery, a unified force which is the tenfold multiple of the simple average force."

Hilferding's claim that one skilled laborer can produce a sum total of new value equal to that of ten unskilled laborers simultaneously is a rather startling interpretation of Marx's process of creating value. The labor power consumed in producing specialized skills is materialized in a product; it is no longer a vital force, and it cannot be revived or expended a second time. Skills can be exercised only through the living energies of skilled laborers. Although expended energy can be reproduced in another human being in the form of special skills, these constitute a special development of simple labor power and are not themselves expended as living energy. The expenditure of labor power is independent of its special forms. In the example used by Marx in the first chapter of *Capital*: "Tailoring and weaving, though qualitatively different productive activities, are each a productive expenditure of human brains, nerves, and muscles, and in this sense are human labor." The labor expended is vital or physiological energy that is qualitatively the same, notwithstanding the exercise of different skills. Thus, "the value of a commodity represents human labor in the abstract, the expenditure of human labor in general."

Considering Engels's remark that the skilled worker may produce two or three times the value of an unskilled worker, other things being equal, what reason did Hilferding have for citing a tenfold multiple of simple labor? In the case of a skilled worker who receives only twice the wages of an unskilled worker the difference may be accounted for, as we shall see in the discussion of Sweezy's solution in the next section, by the transfer of stored-up labor in the worker's skills to the product of his labor. But in the case of a skilled worker who receives ten times the wage of an unskilled worker, this explanation is completely implausible for the reasons that Sweezy gives.

Marx was far more modest and far more realistic in attributing differences in value productivity to skilled and unskilled workers. The highest differential acknowledged by him was in *A Contribution to the Critique of Political Economy*, where he used an example of a threefold multiple of simple labor. Later, in the authorized French edition of *Capital* (1873), it was deflated to twice the value contributed by unskilled labor. For the most part, Marx and his editor, Engels, were noncommittal. In the first, second, third, and fourth German editions of *Capital* 1.7, the reduction of skilled labor to simple labor was left indeterminate. It was not until after Marx's death in 1883 that the translators of the first English edition, Samuel Moore and Edward Aveling, took certain liberties by interpolating Marx's example. Thus, in the English edition (1886) and the American edition (1906) based upon it, we read the following: "in every process of creating value, the reduction of skilled labor to average social labor, e.g., one day of skilled to *six days* of unskilled labor, is unavoidable" (italics mine). This figure has nothing to bear it out in reality.

The principal support for Hilferding's interpretation is the passage from *Capital* 3.8, where Marx says the higher paid labor of a goldsmith is evidence that he produces more surplus value than an ordinary day laborer. But Marx does not say that the goldsmith sets in motion the stored-up living labor of other workers incorporated in his unique skills. He has only his own labor power to set in motion. In Hilferding's example, more labor is expended by the skilled worker than by the unskilled in a given time; hence, his labor is more intense. Marx denied this to be the case. Skilled labor merely "counts" as multiplied simple labor.

Marx's statement is no more helpful than Hilferding's. How can skilled labor *count* as the work of several unskilled laborers if it is the labor of only a single skilled worker? The fact that the skilled worker receives a wage several times that of the unskilled worker through the invisible operation of market forces is irrelevant to the amount of value he produces. Hilferding was confused because Marx himself took too much for granted.

Marx's example of the goldsmith is plausible only on the premise of perfect competition and mobility of labor, which results in equal wages for equal work. As Marx presents this premise in *Capital* 3.8: "although the equalizing of wages and working-days and thereby of the rate of surplus value among different spheres of production . . . is checked by all kinds of local obstacles, it is nevertheless taking place more and more with the advance of capitalist production." The exceptions to this general tendency he dismissed as "incidental and irrelevant" frictions; but this tendency today is the exception rather than the rule. In reality wage differences result from a hierarchy of rates of exploitation. These vary from a ceiling for superexploited workers down to the infinitely small rates marking the difference between highly skilled manual workers and the privileged stratum of professional workers whose high salaries preclude them from being exploited at all.

To use a variation on Marx's example, let us suppose the rate of exploitation of unskilled workers during an eight-hour day is such that common laborers replace their cost of subsistence during four hours and contribute the remainder gratis to their employers. In the case of sweatshops the rate would be higher, say, two hours and forty minutes of necessary labor and five hours and twenty minutes of surplus labor. Here the rate of exploitation has jumped from 100 to 200 percent. For skilled workers the rate would vary in the opposite direction. At five hours and twenty minutes of necessary labor and two hours and forty minutes of surplus labor, the rate of exploitation would have fallen to 50 percent.

In these examples the rate of exploitation varies and so does the spread in wage rates, from the monetary equivalent of two hours and forty minutes for sweatshop workers to five hours and twenty minutes for skilled workers. We have here a ratio of the wages of skilled to unskilled sweatshop workers of 2:1 predicated on a difference in rates of exploitation of 1:4. Because skilled workers are comparatively scarce and are also better organized than unskilled workers, these ratios reflect not so much differences in value between skilled and unskilled workers as differences in their respective prices. In these examples skilled workers are not paid more because they are worth more; they are worth more because they are paid more.

Sweezy's Machine in the Head

For the second interpretation of Marx's passage on multiplied simple labor, we may consider Paul Sweezy's account in *The Theory of Capitalist Development* (1942). In chapter 3 he considers two possible cases: the skilled worker is more proficient than the unskilled because of either superior natural ability or superior training. In the first case, he can produce more than an unskilled worker doing the same job. Here piecework is a measure not of different intensities of labor, which may be assumed as constant, but of different value-creating capacities. The skilled worker is endowed by nature with a monopoly of talent that enables him to produce more values than the unskilled worker. The value of their labor power may be the same, but the more gifted worker can command a higher wage in proportion to his superior productivity when paid by the piece.

In the second case, the value of skilled labor power is greater than that of unskilled labor power because it incorporates the costs of a superior education. As a result, "the superior worker expends in production not only his own labor (which we can assume would have the quality of simple labor in the absence of training) but also indirectly that part of the labor of his teachers which is responsible for his superior productivity." Sweezy has in mind not the living labor of his teachers, as if it could be stored up and later revived, but rather their materialized labor in the form of special skills. Example: "If the productive life of a worker is, say, 100,000 hours, and if into his training went the equivalent of 50,000 hours of simple labor (including his own efforts during the training period), then each hour of his labor will count as one and one-half hours of simple labor." Because this is also the way one calculates the depreciation of machines, it seems fair to say that Sweezy's model is patterned on that of a machine in the head.

This interpretation has been upheld by Ronald Meek who, while throwing his weight behind Sweezy, still cites Hilferding for support. In chapter 5 of *Studies in the Labour Theory of Value*, Meek agrees with Hilferding that the expenditure of skilled labor "signifies the expenditure of all the different unskilled labors which are simultaneously condensed therein." However, he misses the inconsistency between this interpretation of the expenditure of skilled labor and his mode of calculating it, which is derived from Sweezy: "One may simply calculate the amount of simple labor (including his own) which was expended in training the laborer, and then average this out over the whole of his expected productive life." Example: "If p hours is his expected productive life, and t hours of simple labor have been expended upon him and by him during the training period, then when he starts work each hour of his labor will count (for the purpose of estimating the value of the commodity he produces) as $1 + t/p$ hours of simple labor." Again, this expression is the same as that used for calculating the depreciation of constant capital in plant and machinery.

The notion that a specialized skill is analogous to a machine in the worker's head can be traced to Adam Smith. Smith's method of calculating the value of skilled manpower was also predicated on this analogy. In book 1, chapter 10, of *The Wealth of Nations*, he notes that investment in an expensive machine is likely to be made only if its employment enables the owner to recover the original capital and the ordinary profit on his investment; furthermore, that a skilled worker, "educated at the expense of much labor and time to any of those employments which require extraordinary dexterity and skill, may be compared to one of those expensive machines." Consequently, it may also be expected that his work, "over and above the usual wages of common labor, will replace to him the whole expense of his education, with at least the ordinary profits of an equally valuable capital." And it must do this, Smith concludes, in a reasonable time, "regard being had to the very uncertain duration of human life, in the same manner as to the more certain duration of the machine." In effect, Smith conceived of skills as a species of human capital, that is, constant capital in Marxist terms.

Marx seems to have been influenced by Smith's interpretation. The price of the commodity labor power includes, besides means of subsistence for restoring the amount of energy expended, an additional sum for the reproduction of this labor power plus a small increment to recover the prorated cost of specialized training and education. In calculating the cost of subsistence, Marx says in *Capital* 1.6, it is essential to determine the "quantity of human muscle, nerve, brain, etc. [that] is wasted, and . . . [has] to be restored." Increased expenditure of physiological energy, he concludes, demands a larger income. The cost of restoring this energy is greatest in the case of extra heavy work, diminishes proportionately for heavy work, moderate work, light work, and reaches its minimum in sedentary work.

The costs of special training are calculated in an altogether different manner. These expenses enter *pro tanto* into the total cost of producing a particular skill and are recovered by the laborer, not all at once but over a normal working life. The way they are recovered is explained by Marx in his essay, *Wage-Labor and Capital*. At the end of section 2 he writes: "The manufacturer in calculating his cost of production . . . takes into account the wear and tear of the instruments of labor. If, for example, a machine costs him 1,000 marks and wears out in ten years, he adds 100 marks annually to the price of the commodities so as to be able to replace the worn-out machine by a new one at the end of ten years. . . . *Thus the depreciation of the worker is taken into account in the same way as the depreciation of the machine*" (italics mine). This method of calculating the reproduction or replacement costs of simple labor power applies also—though Marx never directly says so—to the costs of skills acquired during a lifetime. Here we have in Marx's own texts a basis for Sweezy's interpretation of compound labor in terms of a machine in the head.

Marxist political economists have taken over this interpretation of skilled manpower, ridding it of the stigma of human capital. Only a minority of skilled workers invest in special training programs with a view to capitalizing on them. What motivates them is the anticipation that their investment will be recovered not with interest but with the advantage of working in an occupation that is more interesting at higher pay. If it were profit that motivated them, they would invest where there was a sure return or at least an immediate one while continuing to exercise their old jobs. Profit is only one kind of material incentive; a higher wage or salary is another. Besides, whether a skilled worker does or does not command a salary in return for his investment in specialized skills has nothing to do with their value. Within a Marxist framework the value of those skills is determined by their cost of production.

We have seen the mistakes in Hilferding's interpretation of the comparative value of skilled and unskilled manpower. Does Sweezy's interpretation fare any better? According to his model, no new value is created through specialized skills; it is their already existing value that is transferred in quotas to the worker's product. But in the process of transferring old value the skilled worker also adds new value to those skills. His skills are not used up in the same way that machinery depreciates. Every hour of expended labor power produces value by adding to the experience of the skilled worker in the course of adding to the value of his product. This return is not produced by "human capital," nor does it constitute a special kind of surplus value.

Like capital, expertise is self-expanding value. How, then, does this self-expanding value differ from capital?

First, the owner of expertise appropriates surplus value in the form of high salaries. This is effected through the exploitation of manual workers and the transfer of the surplus they produce into expert hands. Just as high wages help skilled manual workers to recover part of the surplus lost through the exploitation of their labor power by the capitalist, so high salaries enable the intellectual worker to recover the cost of his particular skills along with the entire surplus that might otherwise have accrued to his employer. But that is not all. Unlike the skilled manual worker, he also appropriates an additional sum consisting of a portion of the surplus value produced by other workers.

Second, the value of expertise increases because of the labor required to exercise superior skills. Unlike the stored-up labor in machinery that depreciates through use and from having labor expended on it, the exercise of these skills preserves their value and also adds to the amount of stored-up labor incorporated in them. In this respect this labor functions like the labor of maintenance, repairs, and improvements in machinery. To search for an appropriate metaphor, expertise resembles a *sponge* that soaks up every bit of labor involved in using it. Because the expert soaks up new values in the process of consuming old ones, he can "have his cake and also eat it."

As skills appreciate in value their prices may increase without any corresponding increase in costs for their owners. That is because every expenditure of labor power involving those skills contributes to a dual product: the expert preserves and adds to the value of his skills at the same time that he adds to the value of other commodities. Because his labor costs are paid for in salaries by the capitalist, it does not cost him additional labor to increase the value of his skills.

Marx argued that precisely because labor power tends to exchange at its value, it yields a surplus for the capitalist. We know that expertise does *not* exchange at its value. Unlike the value paid for labor power, which is less than the values it produces, the value paid for expert skills exceeds the values they yield. The manual worker is exploited by the capitalist; the intellectual worker shares in the exploitation of the manual worker through the intermediary of the capitalist. Unlike the manual worker, he gets back more than he gives.

Within the framework of Marx's theory of value, only labor power has the unique property of producing surplus value; but it can produce a surplus in more than one way. We are familiar with the way in which, in its capacity as variable capital, it produces surplus value for the capitalist. It also produces a surplus for the owner of scientific and organizing skills. Brainpower alone does not set these skills in motion. The amount of hourly energy expended by the brain in the most difficult scientific work has been estimated by industrial physiologists as approximately four calories, but it takes an additional hundred calories of muscle power merely to maintain the body in an upright position for carrying on this scientific work. Only in combination with labor power is scientific expertise effective.

Sweezy is right in likening the brain to a machine in the head put into operation with the help of the body's own labor. He is wrong in assuming that the value of this machine depreciates in the same way as ordinary machinery. Unlike constant capital, which loses its value in the course of transferring value to its products, labor preserves and adds to the value of expertise when exercising qualified skills. The brain alone cannot do it; we have seen that its expenditure of energy is minimal. The source of this surplus value is labor, including the four calories hourly expended by the brain. The beneficiary of this surplus is the owner of expertise, not Marx's capitalist.

The Concept of "Human Capital"

The conventional Marxist theory of intellectual labor is incapable of either describing accurately the nature of salaries for intellectual services or explaining the exploitation of manual workers by intellectual workers. In the effort to overcome these theoretical limitations of orthodox Marxist theory, I presented the arguments for a fourth factor of production. Although based on Marxist texts, this new theory goes beyond them in defining organization not only as a distinct factor of production but also as an independent factor having the same status as land, labor, and instruments. I then showed how this revision or correction of Marx's theory fits into the framework of his labor theory of value. But there are other ways of accounting for the expert's getting "something for nothing" than in terms of Marx's value theory. One advantage of the theory of "human capital," for example, is that it faces squarely the fact of intellectual exploitation and offers an explanation of its own.

That science is a form of "human capital" or "cultural capital" is a major theme of Alvin Gouldner's *Future of Intellectuals and the Rise of the New Class*. The thesis that the possessors of higher education are the owners of a stock of capital distinct from moneyed capital is his alternative to the conventional Marxist view that reduces science to an aspect of intellectual labor. Capital is defined as "any produced object used to make saleable utilities, thus providing its possessor with *incomes*, or claims to incomes defined as legitimate because of their imputed contribution to economic productivity." The key to understanding this academic gobbledygook is the word "imputed." Following Thorstein Veblen, Gouldner argues that capital will always, if it can, increase its income even when this does not increase productivity. In short, capital seeks "something for nothing." In this perspective science becomes a stock of capital, becomes "capitalized" as soon as it generates a stream of income. The class that owns this stock constitutes a new intellectual or cultural bourgeoisie whose capital is not its money but its private appropriation of the specialized knowledge transmitted by the system of public education.

This theory has revolutionary antecedents going back to the Polish anarcho-Marxist Jan Waclaw Machajski (1886–1926). During the period of the first Russian Revolution he published *The Intellectual Worker* (1905) that was to have an important influence on Trotsky's later criticism of the Soviet bureaucracy. Machajski, under the influence of Bakunin's criticism of Marx, argued that the professed champions of the proletariat were subtly undermining the structure of private capitalism in the interests of the intelligentsia, a rising new middle class fighting for a place in the sun against the old privileged classes, the landowners and capitalists. The professed dictatorship of the proletariat was a subtle cover up for a system of state capitalism in which government ownership of the means of production would benefit not the people but educated officeholders, managers, and intellectuals. Under capitalism these neobourgeois "privileged employees of capital" share in the economic surplus in the form of high salaries instead of profits. Although their higher education is a kind of capital—the source of their actual or potential higher incomes—they are bourgeois without being capitalists.

Gouldner is not alone in testifying to Machajski's influence. Johannes Alasco also testifies to it in a much neglected book, *Intellectual Capitalism.* His opening chapter quotes at length from Machajski's own works: "The expropriation of the capitalist class by no means signifies the expropriation of the entire privileged population. The national surplus value . . . passes into the hands of the state, as the fund for the parasitic existence of all exploiters, of the entire bourgeois class." The elimination of the capitalist owners of means of production does not imply the elimination of the bourgeoisie as a whole. In a different form it remains "the same ruling class as it was before . . . , the owner of the national surplus value which is distributed in the form of high salaries paid to intellectual workers."

The scientific-technical-managerial elite, Alasco argues, makes up a new class of capitalists: "The new capitalists, the owners of knowledge, i.e., the professional intelligentsia, can be expected to continue the ventures of their predecessors . . . , to expand the field of opportunity for the profitable investment of intellectual capital . . . [and] to revolutionize the Western world for this sole purpose." The major conflict of the twentieth century involves the issue of economic growth expressed as the struggle between two social classes: "One is the class of stockholders, the capitalists of our time . . . , the other is the class of jobholders, the executive class." Unlike the stockholders, who are concerned with the revenue from their investments, the executives are moved by what Alasco calls a passion for growth. The conflict between them is limited to competition between two different forms of capitalism: finance capitalism, in which an investment of money is the controlling asset, and intellectual capitalism, in which productive knowledge and expertise accumulated in industry become the controlling asset. Although intellectual capitalism, otherwise known as socialism, eliminates intangible assets that are the source of profits, "it does not eliminate intangibles productive of goods and services." On the contrary, ownership of human capital invested in superior skills becomes the principal source of earning power.

The evolution of capital, Alasco argues, has undermined the rationale for communism. Departing from Machajski in essential respects, he denies that capital is the exclusive product of manual workers. Capital values also take the form of intangible assets such as patents, trademarks, commercial patronage, monopoly positions, and technical expertise. Unlike the physical means of production created by Marx's proletariat, this intangible or intellectual capital is created "by the joint effort of highly paid specialists . . . engineers, research workers, business executives, lawyers." Even if the corporations were nationalized, "this capital could be expanded only by their effort." Thus, if social justice requires the expropriation of the capitalists, mainly stockholders and bondholders, then "their capital should be appropriated by the intellectual workers who have created it."

In Alasco's non-Marxist usage, "capital" is much broader than the ownership of the material means of production: "Capital is anything which can be defined in terms of legal ownership and may become a source of income." Accordingly, history shows five principal types of economic organization: feudal capitalism in which land was the controlling asset; commercial capitalism in which raw materials were decisive; followed by industrial, financial, and intellectual capitalism in that order. It is this broad usage that permits him to make distinctions between different capitalist classes.

The limitation of this theory of human capital is that, even when the theory takes account of human exploitation, it can explain exploitation only in the most general terms. The material privileges of intellectual workers are explained in terms of the monopoly of a scarce asset or factor of production—an explanation that applies equally to other forms of privilege in other social formations. The weakness of what Gouldner calls a "general theory of capital" is precisely its lack of specificity, its superficiality, its failure to explore the distinctive characteristics of different modes and mechanisms of exploitation. It is not enough to know that intellectual workers share in the economic surplus because of their monopoly of a scarce resource. For a full explanation we need to know what else is involved: the specific social relations of production, exchange, and distribution governing the combination and subordination of different factors of production.

Behind the common language of "capital" used to describe and explain exploitation under all social formations is the conviction that exploitation is somehow natural and common to all modes of production. This general theory of capital repeats a century later the same mistakes as Proudhon's *Philosophy of Poverty*. As Marx notes in a letter to P. V. Annenkov (28 December 1846), Proudhon's theory suffers from excessive abstractness: "He has not perceived that *economic categories* are only *abstractions* of actual relations. . . . He therefore falls into the error of the bourgeois economists who regard these economic categories as eternal and not as historical laws, which are only laws for a particular historical development." Proudhon's categories, Marx continues, are common to all modes of production, whereas the relations they express are but historical and transitory phenomena. Phrased in another way, "Proudhon does not directly state that *bourgeois life* is to him an *eternal verity*; he states it indirectly by deifying [dignifying] the categories which express bourgeois relations." Consequently, he can see only as far as the bourgeois horizon.

This general theory of capital reads back into history features of the bourgeois mode of production of the nineteenth century, while anticipating that the future will resemble in fundamental respects the bourgeois past. Operating with bourgeois ideas, this theory minimizes the structural and human differences between capitalism and socialism, while scoffing at the possibility of a future postsocialist or communist mode of production. It takes for granted that the general category of capital is applicable to *all* economic formations.

There is a tendency for political economists to confuse historically concrete conditions of production with conditions of production in general. The concept of "capitalism" emerged in an effort to explain the modern bourgeois mode of production but has been abstracted out of its bourgeois context, generalized, and applied to all modes of production. The corresponding concept of "capital" has been transformed from a historically limited category into a general category of production. The result is, to say the least, misleading. The result is that capital ceases to be defined as a specific social relation of production and becomes a general relation by which people get "something for nothing" under all economic conditions. It is precisely this indifference to historically concrete conditions that underlies the indiscriminate mixing together of capital with land and labor as natural and elementary factors of the labor process.

4

The Bureaucratic Class

Basic to Marx's concept of class is his distinction between a class in itself and a class for itself. The first underlies his political economy; the second his economic interpretation of politics and the state.

The elements of this distinction were first formulated in the final section of *The Poverty of Philosophy*. Referring to those workers who had organized themselves into trade unions to fight for higher wages, Marx says: "The domination of capital had created in the mass of workers a common situation, common interests. Thus this mass already constitutes a class confronting capital, but is not yet for itself."

At this stage, we read in the *Communist Manifesto*, the workers face up to capital in a disorganized way in a contest carried on by individual workers, then by workers in a single factory, then by workers in a particular locality. But their struggle lacks a national dimension and is directed against individual bourgeois rather than against the entire bourgeoisie. On a national scale these workers make up a class in itself, but politically they "still form an incoherent mass." They become a class for itself when they begin to form combinations or trade unions, when they club together to keep up the rate of wages, when they make provision beforehand for their occasional acts of revolt. These associations of workers in defense of their common interests against the bourgeoisie are needed "to centralize the numerous local struggles, all of the same character, into one national struggle between classes." Then comes the punch line: "But every class struggle is a political struggle."

The principal classes for themselves are the political forces that explain political life within the state and the struggles between states. Classes are the basic factors of political life corresponding to the fundamental factors of production. Just as the domination of a particular productive force, such as capital, determines the character of an entire mode of production, so the political hegemony of a particular class determines the nature of the corresponding state. The elements of Marx's theory of the state are to be found in his theory of social classes.

The same mistake recurs in Marx's political theory, however, that sprang from his blind spot in political economy: there are not just three factors of production and corresponding production relations but four. Because the owners of expertise cannot be included in any of Marx's three great classes, we may include them in a fourth great class. As we shall see, the role of this fourth great class under capitalism conditions the transition to a new social formation.

This fourth class does not have to be politically organized or conscious of its separate interests on a national scale to make up a class in itself. Neither in the advanced capitalist countries nor under socialism do the owners of expertise have their own political party with the express purpose of seizing political power and transforming the state into their own self-image. It is enough that the relationship to a fourth factor of production sets them apart from other classes and contributes to their organization on a local scale.

The ownership of science in the form of expertise defines membership in this fourth great class. *Like workers under capitalism whose special commodity is labor power rather than the productive factor of labor itself, the members of this fourth class do not own the factor of organization, but they own the expertise that makes it possible.* Expertise is their power of organization corresponding to the worker's labor power. This fourth great class controls the organization of social labor even though it does not own it. I call it the bureaucratic class.

Bureaucracy or Intelligentsia?

The term "bureaucracy" covers a wide range of meanings and has led some Marxists to prefer "intelligentsia" as a name for this fourth great class. In certain respects these terms are too broad. Bureaucracy includes government by bureaus or offices hierarchically structured and administered according to formal rules. In this usage it is not a class but an administrative apparatus in military, political, business, educational, and labor organizations. The intelligentsia comprises those with a monopoly of human knowledge whose members derive from different classes or represent different political movements. Thus, we can speak of an aristocratic intelligentsia, a bourgeois intelligentsia, a liberal intelligentsia, and a socialist intelligentsia.

In other respects these terms are too narrow. Bureaucracy conjures up government officials to the exclusion of their counterparts in industry, labor, education, and so on, with roughly the same expertise and functions of organization and administration. It excludes unattached intellectuals who have no official function. Intelligentsia narrowly limits it-self to highbrow professional cadres with a higher education. It excludes lowbrow "burrocrats" who shuffle paper and rise from the ranks of or-dinary office clerks. For designating the class we have in mind, one term is as misleading as the other. Yet this dispute over terminology is more than a verbal quarrel because behind it we find different interpretations of the nature of the so-called new class.

The term "bureaucracy" is used to identify the ruling class in post-capitalist societies with those who effectively "own" the state that owns the means of production. It is the party bureaucrats, not the intel-lectuals, who have a monopoly of decision making in the new order. Many of them are professional revolutionaries; others are labor bureau-crats whose authority derives not from their education but from their role as organizers. Because many of them never had a college education, never dedicated themselves to intellectual activities, they fall outside the concept of an intelligentsia. But precisely they, rather than their in-tellectual sidekicks, are said to be the new men of power.

The term "intelligentsia" identifies the ruling class in postcapitalist societies not with those who directly govern through the party appara-tus but with the thinking community that makes the fundamental de-cisions. The possession of "intelligence" is singled out as the principal means of sharing in the economic surplus. Knowledge is power; but knowledge is narrowly interpreted as requiring a higher education, as requiring intellectual skills distinct from organizational and adminis-trative know-how that can be learned from experience in a given job. In this interpretation the privileges and high salaries of burrocrats are re-garded as an anomaly.

This dispute over words expresses a factual disagreement over whether the bureaucracy of party, labor, and government officials or the intelligentsia of university-trained intellectuals and technical experts constitutes the core of the new ruling class. The result of this contro-versy has been the bifurcation of the new class into bureaucrats and in-telligentsia. Some writers have interpreted this bifurcation as a class difference. In Gouldner's *Future of the Intellectuals and the Rise of the New Class*, the conflict between bureaucrats and technocrats is pre-sented not as a conflict within the new class in socialist societies but as a conflict between the class in power and the new class.

What is this class in power? Gouldner says that in the USSR and East-ern Europe it is tantamount to the *state class*, the de facto if not de jure owners of the state-owned means of production. Its fractions are the government and political bureaucrats, on the one hand, and the top managers of state-owned enterprises, on the other. In contrast, Gouldner's new class consists exclusively of the owners of higher education divided into two fractions: the intellectuals consisting of "pure" scientists, researchers, artists, and so on, and the technical or applied intelligentsia. Gouldner's interpretation is fairly influential, and we should consider it in some detail.

The new class is on the rise, he contends, but it has yet to become the dominant class under socialism. The technical intelligentsia manages the nationalized and collectivized means of production but does not own them. Effective ownership is in the hands of another class—the class of party bureaucrats. On the basis of this split between ownership and management, which Gouldner claims is no less typical of socialism than of capitalism, he drives a wedge between the class in power and the new class.

These classes are not homogeneous. Gouldner analyzes the class in power into three distinct strata: party leaders and officials above the bureaucratic apparatus of the state who nonetheless control it; "politically reliable commissars" or "top managing directors" of government and industry appointed by the party leaders; and "bureaucratic line officials" who carry out the directives of the political commissars. He divides the new class into a subgroup of "experts" who are directly under the thumb of these old-line bureaucrats and a subgroup of "intellectuals" who are critical, creative, and inclined to revolution because they work outside the boundaries of what Gouldner calls normal science. Here we have two classes based on the ownership, respectively, of two different factors of production: the physical means of production or state capital in the collective possession of the class in power, and expertise or human capital individually owned by members of the new class.

Gouldner's description of party bureaucrats borders on the perverse, and he barely disguises his contempt for them. Those at the top hand down orders without giving any reason; those at the bottom carry them out unquestioningly. The "impluse of domination" lies at the root of the organization's "snake brain" or "brute part of bureaucracy." The culture of these party bureaucrats places them beyond the domain of critical discourse. They do not have "extensive cultural capital." Gouldner describes their skills in the most denigrating terms, skills that include "little more than being able to read, write, file." Bureaucrats are said to employ a control apparatus based on ordering, forbidding, and the threat of punishment, whereas the technical intelligentsia relies on reason, conviction, and material incentives to get things done.

Is it true that party bureaucrats are less expert than the technical intelligentsia? Only in a narrow and formal use of the concept "expertise." The expertise of party bureaucrats is based mainly on experience in coordinating and motivating the work of others; it is more of an art than a science; it cannot be learned by rote from taking courses in the university. Leadership requires talents of its own, including a knowledge of people and the ability to get along with them. To say that organizers lack extensive cultural capital is to acknowledge that they are not bookworms. Experience indicates that organizational expertise is actually more scarce than technical intelligence. It is no longer accurate to describe bureaucratic methods in such simple terms as issuing and obeying commands.

It is another gross caricature to claim that party bureaucrats collectively own the nationalized or collectivized means of production. To be sure, the bureaucrats are in possession and effectively control them. Their control of the means of production, however, is not based on ownership. Control over the means of production and administration is based neither on legal writs nor on brute domination. Its basis is a particular kind of expertise that typically eludes the university intellectual and the compartmentalized intelligence of scientists and technicians. It is the expertise directly associated with the tasks of leadership and organization.

This thesis of a fundamental cleavage between bureaucrats and intelligentsia is novel only because Gouldner interprets it as a conflict between classes. The more conventional view, presented in Albert Parry's *New Class Divided*, is that bureaucrats and intelligentsia belong to incompatible fractions of the same class. Thus, Parry sees a clash between the Communist party central bureaucracy and the scientific-technical-managerial elite, between communists who do not qualify as specialists and specialists who are typically indifferent to politics. As Parry puts it in his chapter called "The Managerial Evolution," the interests of scientific and technical development run counter to party dogma. This conflict is accentuated by an economic disparity. The party continues to raise obstacles to the accumulation of tangible assets by party members: "The Party bosses use state property, but less often do they own houses . . . their enjoyment of state-owned villas is in essence ephemeral." In contrast, the intelligentsia not only enjoys higher salaries than the party elite but also is free to spend them on privately owned dachas, automobiles, and servants.

In criticism of these two theses we have the argument of the Hungarian sociologist-in-exile, Ivan Szelényi. In a book written in 1974 with George Konrád but only recently published in English, *The Intellectuals on the Road to Class Power*, he documents at length the formation of the class power of the intelligentsia in Eastern Europe. Of even more relevance to our purpose is his recent essay, "The Position of the Intelligentsia in the Class Structure of State Socialist Societies," in which he analyzes some of the limitations of the definition of the intelligentsia as a class and criticizes the thesis of a bifurcation between bureaucrats and intellectuals.

His own research as an empirical sociologist, he tells us, convinced him that the bureaucracy cannot be accurately defined as an ownership class. Although it possesses the means of production, it does not legally own them nor does its progeny have a right or claim to inherit them. At the same time it is a mistake to exclude the bureaucracy from the intelligentsia as a whole, Szelényi argues, because the alleged bifurcation between them is disconfirmed in practice. In the Soviet Union and Eastern Europe bureaucratic positions are staffed by academic intellectuals, whereas university posts are occupied by party bureaucrats. Even more important, their training and scientific education are comparable, as are their salaries. Both fractions receive their income in the same form through the state redistributive mechanism. This is further evidence that they belong to the same class. Experts under socialism are recruited as bureaucrats, which makes most bureaucrats experts. In our terminology, both are the private owners of science in its personalized form of expertise. Thus, it is a mistake to regard only the expert as personified science and only the bureaucrat as personified organization. Each personifies both. Although together they constitute a single class, Szelényi concludes that it is a class defined not by *ownership* of a factor of production but by similar claims on the economic surplus made possible by *control* over the redistributive mechanism.

We agree with Szelényi that there is no unbridgeable gulf separating organization and expertise. On the one hand, the organizers are experts; on the other hand, scientists, technicians, even ivory-tower intellectuals are organizers. Scientists organize experiments, technicians organize and design tools and machinery, intellectuals organize a variety of data in the form of theories. Only in a very narrow use of the term is expertise equivalent to the specialized knowledge of scientists and technicians. This narrow usage excludes not only bureaucrats from the category of experts but also intellectuals because of their broad interests. With respect to breadth of knowledge, intellectuals have actually more in common with bureaucrats. Expertise is the capacity to manipulate and combine human beings, materials, tools, symbols, and information. Expertise is organized intelligence; organization is applied expertise. This discussion should suffice to bury the claim that bureaucrats and intelligentsia make up two separate classes.

Where we part company with Szelényi is in defining the bureaucracy-intelligentsia as an ownership class in the Marxist tradition. He believes that, in state socialist societies that have abolished private ownership of the means of production, "we have to go beyond this formal Marxism and beyond the analysis of ownership if we want to find the economic foundation of class antagonism." We have to fight, Szelényi says, the concept of ownership as fundamental to the definition of social classes. But do we? Only if we stick with Marx's three great classes and do not reconstruct Marxist theory by including organization as a fourth factor of production and by adding a fourth great class as the owner of expertise.

The fundamental question is not what to call this new class, but it does need a name and we have seen that the two principal labels are misleading. Is either one a distinct improvement on the other? I do not think so. Although the term "intelligentsia" focuses directly on the expertise of the new class, the term "bureaucracy" focuses on the productive factor of organization that ultimately defines expertise. "Bureaucracy" names what is fundamental to the new class—its dependence on a fourth factor of production. For this reason I prefer it. But "intelligentsia" will also do. These terms may be used interchangeably.

Bureaucrats and Petty Bureaucrats

The protagonists of the concept of a new class take for granted that all who possess expertise belong to it. There are compelling reasons for including high-grade functionaries and highly qualified experts in a single class. But should we include with them low-grade functionaries and ordinary technicians? On the supposition that the bureaucracy is not a class but an administrative apparatus, it is reasonable to include all functionaries together because they perform the same kind of administrative and professional services. In a class analysis, however, other factors must be considered.

The most important of these is the factor of exploitation. High-qualified workers receive high salaries for their services; low-qualified workers receive low salaries. Is this distinction merely a matter of degree?

The price of administrative, professional, and scientific expertise, we have seen, is covered by salaries that in an average lifetime more than recover the initial outlay invested in a higher education. The monopoly and nature of expertise make the difference. On Marx's premise that all wage labor is exploited, it follows that owners of expertise are not wage earners. On the contrary, they recover through salaries the full equivalent of the labor they expend plus a share in the direct or indirect exploitation of other workers.

This share in the fruits of exploitation has a lower but not an upper limit. The lower limit is precisely what distinguishes the owners of expertise from the class of wage laborers who are exploited in varying degrees. Within sight of this threshold the owners of expertise resemble skilled wage earners in being paid mainly for the labor they perform. Although they differ from wage earners in pocketing a share of surplus value, they also differ from owners of high-qualified expertise who receive the bulk of their salaries from exploitation. Thus, we may distinguish between a class of major exploiters that receives the bulk of its income from the labor of others and an intermediate or transitional class, a class of petty exploiters that receives the smaller part of its income in this manner.

Unlike a great exploiting class, a class of petty exploiters has an upper as well as a lower limit to its sharing in surplus value. Within the framework of Marx's labor theory of value, let us suppose x is the average wage for manual workers at a rate of exploitation of 100 percent. During an eight-hour day a manual worker produces a commodity worth x in four hours, but he works another four hours to produce a second x for the exploiters. Then $2x$ will be the lower limit separating the intermediate class of petty exploiters from the workers below, and $4x$ will be the upper limit separating it from the exploiting class above. Here we have the economic basis for distinguishing between a petty-bureaucratic and a bureaucratic class. As we shall see, this was also the basis for Marx's distinction between the petty bourgeoisie and the bourgeoisie.

In real life, there are people difficult to classify in watertight compartments. This is the case of all members of intermediate classes but occasionally also of members of other social classes. Here is an ordinary wage earner who has invested all his savings in General Motors stock. Does that make him a capitalist? There is a small landowner who has done the same thing. What class does he belong to? Marx was cognizant of these difficulties. Though defining the various classes by ownership of a particular factor of production, he also recognized the need for additional criteria for classifying those owning more than one factor.

Consider the genesis of the capitalist out of the small property owner. A moment arrives when the small owner hires his first assistant and begins paying wages. Suppose the rate of exploitation is 100 percent —Marx's standard assumption. If the assistant works eight hours each day, he will be recovering the equivalent of four hours to support himself and his family. Does the owner become a capitalist by exploiting this single laborer? Considering that the bulk of his income is derived from his own eight hours of work rather than from the surplus labor of four hours sucked from his unsuspecting victim, it would seem more reasonable to classify him in an intermediate class. Intermediate to what? To the class of self-employed workers at the lower limit and to the class of capitalists or full-fledged bourgeois at the upper.

In *Capital* 1.7 Marx writes: "If we now compare the two processes of producing value and of creating surplus value, we see that the latter is nothing but the continuation of the former beyond a definite point." In paying himself the full value of what he has produced, Mr. Pettigrew is not creating surplus value; he derives surplus value exclusively from his single assistant. Consequently, we have to ask: What is the dominant process of production in this mix? Is it the process of simple commodity production aimed at producing values? Or is it the emerging process of capitalist production aimed at extracting surplus value? In this case the answer is clear. Our protagonist is engaged mainly in the production of values, not surplus value. The mode of petty commodity production continues to dwarf the invading capitalist elements.

Now suppose he adds a second assistant. The two modes of production are now in perfect equilibrium—neither one definitely prevails. Mr. Pettigrew has grown in stature. He is no longer a petty producer but is on the frontier of something greater. Now he threatens to become a capitalist. With only one assistant he was at most the member of a transition class. As Marx defines this class in part 3 of the *Eighteenth Brumaire,* a *"transition class* [is one] in which the interests of two classes are simultaneously mutually blunted."

The turning point arrives when Mr. Pettigrew adds a third assistant. Henceforth he will be occupied mainly with producing surplus value and converting it into profit. We have thus determined the lower and upper thresholds for membership in the class of petty bourgeois and the lower limit for membership in the bourgeoisie. The bourgeois or capitalist class has no upper limit.

Now let us consider the comparable case of the genesis of the bureaucrat out of the petty bureaucrat. Formerly a skilled manual worker, Mr. Driver is today a foreman in the bottom ranks of Galbraith's "technostructure." He is the proud possessor of expertise in addition to skilled labor power. For that he receives an annual salary in monthly installments instead of wages by the hour or piece. He is no longer a productive laborer producing surplus value for the capitalists, because the values he produces he retrieves for himself. In addition, he gets something extra from pumping surplus value from other workers in his capacity as overseer. Although the overall mode of production is capitalist, his role within it is that of neither wage laborer nor capitalist. He belongs to an intermediate class of small managers. I call it the petty-bureaucratic class.

Twenty years later we find that Mr. Driver has climbed the promotional ladder to the rank of assistant manager. At this point he receives a salary several times that he received as foreman. He too has grown in stature. His principal job is now extracting surplus value instead of producing values for the corporation. From having been a petty bureaucrat, he will have crossed the threshold to become a member of the higher class of bureaucrats.

Bureaucrats and petty bureaucrats alike are "functionaries"; but by their rank and station in the overall system of bureaucratic exploitation only the bureaucrats constitute a fourth great class. Membership in the political, military, industrial, educational, and labor bureaucracies is conditional on the work of organizing large numbers of human beings. The most responsible jobs requiring the most expertise go to bureaucrats. Less responsible jobs are those that administer the labor of fewer persons or of lower-grade workers such as secretaries, laboratory and research assistants, apprentices, students, and blue-collar workers. These administrative jobs are typical of the petty bureaucracy. Bureaucrats and petty bureaucrats make up two distinct classes, just like the bourgeoisie and petty bourgeoisie.

Because of their intermediate position in the class structure, petty bureaucrats share traits with the classes immediately above and below them. Economically, they are caught in a vise between the bureaucrats and the workers. Like bureaucrats but unlike wage earners, they share in the exploitation of other workers. Like wage earners but unlike bureaucrats, they have an upper limit to their earnings. But this sharing of traits with other classes is also a source of confusion. On the one hand, we have the tendency to confuse petty bureaucrats with a lower stratum of the bureaucracy. On the other hand, there is the tendency to swallow them up in the "labor aristocracy."

The tendency to confuse petty bureaucrats and bureaucrats is promoted by the similarity of their incomes. Petty bureaucrats are paid salaries instead of wages. This gives the appearance that they belong to the same class as bureaucrats. Unlike wage earners paid by the hour, day, or week, petty bureaucrats receive a yearly sum broken down into monthly or bimonthly payments. Wage earners are carefully supervised by means of time cards that must be punched when arriving at work and again when leaving; petty bureaucrats have considerably more freedom. Unlike wage earners whose wages may be docked for absenteeism, petty bureaucrats are allowed to make up for lost time at their own convenience. Wage earners may be fired at any moment, whereas petty bureaucrats are protected by an individual contract binding upon the employer as well as the employee. Thus, their jobs are more secure.

Petty bureaucrats are a class separate not only from the bureaucratic class directly above them but also from skilled manual workers with whom they are just as often confused. Even Marx misleads us on this score. First, he failed to distinguish between wages and salaries. At most he correctly characterized the high incomes of financial directors and board members of corporations as only nominal wages, indicating that these were really profits in disguise. The nominal wages of superintendence, he says in *Capital* 3.23, are inversely proportional to the actual supervision performed by "nominal directors" for whom supervision and management "serve only as a pretext to plunder the stockholders and amass wealth." Second, he included the cost of managerial skills with that of manual skills under the heading of "variable capital." In the same chapter he says that wages of superintendence "form a part of the invested variable capital much the same as the wages of other laborers." That cannot be. If payment for expertise includes a share of the surplus labor of other workers, as we indicated in the last chapter, then it cannot be equated with variable capital, that is, wage labor that yields a surplus from being exploited by the capitalist. At most we may concede that the labor of supervision yields surplus value to the capitalist from organizing the exploitation of other workers.

This confusion is compounded by the fact that clerical office workers are also paid salaries. This contributes to blurring the distinction between petty bureaucrats and exploited wage earners under their immediate supervision. Beneath the payment of nominal salaries to the secretarial and office staff one can perceive the real wages they receive as exploited workers. Here salaries are a disguised form of wages. Just as Marx distinguished the real profits of financial directors from the nominal form of wages of superintendence, so we can distinguish the real wages of secretaries behind the salaries they nominally receive.

If this mystification were deliberate, its rationale would be the following. It is in the interest of the few financial directors who are actually capitalists to cover up their class affiliation by paying themselves salaries instead of profits. It is in the interest of bureaucrats and petty bureaucrats to disguise the class differences separating themselves from exploited clerical workers through a mode of payment that is nominally the same for both. And it is also in their interest to divide white-collar office workers with whom they must work on a personal basis from the rest of the labor force. This effect is achieved by paying them nominal salaries instead of wages.

The question is what is fundamental from a social point of view.

Should wages and salaries be distinguished by purely technical criteria, such as their bases in different time intervals? Or is it more revealing to distinguish them as payments for different types of services corresponding to different factors of production? Because Marxist as well as non-Marxist usage is confusing, wages and salaries have to be redefined to avoid equivocation. More important than any technical criteria are the social criteria distinguishing wages and salaries. Clearly, exploited office workers paid over the same time intervals as their immediate supervisors have less in common with them from a class standpoint than with exploited blue-collar workers.

The office staff of lower-grade clerical workers is employed at the same general tasks as management, that of exploiting the rest of the labor force. Nominally, salaries are the price of this particular service, but this usage is misleading. Unlike wages, which are the price of a single force of production, salaries constitute payment for two separate forces: the labor power of the office staff and the power of organization belonging exclusively to management. A common mode of payment covers over the difference between labor of exploiting that is itself exploited, in the case of the office staff, and exploiting labor that is not exploited, in the case of management. This distinction demands a corresponding breakdown in types of salaries: real salaries for management as distinct from the fictitious salaries of the office staff. Because nominal salaries are paid only to this clerical subclass of exploited workers, confusion is minimized by abandoning ordinary usage and applying the term "wages" instead.

The mystifying character of salaries is thus overcome. In this perspective a worker is paid a wage regardless of the type of labor he performs, up to the point that he ceases to be exploited and entirely recovers his own surplus. In excess of that amount the price of his labor power, not to mention the price of superintendence or organizational abilities, is converted into a salary. Suppose that, prior to promotion to a foreman's job, Mr. Driver's wages were five dollars an hour for a weekly payment of $200 at a rate of exploitation of barely 10 percent. After promotion, suppose that he receives the equivalent of six dollars an hour, although the actual pay of $240 weekly is calculated on a monthly instead of an hourly rate—that is, he is now paid a salary instead of a wage. Is the salary nominal or real? It is a real salary because, far from contributing the equivalent of more standard man-hours than he receives as a wage earner, he now appropriates the equivalent of more man-hours than he actually works. His raise of 20 percent puts him in the same privileged category as management.

When Marx extends the meaning of wages to cover the price of superintendence, this term is misapplied. Salaries, not wages, are the price of this particular service. We need a term distinct from wages to cover the price of expertise, the payment for the specialized skills involving supervision that appreciate instead of depreciate over time. To use the term "wages" for both is to play down the fundamental difference between the petty-bureaucratic and laboring classes. To use the term "salary" for petty bureaucrats and low-grade office workers is to fall into the same trap.

In defining these several classes, the relations of production and the form of extracting the economic surplus are of first consideration. But the form this surplus takes in distribution is also an indicator of class membership. Here we can agree with Engels in *Anti-Dühring* 2.1: "with differences in distribution, *class differences* emerge."

Digression on Bourgeois and Petty Bourgeois
The foregoing distinction between bureaucrats and petty bureaucrats parallels Marx's own distinction between bourgeois and petty bourgeois. The bourgeoisie is the dominant class under capitalism; the petty bourgeoisie provides a class of auxiliaries to the ruling class. The bureaucracy is the dominant class under socialism; the petty bureaucracy provides it with a class of auxiliaries. There are more petty bourgeois than full-fledged bourgeois benefiting from capitalist exploitation. There are likewise more petty bureaucrats than bureaucrats benefiting from bureaucratic exploitation. The capitalist mechanism pumps out surplus value in the form of profits for the bourgeois and petty bourgeois. The bureaucratic mechanism sucks out surplus value in the form of salaries for the bureaucratic and petty-bureaucratic classes.

Marxist critics of capitalism overlook its mass basis in the petty bourgeoisie—the principal class that sustains it. Mistakenly, they believe that capitalism has no popular support except in the irrational behavior of a working class that is only partly a class for itself. At the same time they mistakenly think of the mass basis of socialism as the working class, when the workers' objective interest is to bring about the postsocialist society called communism. The mass basis of socialism should be sought instead in the petty bureaucracy. Like the petty bourgeoisie in the United States, the petty bureaucracy in the Soviet Union can be counted in the tens of millions. These are not small classes, and in most countries they outnumber Marx's industrial proletariat.

This parallelism of functions is basic to an understanding of both types of society. The rationale for distinguishing bureaucrats from petty bureaucrats consists of the same underlying reasons Marx and Engels gave for distinguishing bourgeois and petty bourgeois as separate classes. What were those reasons? Because of their importance, a digression is in order concerning Marx's and Engels's distinction.

Marx's language of classes is misleading. If we take his language out of context and give it a purely literal interpretation, then the petty bourgeoisie is the lowest stratum of the bourgeoisie; petty bourgeois are simply small capitalists to be distinguished from middle and big capitalists. But this was not Marx's meaning. For him this distinction was more than a matter of degree.

In part 3 of the *Eighteenth Brumaire*, Marx specifically identifies the petty bourgeois with a transition class intermediate to the bourgeoisie and the proletariat. The members of this class aspire to become bourgeois but are not yet bourgeois. We find the same usage in part 1 of the *Communist Manifesto*. There the rising revolutionary bourgeoisie is distinguished from the disappearing and reactionary "lower middle class, the small manufacturer, the shopkeeper, the artisan, the peasant . . . [who] fight against the bourgeoisie to save from extinction their existence as fractions of the middle class." What is this lower middle class if not the petty bourgeoisie?

This distinction is reaffirmed by Engels in *Germany: Revolution and Counter-Revolution*. Engels specifically identifies these fractions of the middle class with the petty bourgeoisie. In the first chapter we read: "The great mass of the nation, which neither belonged to the nobility nor to the bourgeoisie, consisted in the towns of the small trading and shopkeeping class, and the working people." This class is distinguished in the final chapter from the various sections of the bourgeoisie, from the financial and the manufacturing capitalists. The replacement of the financial by the manufacturing fraction of the bourgeoisie stops short of being revolutionary because it does not transfer political or economic power from one class to another. Nonetheless, the revolutionary experience of 1848–49 led Engels to conclude that "at present two more classes claim their turn at domination, the petty trading class and the industrial working class."

Paradoxically, the lower strata of the bourgeoisie comprise small capitalists but not petty bourgeois. Capitalist and bourgeois are interchangeable terms; small capitalist and petty bourgeois are not. This vagueness in Marx's and Engels's language has led more than one Marxist to deny that Marx and Engels ever distinguished the petty bourgeoisie as a separate class.

In the same chapter Engels gives his reason for making this distinction. Speaking of the petty bourgeoisie, he writes: "Its *intermediate position* between the class of larger capitalists, traders and manufacturers, the bourgeoisie properly so-called, and the proletarian class *determines its character*" (italics mine). Although it aspires to raise itself to the level of the first class, "the least adverse turn of fortune hurls the individuals of this class down into the ranks of the second." Economically, it is a dependent class "possessed of small means, the insecurity of the possession of which is in inverse ratio to the amount." Politically, it is likewise dependent and "extremely vacillating in its views." The petty bourgeoisie flexes its muscles with democratic courage when the bourgeoisie establishes itself in power but "falls back into the abject despondency of fear as soon as the class below itself, the proletarians, attempt an independent movement."

Petty bourgeois constitute a class separate not only from the bourgeoisie but also from the class of independent craftsmen and shopkeepers who are too poor to hire assistants. Both own and operate their individual means of production and the corresponding commodities; but unlike the independent craftsman or small shopkeeper, the petty bourgeois also owns some capital. As Marx comments in the first volume of *Theories of Surplus Value* in an addendum on the labor of independent, self-employed workers in capitalist society: "They [independent craftsmen and peasants who employ no laborers] therefore belong neither to the category of *productive* nor of *unproductive laborers*." Although they are producers of commodities, "their production does not fall under the capitalist mode of production." Unlike independent craftsmen and peasants who have an economic system of their own—the system of petty commodity production—the petty bourgeois benefit from the ownership of capital. If they tend to be confused with self-employed workers it is because they also labor alongside their assistants. Actually, they operate outside the framework of simple commodity production.

Class versus Caste

Marx's own treatment of state bureaucrats and petty bureaucrats did not follow the lines of this parallelism with the bourgeoisie and petty bourgeoisie. That is because he identified state bureaucrats and petty bureaucrats with privileged but independent strata in society rather than with separate classes. For Marx, these strata are neither productive nor unproductive but completely removed from the process of production. Other functionaries with similar qualifications are productive or unproductive, but they are functionaries of the capitalists as distinct from state functionaries. Why did Marx artificially separate them, including some in the upper stratum of the working class and others in a separate caste? Because he lacked the concept of a fourth factor of production and did not regard the ownership of expertise as the basis of a fourth great class.

Marx refers to the bureaucracy of government officials in general as an artificial caste. In a classic comment from the concluding part of the *Eighteenth Brumaire,* he speaks of an enormous bureaucracy, well fed and well dressed, as the Napoleonic idea most appealing to the second Bonaparte. "How could it be otherwise, seeing that alongside the actual classes of society he is forced to create an artificial caste for which the maintenance of his regime becomes a bread-and-butter question?"

The members of this caste, he says in *Theories of Surplus Value* 1.4, include "state officials, military people, artists, doctors, priests, judges, lawyers, etc.—some of whom . . . know how to appropriate for themselves a very great part of the 'material' wealth partly though the sale of their 'immaterial' commodities and partly by forcibly imposing these services on other people." The remainder are not so well paid; they are only partly privileged. They correspond to our category of lower-grade experts and functionaries.

What is important for Marx is the peculiar type of work done by high- and low- grade functionaries that excludes them from capitalist relations of production. Unlike unproductive wage earners in commercial and financial enterprises—workers whose labor does not produce surplus value but converts it into money through the market mechanism—the labor of Marx's functionaries does neither. Unproductive wage earners exchange their labor power for capital; state functionaries exchange their labor directly for income. As Marx notes in an addendum to part 1 of *Theories of Surplus Value:* "Where the direct exchange of money for labor takes place without the latter producing capital, where it is therefore *not productive* labor [and it is *not unproductive* labor performed for a capitalist], it is bought as *service,* which in general is nothing but a term for the particular use-value that the labor provides." These services have value independent of the commodity labor power.

In Marx's account there are two principal categories of service workers. First, there are "higher-grade workers," consisting of self-employed professional people and "*servants* of the public"—a category underscored in *Theories of Surplus Value* 1.4, section 20. Second, there is the "horde of flunkies," from soldiers, sailors, police, and lower officials to mistresses, grooms, clowns and jugglers—a distinction made in section 9 of the same chapter. Marx claims that this second category, which also includes domestic servants, performs the same kind of labor as the first.

Marx's treatment of higher-grade functionaries and "flunkies" may be criticized on several counts. Exploitation under capitalism is not limited to the private ownership of capital essential to this mode of production or to the private ownership of land that is superfluous to it. In addition, there is bureaucratic exploitation of the "horde of flunkies" by higher-grade functionaries. Contrary to Marx, the similarities between functionaries of capitalists and state functionaries are more important from a social standpoint than the dissimilarities. Only when technical and occupational differences are given priority over the social relations of exploitation is there a case for treating these different functionaries separately. But this is not a Marxist approach.

That other kinds of workers, not just productive workers, can be exploited is demonstrated by Marx in *Capital* 2.6. To be exploited it is necessary only to give more labor for less. For example, the sales clerk may have to work ten hours to be paid the equivalent of eight. Because his employer pays no equivalent for this one-fifth of which he is the agent, Marx says, this is evidently a form of exploitation. It is capitalist exploitation when the capitalist does the appropriating. Replace the capitalist with a functionary, however, and the relationship of exploitation becomes a bureaucratic one. In the case of Marx's higher-grade state functionaries, the surplus labor extracted from state flunkies redounds to their benefit alone.

From the standpoint of capitalist relations of production, public functionaries do not belong to the same economic category as private functionaries of the capitalists. On the supposition of bureaucratic exploitation, they do.

There is an ambivalence in Marx's discussion of these capitalist functionaries. In *Capital* 3.23 he argues that "it is quite proper to compel the wage-laborer to produce his own wages and also the wages of supervision as compensation for the labor of ruling and supervising him." By implication, supervisors and managers share in the exploitation of productive workers and in the distribution of surplus value. They are paid "wages of superintendence," but these wages conceal a share in the exploitation of other workers. In capitalist stock companies the capitalist is replaced by hired managers who, although distinct from Marx's category of "functioning capitalists," appear to share attributes of both capital and wage labor.

In the same chapter Marx speaks of a "class of industrial and commercial managers", but his treatment of this "class" is no less mistaken than his treatment of state functionaries as members of an independent "caste." First, industrial and commercial managers, like their nonproductive counterparts in government, sell their expertise and organizational abilities, which is to say that they are paid salaries instead of wages. Second, it is not true that, as Marx argues in chapter 23, the salaries of managers tend to fall with the economic development of capitalism—they tend to rise until they reach a plateau under socialism and then begin to fall. And, third, even if it were true that economic development "reduces the cost of production of specially trained labor-power," the salaries of managers fluctuate independently of the cost of managerial skills owing to the monopoly and nature of expertise.

In an unintended parody of Marx's views, Oscar Lange argues that the dissimilarities between industrial, financial, and commercial capitalists are more important than the similarities; therefore, they do not belong to the same class. In his essay, "The Political Economy of Socialism", he conceives of the owners of banking capital and commercial capital as members of social strata after the manner of Marx's state functionaries. In his own words, " 'classes' receive income through the process of the primary distribution of income, such as wages and surplus value, while 'social strata' derive their income from a secondary distribution."

As Marx also noted, bankers and merchants do not share directly but only indirectly in surplus value through the averaging of the rate of profit and the deductions for interest and commercial profit from the gross profits of industrial capitalists. Yet bankers and merchants are also capitalists. Even less do passive stockholders and bondholders participate in the productive process; but Marx did not exclude them from the capitalist class. Within each class some members are involved in production, others in the process of exchange. Following Lange's logic, should we also include wage earners in banks and department stores in a different class from Marx's industrial proletariat? Besides the primary distribution of income typical of productive workers, there is a secondary distribution defining unproductive workers whose wages are deductions from gross profits along with the interest owed to financial capitalists. Taxes constitute a tertiary distribution for paying the salaries of state functionaries, who are neither productive nor unproductive in Marx's sense of these terms. But here again the directness or indirectness of distribution is not a strong enough reason for classifying these functionaries separately.

A Class for Itself?
We have seen that Szelényi denies that the Soviet and East European intelligentsia constitutes a class for itself. That is because "it has not developed a class consciousness." But Szelényi defines class consciousness in extremely narrow, almost sectarian terms. In the article already cited, he says of the East European intelligentsia: "Not only does it not

recognize the class nature of its own power, but it promotes the ideology of classlessness and consensus, and even more paradoxically, claims that the power exercised by the intellectuals is in fact the power of the proletariat." For these three reasons it is not a class for itself, to which Szelényi adds that in orthodox Marxist class theory "class" does not make sociological sense without class consciousness.

After making this case in the strongest terms, he appends a few qualifications. Dominating classes are not too keen on promoting the awareness of class interests, and they always promote ideologies of consensus. These concessions practically undermine the foregoing argument. In effect, Szelényi revises his original thesis by acknowledging that "class consciousness, or even, more generally speaking, social consciousness in contemporary Eastern Europe exists at a very low level." This means that the intelligentsia is a class for itself but, to use his own words, in *statu nascendi*.

There follows a series of unsubstantiated claims that social consciousness is less articulate in Eastern Europe today than it was in bourgeois society at an early stage of its development. Szelényi explains this anomaly by noting that for the first time in history the intelligentsia is rising to a position of class power that prevents the development of opposing class ideologies. When the bourgeoisie was an ascending class, the intelligentsia occupied an intermediary position between two great classes; it was in a position to articulate and represent the interests of both. In a capitalist society the intelligentsia is a class neither for nor in itself, he tells us; it is "only a stratum." Ironically, when it is not a class it is in a condition to develop class consciousness in other classes; but when it is a class in itself struggling to become for itself it cannot perform this vital role. "It only promotes ideologies which are in its own basic class interest, the most important one being the ideology of classlessness."

Next, we have a further series of self-inflicted blows—these aimed at his revised thesis. First, he concedes that conflicting class interest may become more articulate at a higher stage of socialism. Second, he notes that it took the bourgeoisie 250 years after the English Revolution of 1640, and 100 years after the French Revolution of 1789, to permit the articulation of an opposing working-class consciousness and corresponding independent organizations of the proletariat. Third, he says there are signs that the East European intelligentsia is already becoming more tolerant of dissidents within its own ranks. Fourth, he acknowledges that during the last decade the East European working class has produced its own dissidents. Fifth, he declares that the myth of the dictatorship of the proletariat is being demystified through the articulation of the real interests of the working class by "marginal intellectuals" who are prepared to betray their own class. I interpret these additional concessions as a refutation also of his revised thesis.

The question is how the bureaucracy can be a class for itself when it has yet to acknowledge its independent status as a class. There can be no class for itself, Marx believed, without a distinct political party through which it upholds its class interests. Referring in part 7 of the *Eighteenth Brumaire* to the small-holding French peasants, he says that with "no political organization among them, they do not form a class." Because they are incapable of representing themselves, they must be represented. To represent themselves on a continuing basis, they need to be organized for more than sporadic acts of protest. This condition also applies to the modern working class, Marx's chief concern. "In its struggle against the collective power of the possessing classes," we read in article 7 of the Statutes of the First International, "the proletariat can act as a class only by constituting itself a distinct political party." Presumably, the intelligentsia or bureaucratic class likewise requires a party of its own.

What is meant by a distinct political party? It is a party that not only represents the interest of a particular class but also belongs in some sense to that class. Does this mean that communists must organize their own separate party? Not at all. In part 2 of the *Communist Manifesto* the authors write that communists "do not form a separate party opposed to other working class parties." If they form a separate party at all, it is for the purpose of representing the interests of the proletariat as a whole. Otherwise, they constitute "the most advanced and resolute section of the working class parties of every country, that section which pushes forward all others."

The working class may have several parties of its own or only one. It may also ally itself with other classes in a multiclass party with workers sharing the leadership. "In France the communists ally themselves with the social democrats against the conservative and radical bourgeoisie." And in the same concluding part of the *Manifesto* we are told that in Switzerland they support the radicals "without losing sight of the fact that this party consists of antagonistic elements, partly of democratic socialists in the French sense, partly of radical bourgeois." Although a single party may be the optimum form of political organization, a class has also these other forms of political organization for advancing its particular interests.

Not every political act requires the intervention of a political party. To act politically it is enough to confront in an organized way and on a national scale the interests of the dominant class. In a letter to Bolte (23

November 1871), Marx gives an example: "the effort to force isolated capitalists by means of strikes to reduce the working day in a given factory or branch of industry is a purely economic movement; on the contrary, a movement aimed at forcing through the eight-hour day as law, etc., is a class movement." He concludes that a political movement is any class movement whose objective is "to satisfy its interests in a *general form*, that is, in a form that would make it obligatory for all of society."

By class consciousness Marx means a class aware of its own interests. He does not say that a necessary condition of this awareness is the formulation of its interests in specifically class terms. To be a class for itself, Marx tells us, it is enough for a class in itself to confront its class enemies through an organized political struggle on a national scale. This presupposes the capacity to act politically in its own interests. Does this mean that it must also have an articulate class ideology, that it must be conscious of itself precisely as a class? No, it is enough that it becomes conscious of its common interests as a group, whatever it happens to call itself. Certainly, the Soviet and East European intelligentsia is aware of its common interests in the political struggle against the international bourgeoisie. Although it calls itself a stratum, the nomenclature is unimportant. It is not the word used to identify itself but the consciousness of its common interests that counts. After all, the bourgeoisie in the United States still refuses to acknowledge its own existence as a class. In this perspective Marx's criteria of a class for itself are in fact present not only in every East European country but also throughout the socialist camp.

To constitute a class for itself, Marx says, its members must unite in struggle against some other class. Thus, the bourgeoisie became a class in struggle against the landowning aristocracy; the proletariat became a class in struggle against the bourgeoisie. The fact that the bourgeoisie became a class before confronting the proletariat suggests that the bureaucracy may become a class for itself before confronting its own working class. One may also argue that the East European workers constitute a class for itself in their opposition to imperialism and the bourgeoisie of other countries. Although neither workers nor bureaucrats are organized in a separate party of their own, the point is that they are politically organized in the same vanguard party against a common enemy. At most, one may concede that neither constitutes a class for itself in relation to each other.

Subjectively considered, the Soviet and East European bureaucratic and working classes are nonantagonistic. They are not yet organized in a political struggle of national dimensions against one another, though they are aware of their separate interests and struggle to defend them through a multiclass communist party. The purpose of such a party is to present a common front against the dominant capitalist class—their enemy on a world scale if no longer on a national one. Marx does not say that to become a class for itself the workers must unite in struggle against *all* classes hostile to their interests. It is enough that they are united against their immediate enemy. But under bureaucratic capitalism as well as socialism their immediate enemy is no longer the bourgeoisie. Once again we find the proletariat engaged in struggle against the enemy of its enemy. Because today its immediate enemy is the bureaucratic class, the enemy of its enemy is the bourgeoisie. Does this mean that the proletariat has ceased to be a class for itself? Not at all. In this new situation unforeseen by Marx, the fundamental enemy of the proletariat—the bourgeoisie—is no longer its immediate enemy. Because the revolution of the twentieth century is directed against this fundamental enemy, to make the revolution it is inadvisable for workers and bureaucrats to fight one another and to be organized into separate parties—even though objectively their interests are antagonistic.

The alternative is to hold that the international working class lost the class consciousness it acquired during the nineteenth century and reverted to a mere class in itself. This is not true of the Russian working class and it is not true of French and Italian workers, who exhibit more class militancy today than they did a century ago. The change in their immediate enemy may have disoriented workers in Eastern and Western Europe, but they have not lost sight of their long-range objectives. Although the working classes in former settler colonies, such as the United States, are known for their present lack of class consciousness, this would suggest that they never really had any and never became a class for itself.

Whatever we may conclude concerning the new working class, the bureaucracy is a class for itself. It is a myth that there are no political struggles internal to socialist societies and that all expressions of opposition to the existing regime are mercilessly crushed. Within the bureaucratic class different fractions have contended for power: the revolutionary intellectuals or Bolshevik Old Guard against the Stalinist central political apparatus; and this political apparatus in turn against the new technical intelligentsia committed to "market socialism." The repression of dissidents in the Soviet Union and Eastern Europe testifies to the political bureaucracy's awareness of its common interests as a subclass or fraction of the bureaucratic class. And, as we shall see in later chapters, to this struggle internal to the bureaucracy must be added the struggle between the bureaucracy as a whole and the petty bureaucracy pressing for socialist democracy. It is mainly the new working class that has yet to become involved in a domestic struggle against its own intelligentsia.

The political behavior of the bureaucratic and petty-bureaucratic classes corresponds roughly to that of the bourgeoisie and petty bourgeoisie during the period of the revolutionary overthrow of the landed aristocracy. Initially, the bureaucratic class follows an alliance with the bourgeoisie but, once the bourgeoisie has been defeated, it begins charting an independent course in alliance with the working class. Petty bureaucrats behave like the petty bourgeoisie. They too swing back and forth like a political pendulum, from supporting the bureaucracy against the working class to supporting the workers against the bureaucracy. Does this mean that the petty bureaucracy is not a class for itself? On the contrary, its interests are best advanced in league with the bureaucratic class during the early stage of the struggle against the bourgeoisie, and later with the working class against the bureaucrats in power. In the Soviet Union and Eastern Europe petty bureaucrats constitute a class for itself.

The political relationship between classes is a clue to the nature of a historical epoch. Domination by a landowning aristocracy gave us feudal society; the rise of the bourgeoisie corresponded to the invading capitalist society. "In all the many and complicated political struggles," Engels wrote in his article "Karl Marx" (1877), "the only thing at issue has been the social and political rule of classes, the maintenance of domination by older classes and the overcoming of domination by rising classes." A shift in the power struggle between classes, a change in the correlation of social forces, causes historical transformations. As the Bolshevik party took over the government and the bourgeois were expropriated in revolutionary Russia, a new social formation dawned.

5

The Bureaucratic Social Formation

Rule by a bureaucratic class, not communism, is the imminent wave of the future. The question is what distinguishes the bureaucratic social formation from its capitalist predecessor. Is the abolition of bourgeois property sufficient? Taking the Marxist conceptual framework as a starting point, the answer is no, because the absence of bourgeois property is also a feature of communism. What remains is to describe the new social relations of production set free by the elimination of bourgeois property and to see how these relations differ from those in a prospective communist society.

One social formation differs from another, Marx states in *Capital* 3.42, according to the "specific form in which unpaid surplus labor is pumped out of the direct producers." It is the mechanism of exploitation that determines the relationship of rulers and ruled. This mechanism arises directly out of production and reacts upon it—a relationship corresponding to a definite stage in the development of technology and the capacity of labor to produce a surplus. And it is this relationship that in turn "reveals the innermost secret, the hidden basis of the entire social structure, and with it the political form of the relation of sovereignty and dependence, in short, the corresponding specific form of the state."

The economic structure of society, Marx says in his 1859 preface to *A Contribution to the Critique of Political Economy,* consists of the sum total of its relations of production. The social relations men share with one another in the process of production include: first, their relationship to the factors of production and the role of the various social classes in production; second, the mode of appropriating the economic surplus through particular relations of exchange and distribution. Marx's main thesis was that the distribution of the products of work depends historically on a given relationship to the factors of production. Thus, with the displacement of bourgeois by bureaucratic property relations one may expect new bureaucratic relations of distribution.

How then should one characterize these new property relations? With the removal of the bourgeoisie from power and its divorce from direct control of the means of production, its former functions of management are performed entirely by salaried employees. These employees are not members of the proletariat. But does the proletariat itself survive the capitalist system? Because each social formation is defined by a unique set of social relations and by a different mechanism of exploitation, we are confronted in postcapitalist society with a new ruling and a new working class.

Among its principal claims, modern socialism credits itself with abolishing labor power as a commodity and transforming wages from the price of labor power into payment proportional to the quantity and quality of work. If this new principle were in fact implemented, distribution would be based on the assessment of services by the planning authorities, not on the market value of labor power. What is existing practice in this matter? What precisely is the new mechanism of exploitation by which surplus labor is pumped out of the direct producers?

From Labor Power to Labor Services

In most socialist societies a system of administered prices has replaced the determination of prices by the market mechanism. Among the problems faced by government planning boards is that of fixing artificially low prices for the products of subsidized basic industries, which are compensated by artificially high prices for luxury items. Artificial prices for different grades of skill have also been established in such a manner that the inflated salaries for professional services are compensated by deflated wages for manual labor. In this case, however, subsidies are for comparatively scarce skills rather than for basic ones. The services of artists and ballerinas are among the most highly priced of all; they belong to the category of luxuries; they neither enter habitually into the consumption pattern of ordinary workers nor are necessary to the building of a socialist economy.

The mechanism of exploitation under socialism is different from that of Marx's friend "Moneybags." In *Capital* 1.5-6 the problem of Mr. Moneybags is to find within the sphere of circulation a commodity whose consumption yields a value greater than its own. The only commodity with this unique property, Marx argued, is "abstract" or undifferentiated labor power. In contrast, the managers of socialist enterprises are on the lookout for a commodity that the planning authorities have priced conveniently below its value and whose consumption may yield a value equal to itself. Such are the services of most unskilled and semiskilled manual workers whose below-average wages contribute to subsidizing the above-average salaries of professional workers.

Consider Marx's depiction of the principal actors. For Mr. Moneybags the production of use values is only a means: "The restless never-ending process of profit-making alone is what he aims at." The passionate chase after money and more money is common to both the capitalist and the miser; but though "the miser is merely a capitalist gone mad, the capitalist is a rational miser." This Shylock demands his pound of flesh.

At the opposite pole is the wage earner, "a machine for the production of surplus value." Marx also likens him to an animal, "timid and holding back, like one who is bringing his own hide to the market and has nothing to expect but—a hiding." If he could, the capitalist would reduce the worker's individual consumption to the physiological minimum. The fact that the worker enjoys what he eats is irrelevant to the owner's purpose: "The consumption of food by a beast of burden is nonetheless a necessary factor in the process of production." Later his burden is mechanized; he becomes an "appendage of a machine." Considered by itself, machinery shortens the hours of labor; but in the service of capital it lengthens them. By itself it lightens his burden, "but when employed by capital, [it] heightens the intensity of labor." In the service of a master the mechanized means of production "mutilate the laborer into a fragment of a man . . . , destroy every remnant of charm in his work and turn it into a hated toil . . . ; they transform his life-time into working-time, and drag his wife and child beneath the wheels of the Juggernaut of capital." So conceived, the worker's lot is an "accumulation of misery, agony of toil, slavery, ignorance, brutality, mental degradation." Whether his payment is high or low, Marx concludes, his lot is a miserable one.

What kind of workers are those who typically sell labor power to the capitalists? Marx's answer is contained in a footnote at the end of chapter 7 in volume 1. Using figures cited in S. Laing's *National Distress*, he calculates that in England in the early 1840s approximately 11 million people were unskilled laborers. On the basis of the remaining population of 7 million, Marx then attempts to estimate the number of skilled workers. After deducting 1 million for the "genteel population" and 1.5 million for paupers, vagrants, criminals, and prostitutes, he is left with a figure slightly smaller than Laing's own estimate of 4,650,000 representing a so-called middle class. Within this class Laing included not only skilled workers but also "people that live on the interest of small investments, officials, men of letters, artists, schoolmasters and the like." It is a safe inference that skilled workers consisted of no more than half of this "middle class," or something less than 20 percent of the total labor force. Hence Marx's conclusion, citing James Mill: "The great class who have nothing to give for food but ordinary labor are the great bulk of the people"—not just the bulk, but the "great bulk."

The wage laborers typical of capitalism when Marx wrote were still the classical "hands," workers who sold their muscle power to the capitalists. Just as horses were valued for their horsepower, these human draft animals were hired mainly for their labor power. Although in chapter 6, volume 1, Marx defines labor power as "the aggregate of those mental and physical capabilities existing in a human being, which he exercises whenever he produces a use-value of any description," the mental capabilities demanded from the ordinary hand seldom exceed his ability to understand and follow orders directly emanating from the capitalist as "master."

The conditions for the transformation of labor power into a commodity no longer exist in postcapitalist societies. What were those conditions? Marx spells them out in volume 1, chapter 6, of *Capital*: first, the worker "must be the *untrammelled owner* of his capacity for labor, i.e., of his own person" (italics mine); second, he "must be obliged to offer for sale as a commodity that very labor-power which exists only in his living self." He must be free in two senses, "that as a free man he can dispose of his labor-power as his own commodity, and that . . . he has no other commodity for sale, is short of everything necessary for the realization of his labor-power—that is, he is free of the means of production. Again, in his chapter entitled "The Secret of Primitive Accumulation," Marx says that capitalism depends for its existence on a supply of free laborers "in the double sense that neither they themselves form part and parcel of the means of production, as in the case of slaves, bondsmen, etc., nor do the means of production belong to them, as in the case of peasant-proprietors." Let us see what each of these conditions implies.

First, to be free, labor power must be mobile. The continuous reproduction of the buyer-seller relationship with respect to the commodity labor power, Marx notes in chapter 6, "demands that the owner of the labor-power should sell it only for a definite period, for if he were to sell it rump and stump, once for all, he would be selling himself from a free man into bondage." Thus, the laborer "must constantly look upon his labor-power as his own property, his own commodity." To become a free seller of his labor power, Marx adds in his chapter on primitive accumulation, the laborer must have been emancipated not only from bondage to the land, from the condition of serfdom, but also from bondage to the medieval guilds in the cities. He "must further have escaped from the regime of the guilds, their rules for apprentices and journeymen, and the impediments of their labor regulations . . . the fetters they laid on the free development of production and the free exploitation of man by man."

Second, the basis of the whole process by which the laborer becomes a wage earner and the free disposer of his labor power, Marx continues, was the forcible separation of the workers from their means of subsistence. The expropriation of the peasants from the soil hurled them upon the labor market as free or "unattached" proletarians, and this pool of free labor contributed to competition with the guilds and ultimately undermined their monopoly of special skills. The result was a transformation of the servitude of the laborer: "The advance consisted in a *change of form of this servitude*, in the transformation of feudal exploitation into capitalist exploitation" (italics mine).

Has there been a change in the form of servitude under the conditions of twentieth-century socialism? Indeed, there has. Wage earners in postcapitalist society are restricted in their mobility and partially endowed with property in nationally and collectively owned means of production. In centrally administered economies they cannot shift freely from one job to another, and public property in the means of production protects them from having to sell their labor power to an individual. In these two important respects they resemble medieval serfs who possessed certain lands in common at the same time that they were tied by customary law to the land. In many other respects, of course, they enjoy great advantages over serfs.

Some critics of postcapitalist society, among them "left communists" like Amadeo Bordiga and Bruno Rizzi, have concluded that the Soviet system represents a form of industrial feudalism—the contemporary equivalent of serfdom. This is as much a distortion of the new social relations of production as the Chinese thesis that the Soviet system is a form of state capitalism. Actually, workers under socialism share features with the working classes under both capitalism and feudalism. In common with Marx's proletariat, they sell a human commodity and are paid wages in compensation. The difference arises over the character of this commodity. Wages are paid for labor services, not for labor power.

Does an administered price for such services rule out the possibility of a labor market under socialism? Traditionally, Marxists have assumed that a labor market cannot exist without the commodity character of labor power. But labor in the form of concrete services is also a commodity, and there may be a market for it as well. Whether there is or is not such a market is largely a matter of definition. In postcapitalist societies a labor market is compatible not only with the abolition of manpower as a commodity but also with centralized planning in which workers are stripped of initiative in wage policy and the salaries for each job are administered from the top. In *The Market in a Socialist Economy*, the Polish Marxist Wladzimierz Bruz contends that a bureaucratically administered labor market has special features of its own. It is subordinate to a plan that adjusts the demand for labor to the supply, and there is a "price for labor" that adjusts the supply of different categories of labor to the demand. Evidently, this presupposes some choice of employment and a form of market socialism in place of the old centrally administered economies.

Quality versus Quantity of Work
It is interesting to reflect on the developing bureaucratic rationale for the inequality of wages and salaries under socialism. Its beginnings may be traced to a historic speech by Stalin, "New Conditions—New Tasks," delivered at a conference of leaders of Soviet industry in 1931: "Marx and Lenin said that the difference between skilled and unskilled labor would continue to exist even under socialism and even after classes had been abolished, that only under communism would their differences disappear and that, therefore, even under socialism 'wages' must be paid according to labor performed and not according to need." So far, this is correct, but consider the inference Stalin draws from this perpetuation of the division of labor into skilled and unskilled. "Who is right, Marx and Lenin, or our equalitarians? We may take it that Marx and Lenin are right. But if so, it follows that whoever draws up wage scales on the 'principle' of equality, and ignores the differences between skilled and unskilled labor, is at loggerheads with Marxism and Leninism."

On the contrary, the "equalitarians" took fewer liberties in interpreting the classical texts than Stalin did. He misinterpreted the sense in which, for Marx and Lenin, differences in wages would persist under socialism. For them the technical gap between skilled and unskilled labor was not an argument for perpetuating wage inequalities. Payment according to the "amount of work," to use their expression, would effectively eliminate differences in pay for skilled and unskilled workers. Inequalities would remain, Marx indicated, but they would be based on the intensity of labor in different occupations and on the number of standard man-hours determined by time and motion studies. The level of skill was simply irrelevant as a measure of the amount of work. Evidently, Stalin added a new criterion for determining differences in wages—one that was entirely foreign to Marx's principle of distribution.

What Stalin was implicitly saying his successors said explicitly: the principle of remuneration under socialism is payment not according to work alone but according to the *quantity and quality* of work. The rationale for paying higher salaries for professional expertise was later to include not only higher qualifications but also the relative scarcity of professional skills. Thus, highly qualified workers are subsidized by the Soviet state in the form of above-average paychecks, whereas unqualified workers subsidize the state by means of below-average paychecks. The first get something for nothing; the others get nothing for something.

The principle of payment according to quantity and quality of work is rooted in a system of priorities interpreted as crucial to the development of a socialist economy. Just as economic priorities in the sphere of production are decided by the planning authorities and by them alone, so are priorities in matters of distribution. Services of a political and supervisory nature are given precedence over labor of a purely mechanical or routine sort. The most important criteria for determining personal incomes are the national importance of the job to the overall direction of the economy, the degree of responsibility as measured by the number of subordinates, the level of skill as determined by years of formal education, and artistic and other exceptional abilities based partly on natural endowments. These criteria have nothing to do with traditional Marxism and constitute a distortion of the relevant writings by Marx, Engels, and Lenin.

The new mode of payment is obviously partial to administrative and professional workers. First, it makes possible a standard of reward in excess of the value of qualified labor power. Second, the valuation of services is turned over to managers and professionals themselves. Applied to less qualified workers, socialist remuneration encourages the fiction that all are workers who are paid salaries and that higher-paid services do not constitute a form of bureaucratic exploitation. Whereas the capitalists had sought to disguise their profits under the name of "wages of superintendence," as if they too were workers like everybody else, under socialism bureaucratic privilege is disguised under the cover of payment according to the "quantity and quality of work."

No one anticipated that the old mode of payment for the value of labor power, although a distinguishing feature of capitalist exploitation, could be a barrier to bureaucratic exploitation. If managers were paid wages equal to the value of specialized labor power, they would be paid more than ordinary laborers but only three or four times as much. By adding to the value of their skills in the course of exercising them, some would be in a position to recover the surplus value that would be appropriated by the capitalists under the old system. But this would not qualify them to be more than petty exploiters. Let us see why this is so.

We have seen that, after the period of training, the skilled worker continues to add value to his specialized skills in the course of applying them. Since the time spent in exercising them also improves them, it counts as an integral part of their accumulated value in the same way as the time spent during the training period. This consideration calls for a revision of Meek's formula that will take into account this additional factor allowing for the appreciation of specialized skills.

We recall that each hour of skilled labor counts as $1 + t/p$ hours of simple labor, where p is the worker's expected productive life and t hours of simple labor have been expended upon him and by him during the training period. In this formula t/p represents not only the amount of stored up labor in skills transferred hourly to a particular product but also the hourly prorated value of those skills—their prorated cost of production. However, t/p does not represent the appreciation of those skills during the worker's productive life. Their expanded value is represented by the additional sum of n/p, where n hours of simple labor have been spent in applying and simultaneously improving those skills. Each hour of skilled labor will continue to transfer t/p hours of the costs of those skills to a particular product, but for the purpose of calculating the hourly prorated value of each skill we must use the expanded expression $(t + n)/p$. Substituting the values in Sweezy's example—where the period of training is 50,000 hours and the worker's productive life is estimated at 100,000 hours—the value of this particular skill will continue to increase until, just prior to retirement, when $n = p$, it reaches its maximum limit of one and one-half times the hourly value created by simple labor. This is an increase of 300 percent compared to Sweezy's own figure of one-half the value produced by simple labor.

That the value of expertise is one and one-half times the *value produced by simple labor* does not mean that it is one and one-half times the *value of simple labor power*. At a rate of surplus value of 100 percent, the value of simple labor power in an eight-hour day will be the equivalent of four hours of living labor. During the worker's last day prior to retirement, his expertise will have a prorated value of four hours of stored up labor representing the cost of training, plus another eight hours representing the 100,000 hours of prorated value added to his expertise throughout his productive life—a total of twelve hours of simple labor or three times the value of simple labor power. We have here an example of the self-expanding value of expertise that appreciates as a force of production distinct from living labor power and adds to the value of the worker's skills rather than to his products.

Are the benefits of this self-expanding value to its owner enough to offset the losses from having his simple labor power exploited by another? The answer to this question hinges on the distinction between the value of simple labor power, the original value of expertise, and its expanded value. At the end of his first eight-hour day the expert will have added eight hours of new value to his product plus four hours of old value transferred by expertise. The appreciation of his expertise will be insignificant and may be ignored at this point. If commodities sell at their value, how much will he get back from his employer?

The value he retrieves will be equal to the value of his simple labor power (v) plus the depreciated or prorated value of his expertise. In this example eight hours of living labor is the sum of $v + s$, of which s is the amount appropriated by his employer. If the rate of surplus value is 100 percent, v will be equal to four hours of simple labor. Since another four hours will be recovered from the amortized value of his expertise, he will receive back the equivalent of the eight hours of new value he produces. Let us assume that the cost of expertise is borne entirely by the state. Then the state recovers this cost in the form of surplus value and the expert recovers the loss of this surplus value in the form of the prorated value of his expertise. His employer does not exploit, and he is not exploited—neither at the beginning of his career nor, as we shall see, at the end.

Throughout most of his productive life, the expert will receive back from society actually more than he gives. The appreciation of expertise during his final eight-hour day will be anything but insignificant. At that point, its hourly value will have risen from one-half hour to one and one-half hours of simple labor—from four hours daily to twelve hours. But these additional eight hours of self-expanded value are not, like the original prorated value of four hours, transferred to the worker's product as a condition of recovering their cost. This self-expanded value costs only what it costs to apply one's skills. Consequently, the qualified worker now receives something for nothing. He expends eight hours of simple labor $(v + s)$ but gets back four hours in wages (v), plus four hours representing the depreciated value of his original skills, plus eight additional hours representing their prorated self-expanded value —sixteen hours in all. As we have seen, the state recovers the remaining four hours of surplus value (s), which is just enough to compensate it for subsidizing the worker's training.

How much can the highly qualified worker get for nothing? If he is paid the value of his compound labor power—the value of simple labor power plus the total prorated value of his expertise—then the maximum salary he can earn at the end of his productive life will be equal to twice his outlay of living labor or four times the value of simple labor power. He will expend eight hours but will get back the equivalent of sixteen hours for a net gain of eight hours. He will share in the exploitation of other workers but, until his last working hour, more than half his salary will represent the equivalent of his own labors. That makes him at best a petty bureaucrat, not a bureaucrat. *Given our assumption that expertise exchanges at its value, it is impossible to account for the high salaries of bureaucrats under socialism.*

To account for this discrepancy we assume that the qualified worker sells professional services rather than compound labor power and that his payment conforms to a different principle than wages under capitalism. That new principle, formulated in the *Critique of the Gotha Programme,* is payment according to "work" as redefined by Marx's successors to include its quality as well as its quantity. By their own testimony, professional workers contribute qualified services to their chosen fields; they do not sell their labor power, and it is to their advantage not to. Anyone can measure the quantity of a given service, but its quality can be assessed only by professionals.

Only by the progressive restriction of labor power as a commodity, and the displacement of the capitalist labor market by a bureaucratic market for labor and expert services, is it possible to extend the scope of this new principle of remuneration and the corresponding relations of distribution. At the same time the false appearance is created that all workers are members of the same class because they are remunerated according to the same principle. Actually, there is less room for bureaucratic privilege when all workers are paid for the value of their labor power.

The Mechanism of Bureaucratic Exploitation

Underlying the new forms of domination and exploitation under socialism is the transformation of the forms of property in the elementary factors of production. The factors common to all social formations are land, instruments, labor, and organization. Landed property, capital, labor power, and expertise are the forms of property these take under capitalism. Nationalized land, nationalized or collectivized instruments of labor, labor services, and expert services are the forms they take under socialism. Labor power and expert power or expertise are commodities under capitalism; labor and expert services are at most quasicommodities under socialism because their prices are determined more by administrative decisions than by market forces and they are only partly produced for exchange. Under socialism labor power and expertise are abolished as commodities; workers of all grades and qualifications acquire individual property in their services as well as their service capacities; and they also share in the ownership of their products.

The question is how the mechanism of bureaucratic exploitation operates. We may begin by considering how it differs from the profit mechanism under capitalism.

For Marx the rate of surplus value reveals the mechanism underlying capitalist exploitation. There is a rate for individuals, and there is a rate for the whole economy. The same expression measures both: $s' = s/v$, where s is surplus value, v is variable capital, and s' is the rate of surplus value. In *Capital* 1.9 Marx explains the individual rate: "surplus value bears the same ratio to variable capital that surplus labor does to necessary labor, or in other words the rate of surplus value s/v = surplus labor/necessary labor." Here we have the equation of monetary values s/v, representing the materialized labor in commodities, and the corresponding ratio of surplus to necessary labor representing expenditures of living labor. Necessary labor is that required for wages to keep the worker and his family alive; surplus labor is that which produces gross profits for the capitalist.

In *Capital* 3.17 Marx explains the rate for the whole economy. In this case s consists of the total surplus appropriated by productive capitalists in the form of gross profits. These are divided into their components: industrial and commercial profits of enterprise, interest and dividends for functionless capitalists, rents for the owners of land, and the wages and salaries of unproductive workers whose job is to assist the capitalists in exploiting productive workers and in transforming commodities into money. As for v, it consists of the total wages of productive workers. Here the gross and net rates of exploitation differ. The gross rate has already been given: $s' = s/v$. The net rate is $s' = (s - u)/v$, where u represents the wage and salary bill for unproductive workers.

The capitalist rate of surplus value is a function of labor power in its capacity as variable capital. But labor power ceases to be a commodity under socialism; therefore, the rate of surplus value can no longer be expressed as a function of variable capital. If we use the same expressions to measure bureaucratic exploitation, then v will represent the total wages of productive laborers plus that fraction of the salaries for expert technical services in payment for producing values, s will represent total surplus value as under capitalism, and u will represent wages for unproductive labor services only. Thus $s - u$ is the fat portion of the salaries of bureaucrats and petty bureaucrats covering their share in the exploitation of other workers, while $v + u$ is the total wages for labor services plus that fraction of expert salaries in payment for producing values. Total paychecks are equal to $(s - u) + (v + u) = s + v$. This sum equals the amount of new value created and distributed under conditions of simple reproduction.

Under capitalism, Marx points out in *Capital* 3.9, the collective capitalist dominates the distribution of total surplus value through the formation of a general or average rate of profit. The individual capitalist's share in the total surplus is a function not of his own variable capital but rather of the variable capital of the capitalists as a whole. "The individual capitalist . . . rightly believes that his profit is not derived solely from the labor employed by him, or in his line of production . . . [but] is due to the aggregate exploitation of labor on the part of the total social capital." Each capitalist demands and tends to receive a share of the total surplus value proportional to the amount of capital he owns.

Under socialism the place of the collective capitalist is taken by Marx's collective worker. There everyone is a worker in the general sense of that term; everyone performs a socially useful function for which he demands a share proportional to the quantity and quality of his work. Each demands a share not just of surplus value but of the total new value created. Here the average paycheck takes the place of the average profit under capitalism. Just as the average profit multiplied by the number of capitalists equals the total surplus appropriated by capitalists, so the average paycheck multiplied by the number of workers equals total wages and salaries. *The average paycheck becomes the dividing line between those workers who get something for nothing in the form of above-average paychecks, and those who get nothing for something in the form of below-average paychecks.*

In the perspective of the collective capitalist, the difference between functioning (socially necessary) and functionless (socially unnecessary) capitalists is irrelevant to determining their respective shares of surplus value. It is not the kind of capital they own that is important but the fact that they are all equally capitalists. Similarly, in the perspective of the collective worker under actually existing socialism, the difference between productive and unproductive workers is irrelevant to determining their share of the new value created. What is important is that they are all equally workers, that each fulfills a socially necessary function and a socially assigned task in the collective division of labor.

Under socialism, as under capitalism, the production of surplus value is inextricably tied to the form in which it is appropriated. The source of surplus value is no longer labor power in the form of variable capital but rather the labor services of productive workers who produce more than they consume. The appropriation of this surplus takes the form of above-average paychecks for expert services that are effectively subsidized by below-average paychecks for the services of productive and unproductive wage earners.

That the mechanism of bureaucratic exploitation is a function of the average paycheck is an insight that can be traced to Lenin. Although he denied that the bureaucracy is a class, his critique of its privileged paychecks suggests that it is an exploiting stratum. His critique indicates further that payment in excess of the average paycheck is a form of exploitation that is not capitalist but bureaucratic.

Let us examine what Lenin said on the subject. In chapter 5, section 4, of *The State and Revolution* (1917), he says that popular accounting and control are the *"chief* things necessary for the organizing and correct functioning of the *first phase* of communist society." Their economic importance lies in the fact that they are indispensable in preventing the "intellectual gentry" from acquiring salaries in excess of the wages of average workers. Payment according to the amount of work is interpreted by Lenin to mean that all "should work equally, should regularly do their share of work, and should receive equal pay." A few passages later he reiterates this point: "The whole of society [under the first phase of communism] will have become one office and one factory, with equal work and equal pay." Although unequal pay is required for unequal amounts of work, everyone will be required to work the same amount; therefore, the average wage will be the only paycheck. As there is no reason for believing that bureaucrats and petty bureaucrats work harder than skilled manual workers, above-average paychecks constitute a form of exploitation. And, because it is not capitalist exploitation, it seems reasonable to call it bureaucratic.

Lenin defines bureaucrats in chapter 6, section 3, as "privileged persons detached from the masses and standing over them." He so broadens Marx's definition that it explicitly includes the functionaries of political parties and of trade unions—implicitly, all administrative personnel not involved in the production and circulation of commodities. The privileges that constitute the *"essence* of bureaucracy" are those associated with the functionary's job: first, tenure in office; second, payment in excess of the wages of average workers; third, executive powers independent of the legislative body or other organs of popular sovereignty.

If it were not for these combined privileges, the job of administrator would be like any other working-class job, which is to say that the functionary becomes a bureaucrat only because of such privileges. So argued Lenin in criticizing bureaucratic projections of a new social order:

"From what Kautsky says, one might think that if elective officials remain under socialism [the lowest stage of communism in Lenin's sense], bureaucrats and bureaucracy will also remain! This is entirely incorrect." Marx used the example of the commune to show that under socialism the functionaries cease to be bureaucrats "*in the degree* that election is supplemented by the right of instant recall; when, *besides this*, their pay is brought down to the level of the pay of the average worker; when, *besides this*, parliamentary institutions are replaced by 'working bodies, executive and legislative at the same time' [working bodies of managers, technicians, and accountants directly responsive to the people in arms]." Although the leveling of wages is not in fact a principle of distribution in postcapitalist societies, Lenin was right in believing that above-average paychecks constitute a form of exploitation distinct from capitalist profits, interest, dividends, and rents.

What then is the mechanism of bureaucratic exploitation? The source of surplus value under socialism is not "variable capital"—the capacity of labor power to produce a value greater than its own value —but the assignment of a value to labor services that is less than what they produce. Unlike the capitalist mechanism of exploitation based on the commodity labor power and the operation of market forces, the socialist mechanism is based on an economic plan in which services are assessed according to a hierarchy of ranks within the limits imposed by a fixed budget. The capitalist pumps out a surplus by paying for the full value of labor power; the bureaucrat sucks it out by *not paying* labor services their full value. In each case a different type of exploitation is the source of a different kind of privilege: profits under capitalism, salaries under socialism.

What happens to the bureaucratic and petty bureaucratic classes when capitalism gives way to socialism? They survive in a different form independent of the old relations of production. As capital ceases to be the dominant form of exploitation, functionaries cease to pump out surplus value in its bourgeois form of profit. Under capitalism the mechanism of bureaucratic exploitation operates in an auxiliary capacity alongside the dominant capitalist mechanism; bureaucratic exploitation serves the interest mainly of capitalist exploitation. Under socialism these roles are inverted. Workers are no longer exploited for the sake of capitalists; bureaucrats have their own reasons for exploiting them based on the new and simplified class structure.

Without the capitalists to confront, bureaucrats and petty bureaucrats turn against one another. Beginning with the Bolshevik Revolution the conflicts internal to socialist societies can be traced to the struggles within and between these two classes for a redistribution of the economic surplus. The mechanism of bureaucratic exploitation has yet to be recognized in socialist countries. When that happens the turn will have come for the new working class to become politically active in the struggle against its own ruling class. Then one may expect a new struggle between communists and socialists.

6

The Soviet Stumbling Block

The recognition of a bureaucratic social formation obliges us to recon-
sider the nature of communist regimes. The principal stumbling block
to understanding them is still a distorted perspective of the nature and
destiny of the Soviet Union. Marxist critics of the USSR have put forth
four principal interpretations of Soviet social reality: first, that the Soviet bureaucracy is a sector or fraction of a postrevolutionary state bourgeoisie; second, that it constitutes a nonbourgeois ruling class under
conditions of a bureaucratic capitalist order; third, that it is a postcapitalist ruling class governing on the basis of new bureaucratic but noncapitalist relations of production; and fourth, that it is a new ruling
class or stratum representing a bureaucratic order with roots in a precapitalist "semi-Asiatic" social formation. I exclude from this list the
Trotskyist criticism of the Soviet Union as a "deformed workers' state"
because it rejects the various theses of a "new class," whether bourgeois
or bureaucratic, and reaffirms the original Leninist view of a transitional society between capitalism and communism. Unlike these other
criticisms of the new social order, the Trotskyist critique does not agree
that the Russian Revolution, as a communist one, definitely failed.

The forcible suppression of communist tendencies in the Soviet Union has been interpreted by one group of Marxist critics as not only the
perpetuation or restoration of capitalism but also as the rule of a new
state bourgeoisie. The basis of this new class is found in the collective
possession and control, if not the legal ownership, of nationalized
means of production in the form of "state capital." These critics differ
over the purely political or economic character of the proletarian revolution and subsequent counterrevolution, the dating of each, and the
precise nature of the new ruling class.

Another group of critics agrees that the dictatorship of the proletariat
was overthrown. But they advance a novel thesis of their own: the Sovi-

et Union is a form of "capitalism without capitalists." Although the economic basis of the new ruling class is the collective control of the means of production, the possession of "state capital" does not make its possessors capitalists. On the contrary, the new men of power are said to make up a bureaucratic class.

A third interpretation anticipates my own analysis of Soviet reality. According to it there was both a political and economic revolution in the USSR. Like the preceding criticisms, it finds in the de facto ownership of nationalized means of production the clue to the nature of the new ruling class; but it identifies the new rulers with a managerial- or bureaucratic-collectivist class, while denying that the corresponding economic system is a capitalist one. The new order is a postcapitalist social formation.

Finally, there is the thesis that the Soviet Union is a post-Asiatic rather than postcapitalist bureaucratic order. In this perspective it did not emerge from a struggle between the bourgeoisie and proletariat of capitalist societies but is a parallel social formation at roughly the same level of social and political development as capitalism. Both formations are said to be converging on a future communist society but on the basis of alternative methods of development: the capitalist and noncapitalist roads.

Let us see where each of these interpretations fails.

The New State Bourgeoisie
The theory of a new state bourgeoisie in the socialist countries came in response to the abandonment of centralized planning by Yugoslavia during the 1950s and the scrapping of the dictatorship of the proletariat for a "state of the whole people" by the Soviet Union during the sixties. This two-pronged criticism was first systematically developed by the Chinese Communists in their opening salvo against Yugoslav and Soviet "revisionism" in 1963–64. In two pamphlets, *Is Yugoslavia a Socialist Country?* and *On Khrushchev's Phoney Communism*, the Chinese communists argued that Yugoslavia's adoption of market socialism and the Soviet's adoption of a new program at its party's Twenty-second Congress were tantamount to a peaceful retreat on the road back to capitalism.

In the West the first criticism represented by Paul Sweezy and the second by Charles Bettelheim were aired in the pages of *Monthly Review*. Beginning in the March 1964 issue on Yugoslavia and continuing with his articles on the Soviet Union (November 1967) and Czechoslovakia (October 1968), Sweezy argued that the clue to understanding the tendency toward capitalist restoration in those countries was the retreat from centralized planning. Replying to Sweezy in the March 1969 issue, Bettelheim claimed that the key is the abandonment of the dictatorship of the proletariat. The political rather than the economic factor is decisive, he argued, the loss of power to a new Soviet bourgeoisie. Sweezy then conceded that both factors are decisive: they are related not as cause and effect but dialectically through a process of reciprocal causation.

Bettelheim went on to develop his thesis in a major historical study, *Les luttes de classes en URSS*. The first volume covering the period 1917–23, appeared in 1974, the second on the period 1923–30 appeared in 1977, and other volumes are expected to follow. In his review of the first volume in the November 1974 and January 1975 issues of *Monthly Review*, Sweezy calls it a work of monumental importance for the international socialist movement. At the same time, he admits that nothing in the way of factual evidence or theoretical argument presented by Bettelheim persuades him that economic planning in the Soviet Union is mainly a cover for the laws of capitalist accumulation. Sweezy is especially skeptical of Bettelheim's thesis that centralized planning strengthens rather than weakens the powers of the state bourgeoisie. For Sweezy, writing in 1974–75, these questions were still wide open.

They ceased to be controversial by the time of Sweezy's October 1977 review of the second volume. By then he had accepted Bettelheim's premise that the new industrialization and planning policies initiated as early as 1926 "reflected a sort of alliance between the old Bolsheviks and the nascent state bourgeoisie." In effect, the original labor-peasant alliance basic to Lenin's New Economic Policy was subtly undermined by the party's leaders in favor of an alliance with the new bourgeoisie. Because this rising class "had common interests but was not fully conscious of them," Sweezy interprets it as a class in itself rather than for itself. Nonetheless, he argues that it gradually replaced the working class as the party's social base. When the surplus that could be squeezed out of the peasantry proved to be too little to sustain the projected rate of industrialization, it became necessary "to add the working class itself to the sources of tribute." After that it was only a matter of time for the new class to infiltrate the party and take it over.

What are some of the features of this new class? Turning to a direct discussion of Bettelheim's work, we find in footnote 54 of his preface to the first volume the following characterization of the "bureaucratic state bourgeoisie." These new bourgeois are distinct from the direct producers because "they have effective control of the means of production and of the products that formally belong to the state." But they do not own them. The new ruling class is defined exclusively by economic relations of domination and exploitation.

In defense of this departure from conventional Marxism, Bettelheim claims that the relations of production and appropriation rather than juridical forms of property are basic to the Marxist definition of class. So far we may agree with him, although we should add that ownership is a necessary, if not a sufficient, condition of Marx's definition. The abolition of bourgeois property in the means of production, Bettelheim argues, does not suffice to put an end to antagonistic classes. We can also agree with this claim, except that he interprets it in an un-Marxist way. For him the antagonistic classes that remain are still Marx's bourgeoisie and proletariat, only in a different form. The place of the old bourgeoisie is filled by a new state bourgeoisie that leaves the social production relations of capitalism essentially intact. Thus, in section 2 of the preface, Bettelheim characterizes the Soviet state as a "capitalist state of a particular type."

The composition of the state bourgeoisie is described in part 2 of the first volume. It consists of the managers of state enterprises and the organizers of new industrial branches, plus highly qualified engineers and technicians. Below them are the state petty bourgeois consisting of low-grade administrators and white-collar employees in business and industry, including engineering and technical specialists with comparatively modest qualifications. Bettelheim's choice of terminology is unfortunate and it is a far cry from Marx's own.

For Marx these workers belong to the top and middle strata of the proletariat. At least, Bettelheim is factually correct in arguing that existing income differentials between high-, middle-, and low-qualified workers require that we include them in separate exploiting, semiexploiting, and exploited classes. There is nothing un-Marxist in this effort to reclassify the members of Marx's proletariat whose present composition differs so markedly from what it was a century ago. Bettelheim's categories are misleading, however, as is his notion that control without ownership suffices to define the state bureaucracy as a state bourgeoisie.

Let us concentrate on the positive features of Bettelheim's contribution translated into my terminology of bureaucratic and petty-bureaucratic classes. Bettelheim shows that the elements of a petty-bureaucratic class were present in the Soviet Union from its beginning. The work code adopted by the revolutionary government on 10 October 1918 established that "wages" had to be differentiated on the basis not only of hardship and intensity of labor but also of "degree of responsibility" and "qualification." This was followed by a decree on 21 February

1919 fixing the monthly wage at 600 rubles and establishing a ceiling on administrative salaries of 3,000 rubles. In April of the same year another decree permitted high functionaries of the Soviet Central Executive Committee to receive a monthly salary of 2,000 rubles. As Bettelheim interprets it, this signified "a partial abandonment of *partmax*"—the party maximum prohibiting any member from accepting a wage superior to that of a skilled manual worker.

This wage and salary spread of 5:1 would have been unacceptable to communists prior to the October Revolution. Such income differences were tolerated in 1918–19 only as a temporary measure, as a compromise imposed by the class struggle, by the party's lack of specialized cadres, and by its need for the services of mislabeled "bourgeois specialists." Only much later, Bettelheim notes, did still higher income differences become a permanent institution justified by a distorted application of the Marxist principle, "to each according to his work."

In part 3 of the second volume Bettelheim shows how this wage spread rose to 8:1 in 1924, from there spiraling to 30:1 in 1926. In a survey in March 1924 of a Moscow metallurgical plant the following differentials in pay were reported in terms of the new currency: unskilled worker, 16 rubles; foundry worker, 32 rubles; department head, 77 rubles; director, 116 rubles. Two years later in March 1926, he continues, "the wages of workers were frequently of the order of 13 to 20 rubles per month, while a director could receive up to 400 rubles." At the same time, directors belonging to the party were permitted to receive an average of 188 rubles or approximately fourteen times the minimum wage. As this was several times higher than the maximum for skilled manual workers, here was another exception to the rule of *partmax*.

The year 1926 was a "*decisive year*," says Bettelheim. During the second semester of 1925 the first annual plan was formulated by the State Planning Commission (Gosplan) covering the period 1925–26. Although it contained only guidelines and was not strictly obligatory, it marked the beginning of a new epoch of fixing pay rates and work norms independently of the workers. Prior to 1926, Bettelheim notes, wages and norms of work were established through collective bargaining contracts, but beginning in September 1926 the party's politbureau, after consulting with the Supreme Council of the National Economy and the trade unions, fixed these rates as part of a new overall system of economic planning. Collective bargaining survived in the negotiations between the trade unions and the management of industrial trusts, but only within limits fixed by the plan. Thus, even before the inception of the First Five-Year Plan in 1929, workers had lost control over their relations to the means of production.

Although workers' self-management never took hold in the Soviet Union, before 1926 workers exercised control over the economy through the party and trade unions. The end of effective collective bargaining and the "autonomization" of the administrative apparatus in charge of economic planning undermined these elements of workers' power. The system of one-man management ceased to be provisional and was henceforth justified as an essential condition of economic planning. As a result, the workers remained in the condition of a proletariat, says Bettelheim, while high-paid experts and administrators retained their status as a state bourgeoisie.

Bettelheim does not tell us when the nascent state bourgeoisie dismantled the dictatorship of the proletariat and rose to the position of a new ruling class. At most he indicates that it happened after 1930. We shall have to wait for the third and possibly the fourth volume for an elaboration and dating of the political counterrevolution.

A somewhat different thesis of a state bourgeoisie appeared during the interval between the publication of Bettelheim's first and second volumes: Martin Nicolaus's *Restoration of Capitalism in the USSR.* Also influenced by the Chinese criticism of the Soviet Union, this work differs from Bettelheim's in arguing from the outset that both a political and an economic revolution was made by the Russian proletariat. The first was undermined by a political counterrevolution during the 1950s, the second by an economic counterrevolution during the sixties.

Nicolaus dates the transformation of the Soviet "bureaucratic stratum" into a new "bureaucrat-capitalist class" during the early years of Khrushchev's ascendancy. The stage was set by Khrushchev's anti-Stalin campaign launched at the Twentieth Congress of the CPSU in February 1956. In what follows I present Nicolaus's interpretation of the events that ended with the completion of the "bourgeois counterrevolution" and the launching of the New Economic System by Premier Kosygin in September 1965. Although not a monument of scholarship like Bettelheim's work, Nicolaus's book is deserving of consideration.

Khrushchev's anti-Stalin campaign encouraged a wave of "revisionism" throughout Eastern Europe, culminating in the Polish and Hungarian uprisings in the summer and fall of 1956. Khrushchev also proposed a decentralization package in February 1957 that included such measures as selling the state-owned machine and tractor stations to the collective farms and replacing the central planning ministries for each industry with a territorial reorganization and a hundred or so regional economic councils. However, opposition to his new political line of "peaceful competition," "peaceful coexistence," "peaceful transition," and to his new economic policy of decentralization made him increasingly isolated within the party's top command. To persist in this new course Khrushchev would have to alter the basis of his support within the party and the country.

The tranformation of the Soviet bureaucracy into a new bourgeois class began in June 1957, Nicolaus argues, with a showdown in the party's presidium. By a vote of 7 to 4 Khrushchev was formally removed as the party's first secretary. Instead of resigning he presented his case to the party's central committee, a lower body, and turned for support to Marshal Zhukov, the minister of defense. According to Polish press reports, Zhukov threatened Molotov, Malenkov, and Kaganovich, who dominated the presidium, with the release of incriminating documents concerning their role during the Great Purges. Speaking as he did for the entire Soviet military establishment, his threats were a warning that the armed forces would not tolerate Khrushchev's removal by the Molotov-Malenkov-Kaganovich "antiparty group."

The following events suggest that something like a military coup occurred. Khrushchev mustered the necessary votes, and Zhukov was promoted to full membership in the presidium. Molotov became the new ambassador to Mongolia; Malenkov was reduced to running a power station in Siberia; and their principal supporters were fired from leading posts or expelled from the party and the government. For Nicolaus, the "bourgeois officer corps" had decided the outcome.

This "bourgeois counterrevolution" began with Khrushchev's decisive victory over the Stalinist Old Guard. The seizure of state power by Khrushchev's forces prepared the way for "the expropriation of the Soviet proletariat and the end of the socialist period of Soviet history." The means of production were still predominantly state owned and controlled, but the state had ceased to be the property of the working class. Although the key centers of production continued to function as before, the proletariat had been expropriated at the level of the political superstructure. This bourgeois counterrevolution was not completed until after Khrushchev's fall in October 1964 and the launching of the New Economic System by Premier Kosygin in September 1965. Commodity relations were then restored for the principal factors of production. Only then was the central plan effectively scrapped in favor of the market. As Nicolaus comments at the end of chapter 14: "Instead of subjecting the enterprises to planning, they virtually (and eventually, completely) subjected planning to the enterprises; instead of eliminating the market in means of production and labor power, they expanded, legalized and strengthened it; instead of eliminating profiteering, they raised it to a principle—in short, instead of constructing socialism, the Kosygin reforms restored capitalism."

What kind of capitalism was restored in the USSR? The reform measures introduced by Khrushchev and continued by Kosygin share with Lenin's New Economic Policy (NEP) "the commanding role given to profits, the freedom given managers to engage in commodity exchange." A crucial difference, Nicolaus suggests at the end of chapter 2, was that "Khrushchev and his followers portrayed their policies as an irreversible advance to communism, while Lenin, with the frankness and truthfulness of a Bolshevik, proclaimed openly that NEP was a temporary retreat to state capitalism." Did the New Economic System introduced by Kosygin also involve the restoration of state capitalism? Not according to Nicolaus, who concludes by characterizing it as "state-monopoly capitalism." Kosygin's economic reforms represent a combination of the state capitalism of the NEP and the monopoly capitalism of a still earlier period, "a second edition of the main line in the original development of capitalism in Russia, which Lenin analyzed the first time around in 1899!" At least, national economic planning was not a dead issue under the NEP, whereas Kosygin's New Economic System forecloses on the possibility of centralized state planning. Thus, Nicolaus concludes that the Soviet Union today represents a partially developed, incipient form of state capitalism in which capitalist monopolies make the fundamental decisions.

Three major arguments are advanced in support of this thesis. The first, given in chapter 5, is that capitalist commodity production has been restored in the USSR. Workers have been transformed from owners of the means of production into their appendages and the means of production have been converted from social property into commodities. As a result of the first change, workers no longer have a claim to their jobs, they are deprived of their basic rights at the point of production, and their labor power is turned into a commodity. As a result of the second change, economic planning has been subordinated to the market mechanism. Nicolaus concludes that these fundamental changes have given "free play to the drive by the management of each enterprise to increase 'its' profits to the maximum" and that profits have been placed in command. What Nicolaus overlooks is that commodity production and production for profit are not necessarily capitalist. They also exist under socialism where profit is an index of economic efficiency rather than a major form of distribution.

The second argument is advanced at the beginning of chapter 13. Nicolaus claims that public property loses its socialist character when the state ceases to be the property of the working class. Once workers lose control of the state, they lose control over the means of production; the direct producers are transformed into wage laborers and the means of production into capital. When Khrushchev's "bourgeois forces" succeeded in their palace coup of 1957 they expropriated the Soviet workers and paved the way for a restoration of capitalism. Nicolaus is wrong: the workers were expropriated as early as Stalin's Second Revolution beginning in 1929, and this act of expropriation did not restore capitalism but laid the foundations for bureaucratic socialism.

Nicolaus's third argument is given at the end of chapter 18. Managers of Soviet industry are transformed into capitalists because they perform capitalist functions: "The fact that the director is appointed and removed from above and occupies a definte slot in the bureaucracy does not alter the character of his function." Like Marx's capitalist, the Soviet executive strives for increased profits for reinvestment purposes. Assuming that the professional manager functions as capital personified, Nicolaus insists he must be a capitalist: "He is a bureaucrat-capitalist. . . . put into his post in order to function as a capitalist and, should he fail in this role, the bureaucracy relieves him of his duties." His capitalist function is decisive, not his role as bureaucrat. The "proof" of this claim lies in "the shreds and tatters to which Soviet directors, as capitalists, have reduced the power of the bureaucracy . . . and the central planning machinery." But decentralization is not proof that Soviet managers personify capitalist functions or that they make up a Soviet bourgeoisie.

Further evidence for a capitalist restoration in the USSR is presented in the penultimate chapter in answer to the question, "Who benefits from this 'new economic system?' " Besides underscoring the alleged existence of some 13,000 socialist millionaires, Nicolaus claims that bonuses from the "material incentives fund" amounted after 1965 to approximately 23 percent of the base salaries of directors and their immediate staff. This percentage must have risen during the seventies when Soviet economists acknowledged the simultaneous operation of more than thirty different bonus systems. Because bonuses represent a share in the profits, Nicolaus sees them as a specifically capitalist mode of distribution. Unlike salaries, they reflect the overall performance of the enterprise, not individual skills, and are based on the collective monopoly of the means of production by a particular class. Nicolaus concludes that the bourgeois character of Soviet managers is evident in this specifically capitalist form of sharing in the economic surplus.

Most of the arguments for a new Soviet bourgeoisie mistake profits from state or collective enterprises for profits from the collective ownership of capital. There is a difference. Unlike profits from modern corporations or joint-stock companies, which take a collective form, profits from state-owned or worker-managed enterprises go to rewarding managers rather than owners of the means of production. Shared profits in the form of bonuses are payments for above-standard performance in the exercise of managerial skills; those skills are divorced from property and inheritance rights. Even in Yugoslavia the distributed profits from industrial collectives do not represent a share in collectively owned capital. Factories are "leased" from the state and take the form not of capital but of so-called social property. The possessors of social property do not own it: they cannot liquidate their combined assets or distribute the proceeds among themselves. Soviet managers and Yugoslav factory councils lack a monopoly of the means of production. Such a monopoly, for Marx, is a defining characteristic of capital in its full, concrete sense.

The arguments for a Soviet bourgeoisie miss the fundamental difference between those who traditionally owned the means of production and those who today collectively control them. The terms "capital," "capitalist," and "bourgeois" effectively hide or misrepresent an actual state of affairs by inflating the similarities and by deflating the differences between these two groups. These terms are no less misleading than the definition of socialism as a lower stage of communism. In its doctrinaire use, the term "socialism" is so narrow as to be inapplicable anywhere; the term "capitalism" is so broad as to be applicable everywhere. The interpretations of Soviet reality in terms of a "bureaucratic bourgeoisie" make no distinction between a state bourgeoisie and a state bureaucracy, between state capitalism and bureaucratic statism, between capitalist and bureaucratic exploitation. They must be rejected.

Another mistake of these critics is to assume that salaries as well as profits tend to be maximized under the new order. Collective control of the means of production supposedly guarantees an increasing share of the economic surplus. It is true that in Russia bureaucratic salaries that had become practically extinct during the period of war communism were revived under the New Economic Policy and extended to party members during the thirties. That is because the proletarian revolution was undermined by the First Five-Year Plan launched in 1929. As the Stalinist bureaucracy became entrenched during the plan, its salaries began to escalate. A plateau was reached during the late fifties, however, after which the income spread remained comparatively stable. In 1966 the difference in pay between the highest-paid bureaucrats and the lowest-paid workers in the Soviet Union was approximately 30:1 —roughly what it had been in 1926. If we are to believe Trotsky in *The Revolution Betrayed*, the spread in pay was significantly higher during the thirties when Stalin was campaigning against "wage equalization." But that was an exceptionally critical period in the struggle to give the intelligentsia a material stake in the new order.

The East European experience contrasts sharply with Soviet experience. Because of the role of the Red Army in liberating those countries and their resulting "revolutions from above," there was no proletarian dictatorship to dismantle. Unlike Russia, they passed directly from bourgeois to petty-bureaucratic and bureaucratic forms of domination. In both the German Democratic Republic and Czechoslovakia, two industrially advanced countries with a higher per-capita standard of living than in the Soviet Union, the intelligentsia did not feel threatened by a proletariat intent on leveling incomes. There was no need there for a campaign against "wage equalization." Bureaucratic salaries were reduced with only moderate opposition and have yet to recover their prewar levels. Throughout the rest of Eastern Europe bureaucratic workers also experienced a paring down of the huge salary differentials they enjoyed before the war.

The continuing alliance of the bureaucracy with the working class in the struggle against internal obstacles to development and world capitalist reaction may account in part for the relatively low salaries in most socialist countries compared to what they were before the revolution. The influence of communist ideology has kept in check bureaucratic efforts to obtain a greater share of the economic surplus. After the establishment of socialism, several decades are required before the bureaucracy can firmly consolidate its power. Even if the objective and subjective conditions permitted greater salary differentials, there is no prima facie reason for identifying the cause of such differentials with the bureaucracy's collective possession of the state rather than with its monopoly of a professional education. Each of the interpretations that makes this illicit identification is mistaken.

Capitalism without Capitalists
A more refined interpretation of Soviet reality agrees with the claim of capitalist restoration but identifies the bureaucracy as a new ruling class. This is the thesis of capitalism without capitalists, of new capitalist relations of production without a bourgeoisie.

Tony Cliff's *Russia: A Marxist Analysis* offers the ablest defense of this thesis. Instead of setting the date of the political counterrevolution in 1957, Cliff traces it as far back as 1929. Unlike the other interpreters of capitalist restoration, Cliff holds that the political counterrevolution followed rather than preceded the restoration of capitalism in the USSR. Although designed as a temporary measure, the NEP restored capitalism; the counterrevolution of 1929 went further by abolishing the workers' state. The counterrevolution was basically political in character, but at the same time it transformed a state capitalism under workers' control into what Cliff calls "bureaucratic state capitalism." Thus, a new ruling class emerged consisting of bureaucrats, not bureaucrat-capitalists.

What kind of capitalism is this? In chapter 6 Cliff says it is a capitalism without the capitalist class. It is important to note the differences between this form of state capitalism and one in which the bulk of the surplus is consumed by bondholders. Cliff thinks that in the USSR a bureaucratic class rules on the basis of capitalist relations of production but without the fetters on accumulation imposed by the owners of government bonds; for such owners milk the state as they formerly milked their workers. To qualify the Soviet system either as a bureaucratic state regime or as state capitalism is correct, he concludes, but not sufficient. It combines both features: "The most precise name for the Russian society is therefore Bureaucratic State Capitalism."

Cliff bases his interpretation on three principal points. First, the Stalinist bureaucracy qualifies as a class rather than a stratum. Following Marx's usage of "ideological professions" to designate the priests, lawyers, and so on, who have a monopoly of education, Cliff distinguishes between highly paid bureaucrats and ordinary wage laborers. The bureaucrats are said to have a class monopoly over what Bukharin called the "means of mental production."

This point is reinforced by a second one: the Soviet bureaucracy "owns" the state. Juridically, there is a complete separation in the USSR between the function of ownership and that of management: the state owns, and the bureaucrats manage. In fact, ownership is in the hands of the bureaucrats as a collective body: "it is vested in the state *of* the bureaucracy" (italics mine). The state appears as the employer, the bureaucrats as employees; but in reality only bureaucrats do the hiring and firing. Only they determine the division of surplus value between the state and themselves as individuals.

Cliff's third point is that bureaucrats are the personification of capital without forming part of the capitalist class. Marx had written in *Capital* 1:24: "Except as personified capital, the capitalist has no historical value, and no right to that historical existence. . . . [In] so far as he is personified in capital, it is not values in use and the enjoyment of them but exchange value and its augmentation that spur him into action." Cliff asks: Is it not the same for Soviet managers? Whoever has control of capital and functions as a capitalist is also the personification of capital. What is basic to capitalism is not the appropriation or consumption of surplus value in the traditional forms of profit, interest, dividends, and rents but its accumulation: "Consumption of a part of the surplus product by the exploiters is not specific to capitalism. . . . What *is* specific to capitalism is accumulation for accumulation's sake. . . . Under a state capitalism which evolved gradually from monopoly capitalism, the bondholders would appear mainly as consumers while the state would appear as the accumulator." Although different from the capitalist class, the Soviet bureaucracy personifies the historical mission of accumulation for its own sake, which defines the capitalist mode of production. And it does so in its present form because the "more the relative weight of the factor of *control* increases as against that of bondholding . . . [and] the more the dividends are subordinated to internal accumulation by the corporation or the state-owner, the more purely does capitalism reveal itself." Although state capitalism is a higher form of capitalism than monopoly capitalism, bureaucratic state capitalism is the highest form of all.

Cliff's interpretation is supported by a number of writers who, like Cliff himself, were originally part of the Trotskyist movement but later left the Fourth International. For these defectors Russia was no longer a deformed workers' state but had degenerated into something worse. The USSR had abolished every vestige of workers' control; it had systematically looted the peoples' democracies of Eastern Europe; it had imposed unfavorable terms of trade upon them; it had expelled Yugoslavia from the Cominform and raised an economic blockade against it. These events followed by the organization of the Warsaw Pact and the division of the world into two military blocs suggested that Russia had become an imperialist power.

The most important split from the Fourth International occurred in France where the splitters founded a new journal called *Socialisme ou Barbarie* (1949–65). The second issue contained a 75-page essay by Cornelius Castoriadis (pseudonym: Pierre Chaulieu) entitled "Les rapports de production en Russie"—one of the first attempts to define Soviet economic reality as a system of capitalism without capitalists. Castoriadis argued that capital survived in the USSR in the form of self-expanding value, in the domination of dead or abstract labor over living, and in accumulation for its own sake. He claimed that in Russia the functions of the traditional capitalist were being performed by salaried employees and that the working class in the Soviet Union was being exploited at an even fiercer rate than in the West.

Bureaucrats rather than capitalists, he argued, are the new exploiters. They control the state but do not own it. By virtue of this control, they have a monopoly of the forces of production, which means that those who work for the state really work for the bureaucracy. The workers do not sell their labor power. The Russian worker cannot dispose freely of himself because he is no longer a commodity; his labor power belongs to the state and is nationalized like the other forces of production. Castoriadis cites the role of internal passports and "labor books" that inhibit labor mobility, the forced condition of labor that ties the worker to his job until he is assigned elsewhere or receives permission to move, and the absence of a labor market where wage rates vary with supply and demand. Everyone must work on terms unilaterally imposed by the bureaucracy. This has effectively transformed the Russian proletariat into a class of industrial bondsmen. Ironically, the two great classes essential to capitalism—bourgeoisie and proletariat—have been eliminated without issuing in Marx's communist society. Instead, we have a new working class in addition to a new ruling class.

Castoriadis concluded that the Soviet system is an instance neither of "bureaucratic collectivism" nor of "state capitalism." To call the USSR a bureaucratic collectivist state *underestimates* the extent of capitalist survivals: the role of capital as self-expanding value, the production and accumulation of surplus value, and the struggle over its division. He objected to calling it state capitalism because that *overestimates* the extent of capitalist survivals by negating the fundamental difference between the Russian regime and traditional capitalism. According to Castoriadis, the most accurate characterization of the Soviet system is "bureaucratic capitalism," in which the bureaucracy is the personification of capital or self-expanding value independent of its ownership but in which the capitalist as the traditional owner of the means of production has disappeared.

This last point escapes the predicament faced by Nicolaus: the identification of those who perform a capitalist function as necessarily capitalists. Nicolaus conflates the functionary of the capitalist not only with the functioning capitalist but also with the functionless capitalist, with mere stockholders and bondholders. This was not Marx's view of the matter.

For Marx the capitalist function is neither a necessary nor a sufficient condition of membership in the capitalist class. It is not a necessary condition because, as he notes in *Capital* 3.23, "interest-bearing capital is capital as *property*, as distinct from capital as a *function*"—the owners of mere property in capital are absentee capitalists. It is not a sufficient condition because "the mere manager who has no title whatever to the capital, whether through borrowing it or otherwise, performs all the real functions pertaining to the functioning capitalist, only the functionary remains and the capitalist disappears as superfluous from the productive process."

Here are three different figures commanding as many different forms of revenue. Interest is claimed by *functionless capitalists*; profits of enterprise are pocketed by *functioning capitalists;* salaries are paid to *functionaries of the capitalists.* These are not three persons in one, as Nicolaus would have it. Although the functioning capitalist belongs to the same class as the functionless capitalist, the bureaucrats hired to perform capitalist functions are not capitalists at all. At least, Castoriadis separates these concepts by distinguishing noncapitalists who personify capitalist functions from capitalists who may or may not personify them.

It is enough to own capital for its owner to be a capitalist. What makes the employer of borrowed capital a capitalist is not the function he performs but his limited ownership of other people's capital. As Marx comments in the same chapter, joint-stock companies "separate the work of management as a function from the ownership of capital, *be it self-owned or borrowed"* (italics mine). And in the same paragraph he speaks of a restricted title to capital that comes from borrowing it.

The borrowing of capital by salaried managers of a corporation is unlike the borrowing of capital by an entrepreneur who has his own business—for the corporation is not the collective property of its functionaries. As Marx says in *Capital* 3.27, the formation of stock companies results in the "transformation of the actually functioning capitalist into a mere manager, administrator of other people's capital." Unlike functioning capitalists, these functionaries lack even a limited title to the capital they employ; hence, they are not capitalists.

The principal weakness in these two accounts of the Soviet regime is their excessively abstract use of the term "capital." Contrary to these critics, the terms "capital" and "self-expanding value" are not interchangeable. Expertise is also a form of self-expanding value. What makes self-expanding value "capital" is the private ownership of the means of production used to hire wage labor. As this relation of production is absent in the Soviet Union, so is capital in the strict meaning of the term.

The confusion of self-expanding value with capital lies at the root of several other errors. First, the bureaucrats personify the self-expanding value of expertise, not the self-expanding value of capital. Second, although "accumulation for its own sake" is a necessary condition of capitalism, it is also essential to postcapitalist societies. The fact that the Soviet Union practices accumulation for its own sake does not suffice to characterize the new order as a form of bureaucratic capitalism. Third, those who personify state capital are those who own state capital and receive the bulk of their income from it rather than from expertise. This state capital takes the form *not* of collectively controlled means of production but of state bonds at a fixed rate of interest. Fourth, the owners of state capital are not the ruling bureaucrats but expropriated former owners compensated by these interest-paying bonds. And fifth, there is a conspicuous absence of such capitalists in the Soviet Union.

A Postcapitalist Bureaucratic Order

Among those who broke with Trotsky in 1939–40 were James Burnham and Max Shachtman. They agreed that the Soviet Union was neither capitalist nor communist but a completely new order unforeseen by Marx and Engels. Burnham spoke of a managerial society, Shachtman of bureaucratic collectivism. Both were intellectually indebted to Bruno Rizzi, who had defected from Trotskyism several months before the Soviet-German Pact of August 1939. Later versions of this thesis were developed by Milovan Djilas and Marc Paillet, who acknowledged their indebtedness to Trotsky and to the Trotskyist critique of the Soviet regime. All these interpretations share a common denominator.

These critics argue that the seizure of power by a bureaucrat-manager class was directed against the bourgeoisie as well as the proletariat and that the subsequent transformation of the Soviet economy put an end to capitalism. Thus, they stress the novel features of the Soviet regime and its rupture with the past. They agree that within the Soviet Union there were two competing revolutions: an initial political revolution by the proletariat and the technobureaucratic revolution that eventually prevailed. In the final analysis, they argue that the new bureaucratic class misrepresented Russian national interests and contributed to a deterioration in the conditions of the Soviet people. Although the new regime took a step forward in destroying capitalism, it took two steps backward in subverting the workers' state and replacing it with a totalitarian order. Initially, Rizzi and Burnham believed that the new order represented an improvement in the lot of the masses—but they soon reversed themselves on this score. In the end each of these critics adopted a counterrevolutionary position; each claimed that the new order was worse than the old.

Paillet's *Marx contre Marx: La société technobureaucratique* presents the most recent case for a postcapitalist transformation in the USSR. Like Castoriadis he sees there a new exploited class as well as a new exploiting class. The accumulation of capital and the expansion of surplus value in Russia are dictated not by the old pursuit of profit but by new bureaucratic objectives. Among the most important are an increase in both the volume of production and the rate of economic growth at the national and enterprise levels. Even when profit is put in command, as under the New Economic System, its purpose is to increase wealth by the efficient allocation of resources and new cost-saving techniques. Unlike Castoriadis, however, he distinguishes bureau-cratic accumulation from capitalist accumulation, which is to say that the new class of bureaucrats is not a personification of capital. Self-ex-panding value is common to both technobureaucratic and capitalist so-cieties; but it is not capital in the strict sense unless it confronts a class of wage laborers. Thus, Paillet agrees with Marx's thesis in chapter 3 of *Wage-Labor and Capital* that there is no capital and there are no capital-ists without the traditional proletariat. Because the class of wage labor-ers has been replaced in the USSR by a new working class of "labor sub-jects," according to Paillet, the capitalist class must also have been re-placed by a new ruling class.

Paillet claims that two factors contributed to transforming the old working class into a new one: the existence of a single employer and the omnipresent surveillance of all workers. As the bureaucracy organized in the state is the only major employer, it imposes its own terms on the labor force. The assignment and transfer of jobs and the determination of wage rates are no longer left to the uncertainties of the marketplace. The worker is not in a position to choose one job rather than another, to bargain over the price of labor power or to go on strike. He is subject to penitentiary discipline on the job, and if he is ever fired he loses his lodg-ing as well. He will have difficulty finding new employment because his working papers and certificates will contain a black mark against him. He is completely defenseless in confrontation with the bureaucra-cy; once blacklisted, his condemnation is total; nobody else will hire him, and he will have no place to live. He cannot move freely from one city to another without an internal passport. Surveillance of his actions extends from the workplace to his lodging, to his choice of friends and use of free time. He is tied to his job, and he is tied to the state when off the job. Like the medieval serf bound to his landlord, the labor subject belongs to the bureaucracy. More precisely, Paillet notes, "the subject of the bureaucracy sums up in himself both the feudal and capitalist fea-tures of class exploitation."

Even so, this new working class enjoys several advantages over the old. These include some leveling of incomes, full employment or the right to work subject to the conditions already listed, and free social ser-vices of various kinds. Paillet adds the overcoming of the capitalist mode of production and a renewed impetus to economic growth. But even with these advantages, he asks, can Soviet workers be better off now than they were before the revolution?

The Soviet economy has moved forward, Paillet concedes, but its po-litical and cultural superstructures have suffered a regression. Tyranny over the mind and the body was never so great under capitalism as it has become under Soviet totalitarianism. Political repression is outdone only by ideological mystification. The bourgeoisie never once pretended that the workers had political power, that there was a workers' state; the divorce between political ideals and social reality never before reached such astonishing proportions. Some people still believe that the Stalinist bloodbaths and the liquidation of the revolutionary Old Guard provided the conditions for the first stage of communism! But Paillet denies any overall improvement in the conditions of Soviet workers, because the benefits of economic progress were neutralized by a step backward in other areas.

The bureaucratic revolution is not automatically in the national interest, Paillet concludes, but it will be better or worse than capitalism, depending on what the workers make of it. Hence, he assigns to voluntary factors and to working-class struggles the task of making the conditions of labor more viable in the new society. At the same time, he is skeptical of the outcome. In view of Marx's historical model in which revolutions by ascendant classes have invariably led to a new system of exploitation in place of the old, a communist future constitutes an unlikely rupture in the historical rhythm of societies. On the basis of Marx's own historical method, one is led to predict the emergence of a bureaucratic society rather than a communist one from the capitalist womb. The workers, Paillet concludes, should resist this development.

Admittedly, Paillet's principal intellectual debt was to Milovan Djilas's *New Class*. From Djilas he borrowed the thesis of a cultural and political regression under the bureaucracy. "It would be wrong to think the other forms of discrimination—race, caste, national—are worse than ideological discrimination," Djilas says in his chapter, "Tyranny over the Mind." Brainwashing is only the most obvious example. There is no area of discourse or of art that falls outside the scope of dialectical materialism, the Soviet world view. It permits of no rivals; it is ideologically exclusive and intolerant, accounting for the role of censorship and ideological repression in the USSR. The monopoly of political power by the party is also so encompassing, Djilas writes, that it reaches out even to the courts. There are virtually no means of redress. When judge *and* prosecuting attorney are party members, the citizen is defenseless in the face of the party state. Elections are a farce, he argues in his chapter, "The Party State," they are tantamount to a race with one horse. Dissenters are under constant surveillance by the secret police; the party prohibits political factions and, under the cover of "democratic centralism," it places a ban on internal democracy as well as on the right of opposition.

Djilas went further than a general indictment of the new order: he makes a case for its economic regression. In a chapter entitled "Dogmatism in the Economy," he argues that the Soviet economy "is not the basis for, but a reflection of, the development of the regime itself from a revolutionary dictatorship to a reactionary despotism." Modern technology is in latent conflict with compulsory forms of labor, with the new servile working class that has replaced the old. The new system "leads to low quality of output, a decline in real productivity and technological progress, and deterioration of plant." A decade after the establishment of Communist power in Yugoslavia, Djilas claimed on the basis of official statistics that the standard of living of blue-collar workers was still lower than before World War II. Despite centralized planning, "the Communist economy is perhaps the most wasteful . . . in the history of human society." At that time, the stress of central planners was still on volume of output with little attention to costs, but their most economically reactionary effort was the striving for autarchy in disregard of the international division of labor. The Communist countries not only were producing some goods at several times the cost elsewhere but also were developing new industries when world markets were overstocked with their particular commodities.

Djilas concludes that the tendency toward the unification of world production is the basic tendency of our times and is also the principal condition of economic growth. Even the *Communist Manifesto* contains a panegyric to capitalism, to the development of the world market that compels all nations on pain of extinction to adopt the bourgeois mode of production. In sharp contrast, domination by the new class "creates an isolated political and economic system which impedes the unification of the world . . . [and] causes the weakening of the national potentialities for economic and social progress." Communism, not capitalism, is the fundamental enemy "because the capitalism the Soviet leaders rant about no longer exists." The West continues advancing economically, Djilas maintains, as well as culturally and politically. It too has imposed controls on the anarchy of production and is moving in the direction of statism and nationalization. But the West has not sacrificed social democracy and the basic freedoms that modern technology requires.

Burnham's *Managerial Revolution* is another source of Paillet's thesis of a twentieth-century technobureaucratic revolution. Djilas concentrated on the bureaucratic basis of the Soviet new order, Burnham on its technocratic origins. Although Djilas accepted Burnham's economic approach to the new society, he differed from Burnham in holding that the managing class was spawned by the Communist party. Burnham argued that the managers are not a *new* class but are common to capitalist as well as postcapitalist societies.

Who are the managers? In the chapter of that title Burnham traced their origin to the separation of ownership and control in the modern corporation. It is in the technical direction and coordination of the process of production that the managers are found, not in scientific and engineering work per se or, at the opposite pole, among financial executives, members of the board, bankers, and business agents of the firm. The managerial class consists exclusively of those who have charge of the technical process of production, "the operating executives, production managers, plant superintendents, and their associates . . . [whose job is] to organize the materials, tools, machines, plant facilities, equipment, and labor." This class is the decisive one. From a technical viewpoint, the remaining functions of direction—profit making and financing the company's operations—are "altogether unnecessary . . . [in] the situation to be found throughout *state enterprise.*"

What makes the managers a class? Burnham's answer is, first, control over access to the instruments of production tantamount to de facto ownership; second, preferential treatment in distribution based on such ownership. In the last analysis, ownership means control: "if there is no control, then there is no ownership." This is why the capitalists are being expropriated; their loss of control over production explains the displacement of capitalism by a new managerial society in which local managers and state bureaucrats, concerned with managing the economy as a whole, are fused into a single class with a common interest.

In Burnham's assessment of the Soviet Union, capitalists are seen as the principal losers, but the workers, too, are victimized. In his chapter, "The Economy of Managerial Society," he claims that the labor market has been abolished in favor of compulsory forms of labor and that a new working class has replaced Marx's proletariat of "free workers." To be sure, the old freedom had its limitations. "But proletarian freedom under capitalism also means, to a limited extent, freedom for workers to sell their labor or not to sell it . . . , to sell it to one competing employer as against others, and to bargain over its price." Another major setback for the workers is the loss of faith in the free, classless society of communism. Once they realize that the postrevolutionary new order has introduced a new system of exploitation in place of the old, the chance of achieving Marx's first stage of communism seems more remote than ever. In short, the workers in managerial society are more likely to be demoralized and to submit to exploitation than their forebears under capitalism.

Nonetheless, managerial society is a more rational economic order than the one it displaces. For Burnham, it does not suffer from economic crises based on falling profitability, although it may experience technical and political crises of its own. Second, managerial society abolishes mass unemployment, "the most intolerable of all the difficulties that any economy can face, sufficient, by itself, to guarantee the collapse of an economic system." Third, a managerial economy can produce with the same technical resources a greater volume of goods than capitalism, "a decisive indication of their relative survival value." Fourth, managerial society is in a better position than capitalism to apply new inventions and technology because it is not encumbered by the profit motive. Fifth, it is capable of absorbing the economic surplus by putting excess capital to productive use. Sixth, managerial society is better prepared "to exploit and develop backward peoples and areas in a way that . . . is no longer possible for capitalist economy." Finally, it will be able "to *plan* for and with the economy as a whole in a way that is not possible for capitalist economy."

Managerialism would not be replacing capitalism unless it were capable of solving the principal difficulties that make the continuation of bourgeois society impossible. Its greater productive capacity "would seem to indicate that the masses on the average . . . would have a somewhat higher material standard of living." Although in the same context Burnham concedes that the improved economic conditions of Soviet workers may not always compensate for other, less attractive facets of Soviet society, he finds that systematic planning makes it easier not only to support the privilege, power, and expansionist drive of the new ruling class but also to realize "greater happiness, security, and culture for mankind at large."

In his chapter headed "Totalitarianism and Managerial Society," Burnham argues in the same vein that Soviet totalitarianism is likely to be replaced by some form of nonparliamentary democracy. Despite the absence at the national level of a genuine political opposition, there is a modicum of freedom at the local level through such institutions as trade unions, cooperatives, and technical associations: "In spite of the surface rigidity, it [the localization of political opposition] represents a democratic intrusion, capable of indefinite development, in the totalitarian political systems." It would not endanger the power and privileges of the managers; but, as under capitalism, democracy would improve the quality of life for all.

The picture Burnham painted of Soviet society was a comparatively sober one, but two years later, in *The Machiavellians: Defenders of Freedom*, he negatively revised his original assessment. And less than a decade later he was actively calling for the "liberation" of Eastern Europe by the NATO armies!

In the real world rather than the mythical one of ideologies, democracy implies liberty or juridical defense, "a measure of security for the individual which protects him from the arbitrary and irresponsible exercise of personally held power." Breaking with his earlier thesis that economic factors are decisive for human well-being, Burnham argued that the degree of liberty makes the crucial difference between one society and another. Liberty is a "necessary condition of scientific advance." It is a condition of an advanced level of civilization: "liberty is needed to permit the fullest release of the potential social forces and creative impulses present in society." Liberty is necessary for the maximum development of creativity not only in the arts and sciences but also in economic and political affairs. Finally, liberty means, above all, the right of political opposition: the existence of a public opposition is crucial because only power restrains power; such an opposition is "the only effective check on the power of the governing elite."

This right is of no small importance to the masses; it is a way of benefiting from a cleavage in the ruling class. When there exists such a cleavage, the opposition cannot win without seeking popular support and promising certain reforms. Whoever wins, the masses must benefit because they become capable, though perhaps only indirectly, of limiting the power of their rulers. Under pressure from the masses, the governing elite is compelled to grant certain concessions. Where there is no right of opposition, the concentration of economic power in the state apparatus "tends to unite with control over the other great social forces . . . to destroy the basis for those social oppositions that keep freedom alive." Thus, "there exists more liberty, much more, in England or the United States, than in Germany, Russia, Italy or Japan"—countries in which a managerial revolution had occurred or was in the process of completion.

The same year that Burnham arrived at this indictment of the managerial revolution, Max Shachtman presented a similar thesis in *The Struggle for the New Course*. There he pushed the logic of Trotsky's assessment of the Soviet Union to its ultimate consequences. Beginning with Stalin's Second Revolution in 1928–29, he argued, the bureaucracy developed into a new ruling class, and by 1936–38 it had fully consolidated its power. The workers' state was dismantled; the workers no longer did the planning; they ceased to control production; they lost their influence over the planning agencies; they became "totally disfranchised state-slaves"; the old Bolshevik party was replaced by a new one subservient to the bureaucracy; and the trade unions were transformed into an agency of the state. Before 1929 the workers owned the means of production because they also controlled the state, but by 1936 they were displaced by the bureaucracy, which "owned" the state that had nationalized the means of production. In effect, Russia was transformed from a workers' state into a bureaucratic collectivist one. The bureaucratic class rose to power in response to the developing needs of production, which neither the capitalists nor the isolated Russian workers were able to satisfy.

That was not a revolution, according to Shachtman, but a "counter-revolution." During the period of bourgeois revolutions, "the bourgeoisie was progressive, speaking on the whole, because no other class in society had matured that could take its place and do its job." But today, during the period of bureaucratic ascendancy, "a class already exists *on a world scale* which is fully matured for the task of reorganizing society on a rational basis, a task that can be postponed now only at the imminent risk of a lapse into barbarism." That class is the proletariat. If the Russian workers were not ready for the task, presumably those in Western Europe are. Shachtman's assessment of the new order was negative. Bureaucratic collectivism represents a major setback for the working class at a time when socialism is ripe and revolution is on the historical agenda.

The original source and prototype of these various interpretations of a postcapitalist bureaucratic order was Bruno Rizzi's *La bureaucratisation du monde.* In the new ruling class Rizzi included technicians, specialists, directors, highly skilled and exemplary workers (Stakhanovites), functionaries, and supervisory workers in government as well as in industry. Unlike the bourgeoisie, this new class does not appropriate surplus value directly at the enterprise level but does so indirectly through the state. That the workers are collectively exploited by the entire class of bureaucrats was the basis for Rizzi's description of the new order as a "bureaucratic collectivist" one.

In his chapter titled "The Proletariat" Rizzi argues that a new working class has taken the place of the proletariat under the new postcapitalist system. In place of free labor and a labor market, we find a labor force completely regulated by the state. The Soviet worker has only one employer; he is a virtual prisoner of the regime; he is under direct and continuous surveillance by the bureaucracy; he cannot move without an internal passport; he no longer controls or has legal authority over his own labor power; he is tied to his job and to his employers collectively; he belongs to the state from the cradle to the grave; and he must serve it continually. Thus, the worker shares some of the features of the medieval serf and is closer to being a state subject than a proletarian. In this Rizzi anticipated not only Burnham and Shachtman but also the interpretation of Djilas and Paillet.

The new ruling class has been formed because it has a historically necessary task to play in the progress of mankind, "the task of organizing production on the basis of collective property and state economic planning"; but it has yet to establish a stable international system and to overcome the vast disparities in distribution. For these reasons Rizzi ridiculed the Trotskyist commitment to unconditional defense of the Soviet Union and advised the old and new working classes to pursue an independent line opposed to both capitalism and bureaucratic collectivism. There is little advantage for the workers, he concluded, in having state ownership; their interest is to control the state and thereby the means of production. And this means that the workers should seek new leaders who, rather than being apologists of the Soviet Union, favor an independent strategy for socialism.

The picture Rizzi paints is not entirely black. On the positive side, the bureaucratic collectivist regime overcomes the fetters on production of the dying capitalist society. The contradictions between the social character of production and the bourgeois form of appropriation, between the discipline of the individual workshop and the anarchy of production as a whole, are resolved along with the class antagonism between capitalists and workers. "At the beginning the new order is ferociously exploitative as was the case under capitalism," Rizzi comments, "but the consolidation of the system and the expansion of production make it possible for the ruling class to distribute a greater share to the exploited." Bureaucratic collectivism in the USSR has improved the standard of living of the masses. As a halfway station, an intermediate order between capitalism and socialism, it is a step forward on the road to Marx's classless society.

Rizzi's assessment of Soviet society contained heavy criticism but was on balance favorable. Shortly after the publication of his major work in July 1939, however, he announced that bureaucratic collectivism was not a progressive but a regressive social phenomenon. The reasons for changing his judgment are given in his *In margine al collettivismo burocratico*, published together with an Italian edition of his earlier work. In chapter 4 he says that the Soviet-German Nonaggression Pact destroyed his illusions of a bureaucratic, collectivist stage between capitalist and socialist societies. He began to see that bureaucratic collectivism represented a historical regression, launching the world backward toward fascism and the barbarities of war with the complicity of the Soviet Union. The alternative, he said, was socialism or barbarism: a struggle that was bound to end, in the words of the *Communist Mani-*

festo, "either in a revolutionary reconstitution of society at large or in the common ruin of the contending classes."

Interpretations of Soviet society as neither capitalist nor communist have an advantage over the various theses of a perpetuation or a restoration of capitalism in the Soviet Union, but they share several mistaken claims: first, that collective possession of the state and, through the state, the control of the means of production are the basis of exploitation in postcapitalist societies; second, that oppression in those societies is worse than under capitalism. Together these positions have become the basis for criticizing and for actively opposing the revolutions of the twentieth century.

Despite their differences, the foregoing critics concur that possession of the state is the principal source of material privileges under conditions of public ownership. In common with the critics of the Soviet ruling class as a state bourgeoisie and as a bureaucratic class that is still tied to capitalist conditions, these critics believe that the perpetuation of exploitation may be explained independently of the possession of expertise or a monopoly of higher education.

This belief is unwarranted. It cannot account for the extortionate salaries of bureaucrats under capitalism or for the lower rate of bureaucratic exploitation under socialism—precisely where it should be higher because of the collective and unrestricted possession of the state that formally owns the means of production. The salary spread has been generally lower in socialist than in capitalist countries—significantly so. And one has to account for this discrepancy.

Do high salaries under capitalism result from restricted control of the productive apparatus or from the ownership of expertise? In the case of industrial and commercial managers there would seem to be no direct way of knowing. But consider their professional counterparts—research scientists, for example—who have no influence at all over the means of production. The high salaries of professional workers who are not themselves managers must derive from some other source than collective possession or control. Because managers are also professional workers, there is reason to believe that they have the same source of income. Our problem is to identify that source. It is not capital, it is not land, and it is not labor power as Marx understood it. That leaves the ownership of expertise as the principal, if not the only, explanation of the high level of salaries prior to the advent of a bureaucratic social formation.

The foregoing critics of the new bureaucratic class and bureaucratic postcapitalist order believe that the workers are basically worse off under the new system than under the old. The qualitative character of this judgment makes it extremely difficult to support with hard data and their thesis is insufficiently substantiated by the facts. An abstract conception of freedom underlies the claim that the absence of an organized political opposition in the Soviet Union is a more important index of human well-being than state-subsidized basic necessities, that freedom of expression and association is more important than a guaranteed livelihood, and so forth. In the socialist countries all the basic wants are met from the cradle to the grave. Although man does not live by bread alone, he must have bread before circuses. At least, the priorities followed in socialist countries correspond to fundamental biological needs. In Mexico, for example, where unofficial estimates place half of the population as unemployed or subemployed and there is widespread illiteracy, the suffering underclasses are not impressed with their freedom to buy books they can neither afford nor read. By contrast, in the "totalitarian" USSR everyone receives at least a high school education, and more books are bought and read every year than in any country on earth. Intellectuals like Rizzi, Burnham, and Paillet might prefer to live in Mexico, whereas tens of millions of Mexicans might prefer the USSR.

All of the foregoing critics take issue with Marx's thesis that revolutions represent the people's interest. Revolutions may not be worth the effort, their arguments run, depending on the trade-offs or social costs of securing new benefits. In a loose sense of "revolution," who could disagree? But Marx's usage was more precise, as the *Communist Manifesto* and his 1859 preface make clear: a social revolution overcomes the fetters on the productive forces imposed by a decadent economic system, and it promotes their economic expansion. Because the wealth of nations is the most important single factor in accounting for social well-being, the sacrifices incurred by revolutionary upheavals are dwarfed by advantages in the long run.

What precisely does this mean? Marx's logic of revolutionary transformations, given the definition of social revolution as a transfer of economic power and privilege from one class to another, is the following: if each class rules primarily in its own interest and workers cannot overcome exploitation except by getting rid of exploiting classes one by one, then revolution is in their interest—*but only if a communist revolution is ultimately feasible.* Although revolutions tend to devour their own children, although the price may be extortionate for particular classes and individuals, revolutions signify liberation or a step in that direction for the bulk of humanity. As Marx noted in his "Discourse on Free Trade," support for the bourgeois revolution is necessary for the ultimate victory of the proletariat. For the proletariat this is its *sole* justification. In the short run the costs of the revolution would be devastating, but in the long run workers would enjoy the fruits.

A more positive argument is put forth in part 4 of the *Communist Manifesto:* "The communists fight for the attainment of the immediate aims, for the enforcement of the momentary interests of the working class"—not just their ultimate interests. The presumption is that in defending their immediate interests "they also represent and take care of the future of that movement." Nothing is said about subordinating immediate to future interests; each is important in its own right. The fact that communists in Germany support the bourgeoisie, whenever it acts in a revolutionary way against the feudal squirearchy and petty bourgeoisie, does not mean that they support the bourgeois revolution *solely* as a step toward the emancipation of the proletariat from all exploitation. The intolerable conditions of life under the old order and the prospects of improvement under a new one combine in driving the exploited majority and discontented minorities to search for a revolutionary way out.

Bourgeois revolutions are in the national interest. It is true that in *Capital* Marx voices grave reservations concerning this judgment. The bourgeois social revolution of the nineteenth century not only overcame the feudal fetters on production, it also increased the rate and mass of human exploitation. In England, Marx argues, the revolution signified a step backward for the workers. The more England forged ahead in the adoption of new technology, in the accumulation of capital, in social wealth, the worse became the lot of English laborers. The business cycle is a product of capitalist development; so is the industrial reserve army at the disposal of capitalists. Marx rightly emphasized the tendency toward the degradation of modern wage earners, whether their wages are high or low. His general law of capitalist accumulation underscored both the absolute deterioration in the conditions of labor and the deterioration relative to the increasing wealth of the bourgeoisie. At the same time, Marx acknowledged that this law "is modified in its working by many circumstances." "Like all other laws," it is only a tendency; it can be checked by the freedom of labor to organize and by the growth of political democracy.

In view of the history of modern reform bills, Marx's suggestion concerning countertendencies seems justified. At the end of his chapter, "Machinery and Modern Industry," he notes the tendency for capitalism to create new industries and to revolutionize periodically old methods of production. "Modern Industry . . . through its catastrophes imposes the necessity of recognizing, as a *fundamental law of production,* variation of work, consequently fitness of the laborer for varied work, consequently the greatest possible development of his varied aptitudes" (italics mine). This is no ordinary tendency. "It becomes a question of life and death for society to adapt the mode of production to the normal functioning of this law . . . , to replace the detail-worker of today, crippled by life-long repetition of one and the same technical operation, and thus reduced to the mere fragment of a man, by the fully developed individual, fit for a variety of labors, ready to face any change of production, and to whom the different social functions he performs are but so many modes of giving free scope to his own natural and acquired powers." This is not an augury of a communist future, but it is an augury of the death of capitalism.

Critics of revolution claim that the masses have little to gain from exchanging one exploiting class for another. In fact, revolutions do more than substitute one ruling class for another; they get rid of the most immediately oppressive class. Prior to a social revolution, old and new modes of exploitation coexist in comparative peace. They also reinforce each other. During the revolution, the old mode of exploitation is rapidly or gradually eliminated, and concessions are made to workers as the price of their support. After the revolution, workers have fewer exploiters to contend with; the extent of their exploitation is momentarily reduced with the prospect of being further modified in the long run. Thus, to the premises that each class rules in its own interest and that workers cannot overcome exploitation except by stages may be added a third: the fewer exploiting classes there are, the less is the overall burden of exploitation. Social revolutions are in the interest of exploited classes—even if a communist revolution never materializes.

The three great revolutions of our century—the Russian, Chinese, and Vietnamese—involved extended civil wars and were extremely bloody affairs. Although Rizzi, Burnham, and Shachtman firmly backed the Bolshevik Revolution until they became disillusioned with its consequences, the logic of their analyses of postcapitalist society led them to resist the subsequent Chinese Revolution. By the same logic they and their successors were unable to support the Vietnamese Revolution because it was led by communists. Ironically, the critics claimed to represent the best interests of the Chinese and Vietnamese peoples, although these had voted with their feet against overwhelming odds to break with the old forms of capitalist-colonial oppression.

Brainwashing is supposed to account for mass acceptance of the new social order. But there were also adaptive and acculturation mechanisms under the old system that did not work! Certainly, the Chinese and Vietnamese masses were not brainwashed into revolting against the *ancien régime.* Although the new society may not have lived up to their expectations, the people had no viable alternative but to revolt. The system of capitalist and colonial oppression had become unendurable. Should socialism also become oppressive to that extent, we may anticipate a similar response from the masses. Revolution is the people's choice, and those who resist it are not their friends but their enemies.

It took the Soviet people more than a decade after the Bolshevik Revolution to recover prewar levels of production. A decade later they had to suffer the threat and then the reality of a second world war on their own soil. In that war Soviet casualties outnumbered that of all the belligerents combined. On the heels of this hot war, a cold war followed. Is the new social system to be blamed for the hard times that followed those calamities? Marxist critics of the new order have mistakenly diagnosed its ailments. The October Revolution suffered a setback with the dismantling of workers' power, but it did end capitalist exploitation. At least, Trotsky recognized the historically progressive character of the Soviet Union and the stake of the international working class in its defense.

A Post-Asiatic Bureaucratic Formation

All the Marxist critics of existing socialism thus far examined share a common premise: the new Soviet order is a successor to and an outgrowth of the capitalist system. But there is another group of Marxist critics who reject this premise. According to their analysis, the new social structure is the outgrowth not of capitalism but of a particular form of the Asiatic mode of production or, in the case of certain advanced countries in Eastern Europe and Cuba, the result of the imposition of the Soviet model on an existing capitalist society from outside.

The other interpretations we examined derived from mainly Maoist or Trotskyist sources. In contrast, this interpretation reveals the influence of New Left tendencies in Eastern as well as Western Europe. Here we have a comparatively sober response to the semihysterical depiction of the Soviet Union in Karl Wittfogel's *Oriental Despotism* and to the Cold War analysis of W. W. Rostow's *Stages of Economic Growth*. As an alternative to Europocentric assessments of Western capitalism as a more advanced civilization than the new bureaucratic order in the East, these New Left critics offer an antiimperialist perspective of the revolution of our times focused on the third world. Unlike the Rizzi-Djilas-Paillet critics of the Soviet Union who claim it represents a postcapitalist regression, they argue that it is a positive advance over the semi-Asiatic despotisms it replaced. Thus, the Soviet Union today is as close to reaching the promised land of socialism as are the more industrially advanced nations in the West.

Common to these critics is a Marxist counterpart to Rostow's parallelism-convergence thesis: the thesis of a noncapitalist and a capitalist road to industrial development eventually converging on each other. The Soviet and capitalist systems are depicted as parallel social formations that perform virtually the same function of economic development under different social and historical conditions. Unlike non-Marxist theories of convergence based on the sharing of capitalist and bureaucratic traits, however, their Marxist counterpart envisions a convergence in a future communist society that is both postcapitalist and postbureaucratic.

Underlying the thesis of two parallel social formations and their convergence in Marx's lower stage of communism is a particular interpretation of Marx's concept of the Asiatic mode of production and its relevance to our times. In his 1859 preface Marx sketched what most of his followers mistook for a unilinear scheme of historical development: "In broad outlines Asiatic, ancient, feudal, and modern bourgeois modes of production can be designated as progressive epochs in the economic formation of society." But there is little that suggests from Marx's scattered discussions of these different formations that he intended this order to be a historical progression from one to the next. His followers tended to ignore the geographical and historical peculiarities of the Asiatic mode that led Marx to label it as "Asiatic" in contrast to all the other modes of production that were European.

The Asiatic mode as conceived by Marx and Engels differed significantly from European formations by the stagnant condition of its productive forces, its comparative immobility. In the effort to explain this arrested development, they formulated two basic hypotheses, although they never fully made up their minds concerning which was more important. The first hypothesis was formulated in Marx's letter to Engels on 2 June 1853, with which Engels agreed in response (6 June 1853). It traces the principal cause of stagnation to the absence of private property in land or, what amounts to the same thing, the ownership of the basic means of production by the state. The second hypothesis, formulated in Marx's article "The British Rule in India," in the New York *Daily Tribune* of 25 June 1853, traces the cause to the plight of self-sufficient villages despoiled of their surplus through tribute, to the absence of trade between villages as a consequence of the total expropriation of their surplus by the state. In both hypotheses the cause of social immobility is the political structure of "Oriental despotism," the despotic role of a centralized state bureaucracy that choked off private initiative in its various forms.

Just as capitalism is the outgrowth of a decentralized feudal society that made possible such initiatives, these critics argue, so Soviet society is the outcome of a centralized semi-Asiatic despotism. The Oriental despot occupied the top rung of a ruling class or stratum comprising state officials, mandarins, bureaucrats, and military leaders who appropriated the tribute levied on the village communes. Following a brief interlude of a workers' state with "subjective socialists" in command, the Soviet Union gave birth to an allegedly post-Asiatic mode of production in which a new bureaucracy became the ruling *class* or *stratum*. I emphasize these terms because there are two principal variants of this thesis. The most recent version, represented by Rudolf Bahro's *Alternative in Eastern Europe*, holds that the Soviet bureaucracy includes a pyramidally ordered series of strata capped by a special elite. An earlier version by the Italian sociologist Umberto Melotti in his work, *Marx and the Third World*, argues in the tradition of Rizzi and his successors that the bureaucracy is a new ruling class.

Bahro claims that progress in our epoch proceeds less directly from the internal contradictions of imperialism than from its external contradictions. "The October Revolution," he says in chapter 2, "was and is above all the first *anti-imperialist* revolution in what was still a *predominantly precapitalist* country . . . with a socio-economic structure half feudal, half 'Asiatic.' " It was the first revolt by those "doubly oppressed peoples whom capitalism found at a lower stage of social development." In their condition socialism was premature; the principal problem was to industrialize a backward country by following the "noncapitalist road." Only during the 1970s, Bahro adds, has socialism in the Soviet Union become a feasible goal.

The origin of this noncapitalist road is discovered in the legacy of the Asiatic mode of production. In Bahro's reading of Marx, the Asiatic, slave, and feudal formations represent not a unilinear development from lower to higher stages but three indigenous formations proceeding immediately and along parallel lines from the primitive commune. Although slavery emerged later than the Asiatic mode, and feudalism appeared even later, Bahro maintains that these later formations did not have to go through the earlier forms. The Greeks, for example, developed slavery directly from the same starting point that the Germans developed feudalism and the Eastern peoples developed the Asiatic mode. Thus, Bahro gives his interpretation of Marx's historical schema: "Original slavery existed only where there was no previous economic despotism. Original feudalism existed only where neither slavery nor economic despotism had taken firm hold. . . . Original capitalism, however, has only existed where this feudalism developed beforehand."

At the turn of the twentieth century, Bahro continues in chapter 3, Russian society had three formations superimposed on one another: the

Asiatic formation at the bottom; on top of it a semifeudal formation that had never fully dissociated itself from the older Asiatic formation; and at the very top the modern capitalist formation concentrated in a handful of cities. The question is what survived of this predominantly precapitalist mix when the capitalists were chased out together with the semifeudal landed proprietors. What survived, Bahro tells us, were remnants of the Asiatic mode: a peasant economic base with its petty-bourgeois periphery in the towns and a bureaucratic superstructure. The new order created by Stalin required a restructuring not of Russian capitalism but of a "predominantly patriarchal [peasant] and petty-bourgeois economy" that was never potentially bourgeois.

In this perspective Bahro rejects Lenin's term "state capitalism" as misleading. For Lenin it "meant nothing more than state disposal over all social funds and products, which had been divested by the revolution of their capital character." By the end of the New Economic Policy and the launching of Stalin's Second Revolution the dominant mode of production was still not capitalist but rather *peasant commodity production*—a precapitalist economic formation corresponding to Marx's concept of simple commodity production. "In Soviet Russia the peasants were the strongest class in the population, and up until 1928 the sole class to reap the benefit of the social revolution." The Stalinist transformation that followed, Bahro contends, issued in a post-Asiatic bureaucratic despotism, *not* a postcapitalist one.

The two parallel social formations moving in the same direction toward a socialist future are represented by the capitalist-imperialist first world and by the "precapitalist Second World," alike competing for the allegiance of a third world whose Asiatic legacy inclines it toward the noncapitalist road. This is *"the shortest route to socialism,"* Bahro argues, because it bypasses the capitalist stage of development. Capitalism does not have a monopoly of industrial civilization but shares this industrial basis with the new societies in Eastern Europe. Thus, in chapter 6 Bahro emphasizes *the common historical basis of the two industrial societies and the pledge of their ultimate convergence in socialism.*

Is one of these formations nearer to achieving socialism? Although late capitalism is industrially more advanced, Bahro depicts it as socially more retrograde than the post-Asiatic formation. In the West the state apparatus of late capitalism, he says in chapter 4, "acts as the organizer of productive forces that have outgrown capitalism"—but not to the same extent as the state apparatus in the Soviet Union. The social structure in the Soviet Union is more advanced than that under late capitalism: a horizontal class division based on the private ownership of means of production has been replaced by an essentially classless but vertically stratified society based on economic functions. In chapter 6 he depicts this new social structure as "already beyond the capitalist structure." The relationship between the social structure and the productive forces is "more direct . . . than in late capitalism," which means that there is less room for social parasitism. In chapter 8 he adds that the Soviet state, despite its Asiatic legacy, is "in no position to *enforce* the same intensity of labor as capitalism can." The antagonisms between it and the direct producers are softened, and "the workers have a far greater opportunity to blackmail the 'entire society' than do the trade unions under capitalism." The industrial bureaucracy in the West has yet to emancipate itself from the tutelage of capital, whereas "in our system it has full charge of the entire reproduction process." For the vast majority of people in the third world bureaucratic despotism is preferable to capitalism because it addresses itself to basic human needs. As Bahro comments in chapter 2: "Revolutions such as the Russian and the Chinese are the preconditions for victory over hunger."

Turning now to Melotti, we find him defending the new post-Asiatic order also on the grounds of its antiimperialism. Although he nominally accepts Wittfogel's description of the Soviet Union as a system of general slavery based on industry, he denies that Western capitalism is its Manichaean antithesis. In his conclusion he writes, "The idea of two separate and *unequal lines of development* . . . deserves as little consideration as the prevailing view from positivist ideology in the age of rampant colonialism, that the European line of development must be followed by all nations." He escapes the traps of ethnocentricity and cultural relativism by arguing that capitalist and bureaucratic collectivist societies exhibit both positive and negative features: "In reality, the traditions of the West and the Third World alike contain some elements that enslave them and need to be abolished by a true cultural revolution, and others that are of value and deserve preserving." Among the positive features of capitalism, for example, are the values of critical inquiry and respect for the individual and his personality, while bureaucratic society represents "no less important values, such as the communal ethic, the concept of a proper balance between man and nature, and the integration of the social and natural worlds." In this assessment, the free West is no closer to achieving socialism than the despotic Eastern societies, and "China and the USSR are no further along the road than the West."

The new social formation cannot be understood in terms of an outgrowth of nineteenth-century capitalism. In Russia, Melotti argues in chapter 20, one finds "the reproduction, in a new guise but much the same form, of the State bureaucratic despotism that had survived for centuries in very similar conditions, based on the Asiatic mode of production." Because in Russia there was no feudalism deserving of the name, he calls it a "semi-Eastern society." Capitalism had difficulty emerging and never became predominant because it did not have a decentralized feudal base as in Western Europe. Modern Russia was never subjected to a prolonged and penetrating capitalist development because its capitalism was mainly imported in the form of Western imperialism. Prior to the October Revolution, Russia thus faced a situation similar to that faced by third-world countries today. "For those countries the impact of capitalism was enough to upset their centuries-old stagnation," Melotti concludes in chapter 21, "but not enough to draw them into the Western stream of development."

As he convincingly argues, this was also Marx's and Engels's characterization of Russia in the nineteenth century. This is evident in Engels's article in the New York *Daily Tribune* of 19 April 1853, signed by Marx, and in Marx's own article on 5 August 1853. Not just Plekhanov but all the other major Marxists including Lenin, Melotti claims, adopted the basic principle of Marx's and Engels's interpretation of Russia as a "semi-Asiatic despotism."

In his chapter, "Semi-Asiatic Russian Society," Melotti provides supporting evidence for Marx's and Engels's view. From the ninth century onward the history of Russia remained for centuries "an unbroken succession of conflicts with the Tartars, Turkomans, Turks, Kirghizes and other nomadic peoples of the steppes." Later, between the thirteenth and sixteenth centuries, a large part of Russia came under the rule of the Mongols: "The Mongol hegemony in particular enhanced the semi-Asiatic nature of the country by isolating it from the rest of Europe . . . and by introducing structures and institutions typical of the Oriental autocracies." Ivan the Great (1462–1505), the first independent king of Muscovy and founder of the modern Russian state, adopted the Mongol pattern of rule. As Melotti describes him, he was "a true Oriental despot, holding all the reins of political, economic, military and religious power." Like his Oriental counterparts, Ivan introduced "a new class of military and civilian officials, who were rewarded with grants of land, not in perpetuity but for life only, and conditionally." This was not a semifeudal innovation, Melotti continues to argue, but a semi-Asiatic one. Most important to his argument, there were no groups or institutions, as in the West, capable of setting limits to despotic power.

Capitalism and bureaucratic collectivism, Melotti claims in the final chapter, are "parallel socio-economic formations which in different circumstances perform much the same function: ensuring the maximum development of the social forces of production, the *sine qua non* of the transition to socialism." Both also have the same limitations: each represents an antagonistic class formation replete with exploitation, oppression, and violence. In considering both formations, he places the emphasis not on their differences but on "the far more important difference between the free societies of the future and the societies of the present that are not yet free." But this is the perspective of utopia rather than of actually existing societies. Certainly, Marx never measured the present in terms of an ideal future. On the contrary, whatever future there is in store for mankind he found embodied in the present. For Marx the differences between competing social formations are more important than the similarities.

There are two fundamental weaknesses in Bahro's and Melotti's depiction of the bureaucratic social formation. First, the concept of a post-Asiatic society suffers from all the ailments of the concept of an Asiatic mode of production. Second, it is empirically false that the Soviet Union never experienced a capitalist stage of development, no matter how brief that may have been. Unlike the parallelism-convergence thesis, the thesis of a postcapitalist society explains how in the competition between rival systems the bureaucratic formation has almost invariably been the victor.

The concept of Asiatic despotism is too loose to cover societies as diverse in time and space as the Old, Middle, and New Kingdoms in Egypt (2900–670 B.C.), pre-Columbian civilization from the rise of the Olmecs in 1000 B.C. to the Spanish conquest of Mexico in 1521, Indian civilization from the rise of the Maurya dynasty in 322 B.C. to the British conquest of India in the eighteenth century, Chinese civilization from the emergence of the Chou dynasty in 1000 B.C. to the fall of the Manchu dynasty in 1911, and Russian society from the rise of Ivan the Great at the end of the fifteenth century to the fall of the Romanov dynasty in 1917. The Europocentrism implicit in this concept is no longer acceptable to modern scholarship. The picture of an inert Asia is no more plausible today than the image of the changeless Middle Ages. As Ross Gandy notes in his discussion of the Asiatic mode in *Marx and History*, in Marx's day "the lack of data made a serious knowledge of Egypt and the ancient Middle East impossible." Virtually nothing was known about African history or pre-Columbian civilization in the Americas. Then it made sense to lump together all those civilizations in a single non-European category. It no longer does.

A comparatively accurate picture of Russian despotism is given in George Konrád's and Ivan Szelényi's *Intellectuals on the Road to Class Power*. In chapter 9 they argue that Russia's original feudal organization in the twelfth century gave way, under the influence of Tartar and Turk-ish expansion, to the Asiatic mode of production and the corresponding political form of Oriental despotism but that centuries later feudalism reestablished itself. The result of the Asian influence was the replace-ment of Russia's free and hereditary nobility with a "nonhereditary ser-vice nobility" based on "direct prebendal tenure" from roughly the thir-teenth until the eighteenth century. With the triumph of the Eastern European monarchies over the decaying Turkish and Tartar empires there was then a restoration of the seigneurial economy: patrimonial, hereditary landed property was revived not only in Russia but also in Austria and Prussia. A structural reform of the Asiatic mode was needed to meet the economic challenge of Western Europe; beginning with Peter the Great (1672–1725) the history of Russia began to converge with that of the West. But its feudal status was prolonged even beyond the emancipation of serfs in 1861 through a "system based on a combin-ation of Asiatic redistribution and European feudalism." By the early twentieth century this combination was strengthened by the addition of a third partner—large-scale capital. Although I disagree with the au-thors that the bureaucratic formation is postfeudal rather than postcap-italist, they are right in arguing that it is *not* a direct outcome of a semi-Asiatic society.

The role of capitalism in Russia must not be minimized in the break-up of this predominantly feudal mode of production with Asiatic resi-dues. Stolypin's reforms after 1906 hastened the process. According to the first chapter of the monumental work by the German Marxist his-torian Richard Lorenz, *Sozialgeschichte der Sowjetunion, 1917–1945*, by 1913 the Russian Empire held fifth place in world industrial produc-tion behind England, Germany, France, and the United States. But capi-talism was not yet the dominant mode of production.

In 1916, Lorenz notes, the landed nobility held a fourth of the culti-vated land in giant estates and received rents and indirect payments from millions of peasants. It also held all the important top posts in the state bureaucracy. During 1917 and 1918, the peasants stormed the manor houses of the aristocrats and burned them out, seized the estates of the Church, and divided up the lands of the Treasury and the czar's family. By the middle of 1918 the peasants had cut up these vast hold-ings into tiny plots. According to Lorenz's figures in chapter 2, the peas-ants now owned 98 percent of the cultivated land. Both the landed no-bility and the surplus product had vanished from the countryside. Did another class in a different sector of the economy acquire the lion's share of the surplus *by default*?

During the revolution, the foreign enclaves and many holdings of the native bourgeoisie were nationalized. But in the 1920s a new bourgeoisie emerged in the cities to make money in private trade and the black market: vast fortunes mushroomed in Moscow and were spent with here-today-gone-tomorrow fatalism. In the countryside ambitious peasants gathered land into their hands and reaped new economic surpluses of their own. For a short time this new bourgeoisie of "NEP men" and kulaks pocketed the bulk of the economic surplus. *The immediate outcome of the proletarian revolution of 1917–21 was a bourgeois social revolution under proletarian leadership between 1922 and 1929.*

It was the establishment of capitalism in Russia that prepared the ground for Stalin's Five-Year Plan (1929–33) and the Second Revolution made possible by the plan. The plan expanded the state sector in industry and wiped out the NEP men in the cities; the collectivization of the peasants liquidated the kulaks. Contrary to the critics, Soviet society in the twenties had a capitalist economic basis. Thus, the new society that Stalin built was a postcapitalist bureaucratic order.

7

Getting Rid of Communists under Socialism

It was Stalin's great accomplishment to have constructed the new social order we know as socialism. Yet he was opposed at almost every step by Trotsky, who claimed to represent Marx's original theory of postcapitalist society. Unlike Stalin, who prided himself on being a creative Marxist, Trotsky insisted on the letter of Marx's theory and on Marx's forecasts as defining the postcapitalist social order. Because Stalin's practice was to impose his own definition of socialism, Trotsky denounced him for violating Marx's theory. Stalin then attacked Trotsky for subverting the construction of a new society in the Soviet Union.

What does the Stalin-Trotsky confrontation tell us about Marxist theory and the behavior of Stalin in power? Basically, it was a debate between Stalin and the dead Marx, with Trotsky acting as the principal mouthpiece of Marxist orthodoxy. In effect, the exile of Trotsky from the Soviet Union in 1929 was testimony to Stalin's break with Marx's theory of the lower stage of communism. Stalinist practice triumphed over Marxist orthodoxy because Stalin's redefinition of socialism was more in keeping with actual conditions. Paradoxically, the practice of the Communist party under Stalin was anticommunist. At the same time the champions of communism were out of step with events in advocating measures that could not be implemented.

The Internal Enemy: Trotskyism

The experience of the Soviet Union from October 1917 to the adoption of the new Stalin Constitution in November 1936 shows that the costs of building socialism were staggering. To make a successful political revolution and to construct the foundations of socialism, the Bolshevik party had to accept the shameful peace imposed by the victorious German armies at Brest Litovsk in March 1918. The treaty stripped Russia of Poland, all the Baltic provinces, and the vast Ukraine stretching south and southeast from Poland to the Black Sea. Russia lost 26 percent of its railroads, 27 percent of its arable land, 33 percent of its manufacturing industry, 73 percent of its iron production, and 75 percent of its coal mines in operation. In addition, it was robbed of approximately 44 percent of its population. A civil war followed the treaty; surviving czarist generals supported by allied arms marched through the length and breadth of Russia trying to dislodge the Bolsheviks from power. And in 1920, toward the end of the civil war, the Bolsheviks had to contend with a rash of strikes and demonstrations followed by a mutiny at the Kronstadt naval base by sailors who wanted *Soviets without Communists.*

That was only the beginning. Attacked from both the left and the right, the Bolshevik leadership fractured into left and right factions responsive to pressures from outside the party. After Lenin died the struggle for succession began among the Bolshevik Old Guard, ending with the triumph of Stalin, the banishment of Trotsky to Alma Ata on the Russian-Chinese frontier, and the first major purge of the party's left wing. Stalin then ran into trouble with the party's right wing when his program for collectivizing the countryside encountered armed resistance from the peasants. Although confined to rural areas under conditions in which the Red Army had a clear preponderance of force, this second social upheaval lasted from 1929 to 1933. The party then launched a series of purges aimed at liquidating the entire right wing that had resisted the collectivization program. And in the course of these purges the surviving remnants of the left were eliminated.

It was not just the economic backwardness of Russia that contributed to the practical abandonment of communism by Stalin and his supporters. The hostility of England, France, and Germany after the rise of Hitler had created a situation of "capitalist encirclement" and fascist belligerence threatening the survival of the new regime. In this climate the campaign against Trotskyism acquired hysterical dimensions. In the 1939 *History of the Communist Party of the Soviet Union (Short Course)*, Trotsky was presented as the central villain responsible for the bulk of inner party dissension, sabotage, and treason during the entire period from Lenin's illness in 1923 to the purge and execution of the ranking members of the party's right wing in 1938. The influence of the exiled Trotsky was allegedly discovered in a secret alliance with Bukharin, the most prominent leader of the so-called right deviationists. In the final chapter of the *History*, wilder charges are made: "The trials brought to light the fact that the Trotsky-Bukharin fiends, in obedience to the wishes of their masters—the espionage services of foreign

states—had set out to destroy the Party and the Soviet state, to undermine the defensive power of the country, to assist foreign military intervention, to prepare the way for the defeat of the Red Army . . . , to destroy
the gains of the workers and collective farmers, and to restore capitalist
slavery in the USSR."

Why did this campaign of vilification center upon Trotsky? The
party's right wing was considerably stronger than the handful of Trotsky's followers in the Soviet Union and elsewhere and Bukharin's policies were eliciting a sympathetic response from the old social democratic and socialist parties of Europe. Yet neither Bukharin nor his close
associates ever dreamed of writing an indictment of Stalin's dictatorship as harsh as Trotsky's *Revolution Betrayed*. Trotsky was the first
Bolshevik to call on Russian Communists to prepare for a political revolution against the Soviet bureaucracy as a condition of establishing socialism in the USSR. For that act of treason he was "executed" by an
agent of the Soviet political police in his home in Coyoacán, a suburb of
Mexico City, in August 1940.

In criticism of Stalin, Trotsky argued that exploitation had not been
overcome by 1936. In chapter 6 of *The Revolution Betrayed* he claimed
that shock workers (Stakhanovites) were earning from twenty to thirty
times the basic wage and that specialists were receiving salaries as high
as eighty to a hundred times the wages of unskilled workers. Because
these claims were unsubstantiated, one may suspect they were exaggerated. Trotsky should have distinguished the supersalaries of foreign
specialists from the lower ceilings for native specialists in this generalized estimate. But it is fair to say that during the height of Stalin's
campaign against "egalitarianism in distribution" the ceiling was
somewhere between thirty and fifty times the minimum wage. In any
case, Trotsky was right and Stalin was wrong in claiming that exploitation still weighed heavily on the shoulders of Soviet workers. He was
mistaken mainly in calling it a survival of "bourgeois forms of
appropriation."

Unlike Bukharin, Trotsky had become the personification of the surviving remnants of communism within the Bolshevik party, the cham-
pion of classical Marxism and its Leninist adaptation. These elements
survived through the rival Trotskyist parties of the Fourth International, which was formally organized in 1938 as a counter to the Stalinist Third International. Trotsky was feared because of his "leftism," his
excessive demands on the party's leadership. Bukharin was less to be
feared because of his "go slow" policies. Thus, when Bukharin's followers were purged from the communist parties in Western Europe
they did not organize counterparties of their own, much less a rival

communist international. They returned to their origins, to the social democratic parties that nurtured them.

Trotsky was a thorn in Stalin's side because the conditions of a socialist revolution were too stringent, in Trotsky's view, to be realized in backward Russia. Already, in *The Permanent Revolution* (1929), he had added two conditions of his own to Marx's features of the new society: first, "the subsequent fate of the dictatorship [of the proletariat] and socialism is not only and not so much dependent in the final analysis upon the national production forces, as it is upon the development of the international socialist revolution"; second, "[the] world division of labor, the dependence of Soviet industry upon foreign technology, the dependence of the productive forces of Europe upon Asiatic raw materials, etc., make the construction of socialism in one country impossible." These two premises from the concluding chapter of his book make socialism unrealizable without successful, simultaneous proletarian revolutions in several advanced countries. In effect, Trotsky made the achievement of socialism even more difficult than it had been for Marx.

In *The Revolution Betrayed* Trotsky did not, like Marx, forecast what a postcapitalist industrial order would be like; he prescribed the conditions that would have to be satisfied for it to qualify as socialist. Along with the abolition of bourgeois forms of property, he included among the indispensable conditions of socialism Marx's six corollaries sketched in the *Communist Manifesto:* the overcoming of class antagonisms, of classes generally, of exploitation in all its forms, of commodity production, of national antagonisms, and of political power in the form of the oppressive state. But he also insisted, in chapter 3, that for Marxists this question is not exhausted by a consideration of forms of property and relations of exploitation and oppression. By the lowest stage of communism Trotsky meant a society with a higher degree of labor productivity, "a society which from the very beginning stands higher in its economic development than the most advanced capitalism." Its material premise is "so high a development of the economic power of man that productive labor, having ceased to be a burden, will not require any goad, and the distribution of life's goods existing in continual abundance will not demand . . . any control except that of education, habit, and social opinion." This was not Marx's view. For Marx such a degree of economic development is a condition of the highest, not the lowest, stage of communism.

Trotsky believed that the dearth of consumer goods contributed to the struggle of each against all for capitalist privileges but that in Soviet Russia the object of the struggle was bureaucratic privilege. In Trotsky's judgment, bourgeois norms of labor and distribution still survived in the USSR: Soviet leaders had fashioned an independent principle of distribution at variance with Marx's principle in the *Critique of the Gotha Programme*. Their mistake, he argued, was to make a virtue out of necessity by inflating Marx's principle of bourgeois right—"the exchange of equal values" regulating distribution during the lower stage of communism—into the supposedly socialist principle, "to each according to his work." Such a principle is at best a hangover from bourgeois society, Trotsky believed, not a principle acceptable to communists. For communists, as for Marx, there is only one principle of distribution: "From each according to his abilities, to each according to his needs."

Trotsky concluded that the alleged socialist principle of payment according to work was in reality a cover for the principle: "Get out of everybody as much as you can, and give him in exchange as little as possible." Its complete formulation, "from each according to his abilities, to each according to his work," was interpreted as splitting Marx's communist principle into two unrelated halves. The first half was part of Marx's communist principle; the second was a principle of bourgeois right.

Actually, Marx had formulated only one principle, fully applicable during the highest stage of communism but modified during the lowest stage. Thus, he regarded payment according to work, under the pressure of physical necessity and goaded by material incentives, to be the closest approximation to this principle during the lower stage. Although Lenin, and Stalin after him, had misinterpreted Marx by splitting this principle into halves and then reconstituting them as two separate principles—one for the lower stage and the other for the higher—Trotsky also misinterpreted Marx by failing to recognize Marx's own modifications of this principle. What is important is that, for Trotsky, the lowest stage of communism could not appear until both halves of the principle were at least partially realized. And for that, a society flowing with milk and honey was a virtual prerequisite.

Marx's forecasts of a postcapitalist order were transformed by Trotsky into a series of doctrinal precepts defining its nature. Granted that the Stalinist principle of distribution amounted to a "falsification" of Marx's text, it did give prominence to the form of ownership as the fundamental criterion of a new mode of production. In interpreting Marx, Trotsky stressed the letter of the text, whereas Stalin insisted that only the abolition of bourgeois property was historically feasible.

Among the practical consequences of Trotskyism was a defeatist attitude about the prospects of building socialism in the USSR. In *The October Revolution and the Tactics of the Russian Communists* (1924), Stalin commented that Trotsky's theory of permanent revolution had its practical counterpart in permanent hopelessness: "Lack of faith in the strength and capabilities of our revolution, lack of faith in the strength and capabilities of the Russian proletariat—that is what lies at the root of the theory of 'permanent revolution.' " Here Stalin stretched an otherwise convincing point in suggesting that hopelessness was not a consequence but a condition of Trotsky's theory. In any case, Trotskyism became symbolic of defeatism. Without a continuous series of proletarian revolutions in the West, Trotsky believed, the only choice that remained for the revolution in Russia was either to rot away or to degenerate into a bourgeois state. This was a serious admission. It tended to demoralize the party leadership. It constituted an indictment of Communist practice.

The Stalinist Alternative
In 1924 Stalinism crystallized as a strategy for suppressing communists in Russia. This was not its self-image, but it was in fact its role in creating a new order distinct from the first phase of communism anticipated by Marx and Lenin. The contours of this un-Marxian socialism became visible only after Lenin's death, mainly through the struggle against the emerging Trotskyist opposition.

Whereas Trotskyism defined itself in terms of its opposition to Stalin, Stalinism emerged as a movement of opposition to both social democratic (Bukharinist) and communist (Trotskyist) tendencies within the party. Because Bukharin's followers hoped to grow into socialism peacefully, the only rivalry of revolutionary consequence was between the Stalinist and Trotskyist vanguards. Both departed from Marx's theory of a postcapitalist new order but they did so in different ways: Trotsky through a dogmatic or fundamentalist interpretation of the Marxist classics, Stalin through their historical adaptation to new conditions and tasks. Each in his own way misinterpreted the transformation that had been wrought in the Soviet Union: Trotsky minimized the differences with Western capitalism; Stalin exaggerated them. Socialism was indeed possible and victorious in one country, but it was not the lower stage of communism as understood by Marx and Engels.

What kind of socialism was it? In 1921 there was little difference between the wages of skilled and unskilled workers. But with the introduction of the New Economic Policy (NEP) in 1922 wage scales were revised upward. Until the formulation of the First Five-Year Plan in October 1928, however, no member of the Communist party could earn more than a skilled wage earner without special permission—and that was only three and one-half times the minimum wage. As a general rule, topmost scientists, engineers, and administrative and professional workers could earn no more than eight times as much as unskilled workers. The rule limiting the income of party members was especially important because many of the executives in government and industry were Communists: it signified that there was a proletarian dictatorship from at least 1917 until 1929. But the workers' state was nullified by the transformation of proletarian executives into petty bureaucrats who later became full-fledged bureaucrats. After 1934 Soviet statisticians ceased compiling figures relating to maximum and minimum incomes on different jobs. Did the Soviet executives responsible for this decision have suddenly something to hide?

With the eradication of communist economic tendencies in the Soviet Union also went the dismantling of workers' power. All the benefits that workers had received during the early years of the revolution were eventually undermined. Immediately after the October Revolution workers had the right to defend themselves against the state, but under a law of June 1927 aimed at counterrevolutionary sabotage, strikes and slowdowns became punishable with from one to twenty years in prison. If strikers were not initially prosecuted under this law, it was because no one dared to interpret strikes as sabotage. The worker's freedom to change jobs at will had been guaranteed by article 37 of the 1922 Labor Code but was revoked in July 1932. The right to move freely from one part of the country to another was revoked in December 1932 through the restoration of the use of internal passports. Labor books for industrial workers were first introduced in February 1931 and extended to all workers by December 1938. No worker could be hired without one or rehired without presenting it with the evaluations of his former employers. In November 1932 a law against absenteeism made anyone liable to dismissal who had been absent from work for a whole day without good reason; a decree of December 1938 provided further sanctions against those arriving late to work, leaving before the scheduled time, and idling on the job. After 1932 the seven-hour day was abolished, and the workers ceased to be consulted in the determination of wages. The year 1934 saw the end of all collective-bargaining contracts, and when they were revived in 1947 wages were not covered by them. All the agencies through which the laborer could formerly plead his case, the unions and the courts, had become agencies of the government. Workers' councils that had originally curbed the powers of management were abolished. With the triumph of Stalinism the legal status of labor changed for the worse. Capitalism was eliminated, but at the cost of abolishing the dictatorship of the proletariat.

The principal opposition to the establishment of this brand of socialism was, of course, Trotskyism and its fidelity to the letter of Marx's teachings. But Stalin also could claim to be a Marxist. If Marxism is not a dogma but a guide to action, then it must be periodically revised in the light of the changing events and practical tasks. As the 1939 *History of the Communist Party of the Soviet Union* concluded, "one must not cling to the views of yesterday." What would have happened to the party and to the revolution "if Lenin had been overawed by the letter of Marxism and had not had the courage of theoretical conviction to discard one of the old conclusions of Marxism and to replace it by a new conclusion affirming that the victory of socialism in one country, taken singly, was possible, a conclusion which corresponded to the new historical conditions"? "The Party would have groped in the dark, the proletarian revolution would have been deprived of leadership, . . . Marxist theory would have begun to decay . . . and the enemies of the proletariat would have won."

Surpassing Lenin in his refusal to be overawed by the letter of Marxism, Stalin departed from the classical conception of socialism on a number of important points. For the victory of socialism in one country, it was enough to proceed negatively by abolishing bourgeois property relations. Although the construction of socialism under conditions of capitalist encirclement might require repressive methods, Stalin believed that the abolition of capitalism sufficed to put an end to class struggle and to exploitation in all its forms. By 1936 the "complete victory of socialism in all spheres of the national economy" was more than a wish.

This claim from Stalin's report, "On the Draft Constitution of the USSR" (November 1936), was accompanied by the following observations on the transformation of the class structure of Soviet society: "the draft of the new Constitution of the USSR proceeds from the fact that there are no longer any antagonistic classes in society; that society consists of two friendly classes, of workers and peasants; that it is these classes, the laboring classes, that are in power." The working class is not the old one dispossessed of instruments of production; it is a new one that possesses them jointly with the whole people. And the peasantry is not the old class of small producers relying on their individual labor and on backward technical equipment; it is a new collective-farm peasantry. That these were conceived by Stalin as separate and distinct classes followed from his distinction between different forms of socialist property: nationalized means of production in the case of the new working class; collectivized farm ownership in the case of the new peasant class.

In Stalin's revision of Leninism, a basic point was the reliance on the repressive state apparatus as a condition of building and then preserving socialism in the USSR. Stalin's professed aim was to preserve the dictatorship of the proletariat that Marx and Lenin had considered to be a transitional regime between capitalist and postcapitalist societies. Stalin relied on dictatorial methods to strengthen the party bureaucracy and its monopoly of political power. The bureaucratic state apparatus was to continue with its repressive functions until socialism emerged victorious in a majority of countries, until a socialist encirclement replaced the existing capitalist one, and until the danger of war had been dispelled. In the final part of his "Report on the Work of the Central Committee to the Eighteenth Congress of the Communist Party," we read: "[After] the elimination of the capitalist elements in town and country . . . the function of defending the country from foreign attack fully remained; consequently, the Red Army and Navy also fully remained, as did the punitive organs and the intelligence service, which are indispensable for the detection and punishment of the spies, assassins and wreckers sent into our country by foreign espionage services." Although military suppression inside the country was no longer necessary, police repression continued as before. Political power would survive even under the higher phase of communist society "unless the capitalist encirclement is liquidated, and unless the danger of foreign military attack has disappeared."

Stalin also repudiated Marx's corollary that commodity production would be abolished during the initial or first phase of communism. In *Economic Problems of Socialism in the USSR* (1952), he insisted that this forecast did not apply to the Soviet Union where collective ownership prevailed in the countryside and not all of the means of production had been nationalized. Commenting on a passage from Engels's *Anti-Dühring* predicting that commodity production would be abolished with the socialization of the means of production, Stalin noted that it applied only to countries where capitalism had advanced far enough in agriculture to permit the expropriation and conversion of wealth into state property. But with the exception of Great Britain, no country had achieved such a concentration in agriculture as to permit the expropriation of the fairly numerous class of peasants, including in Russia the owners of collective farms. This point, made in part 1, section 2, of Stalin's essay, indicated that the conditions were still not ripe for the abolition of commodities: "when instead of the two basic production sectors, the state sector and the collective farm sector, there will be only one all-embracing production sector with the right to dispose of all the consumer goods produced in the country, commodity circulation with its 'money economy' will disappear . . . [but] so long as the two basic production sectors remain, commodity production and circulation must remain."

The acceptance of commodity production during the first phase of communism falsified Marx's forecast that workers would be paid not by the value of their work but by the amount—measured by its duration and intensity. Marx's measuring rod ruled out differentials in pay for what Engels called "compound labor." In *Anti-Dühring*, Engels argued that under socialism the educated and highly skilled worker has no claim to extra pay based on the greater values produced by compound labor, because his education and skills are financed by society. For Stalin, however, he can claim extra pay because the measure of work is its quality as well as its quantity. Only in the higher phase of communism would work be measured directly by its duration and intensity: "In the second phase of communist society, the amount of labor expended on the production of goods will be measured not in a roundabout way, not through value and its forms as is the case under commodity production, but directly and immediately—by the amount of time, the number of hours, expended." This measuring rod is for purposes of social accounting only. Thus, in the higher stage of communism distribution would be proportional not to the amount of work but to human needs.

In Marx's theory postcapitalist society is communist society, but the initial phase of communism is still haunted by the past. The *Critique of the Gotha Programme* presents the dictatorship of the proletariat as followed by a lower stage of communism, "not as it has *developed* on its own foundations but, on the contrary, just as it *emerges* from capitalist society; which is thus in every respect, economically, morally and intellectually, still stamped with the birth marks of the old society." This statement is deceptively realistic. Of what did Marx's realism consist? It amounts to the claim that in the lower stage of communist society "the same principle prevails as in the exchange of commodity-equivalents: a given amount of labor in one form is exchanged for an equal amount of labor in another form."

This principle of distribution, of payment equal to the amount of work performed, Marx characterized as a principle of bourgeois right. That the right of the producers is proportional to the labor they supply was criticized by him as a "bourgeois limitation." But is it? In view of Stalinist practice, in which distribution during socialism is characterized by the unequal exchange of labor, it would be more accurate to say that the equal exchange of labor is a postsocialist phenomenon. The limitations on it are not imposed by a fading capitalist society but by a socialist system that is anything but communist. The communist principle that Marx criticized for its bourgeois hangovers is in fact subversive of socialism. Is it any wonder that Stalin tried to get rid of it?

What remains then of Marx's forecasts? According to Stalin, the abolition of bourgeois property, of class antagonisms, and of exploitation were three predictions confirmed by events. But were they? In reality only bourgeois property was abolished. Exploitation was not eliminated except in its bourgeois form. Because exploitation indicates the presence of class antagonisms, this compels us to revise Stalin's theory that two friendly classes survive in the USSR. And it also compels us to reject his conception of bureaucracy inherited from Marx, the conception of a classless stratum independent of production and the class structure.

Evidently, Stalin did not go far enough in his recasting of Marxist theory. His claim that exploitation no longer characterized Soviet society was seen as a "falsification" by Trotsky, which indeed it was. In part 1, section 4, of his 1952 essay, Stalin conceded that in capitalist societies physical workers are exploited by intellectual workers, but he believed that under socialism higher salaries for superior skills is consistent with the abolition of exploitation. Not once did he attempt to substantiate this claim. Although capitalist exploitation is no more, bureaucratic exploitation flourishes in its place. There are strong reasons for interpreting scientific, professional, and administrative workers —Stalin's intelligentsia—as an exploiting class and not merely as a friendly stratum.

Did Stalin contribute anything of positive significance in characterizing the new mode of production? His formulation of the "law of motion" of socialist societies is a case in point. In part 1, section 7, of *Economic Problems of Socialism in the USSR*, he indicates that the development of new production techniques under capitalism is limited by the expectation of obtaining the maximum profit. This is not so under socialism. Thus, his law of motion states: "instead of maximum profits, maximum satisfaction of the material and cultural requirements of society; instead of the development of production with breaks in continuity from boom to crisis and from crisis to boom, unbroken expansion of production; instead of periodic breaks in technical development accompanied by destruction of the productive forces of society, an unbroken process of perfecting production on the basis of higher techniques." Scientific planning and the abolition of the anarchy of production are taken for granted in this somewhat naive characterization of socialist development. At the same time Stalin assumes that commodity production will continue for a long time. Unlike Marx, he believed that unbroken economic growth could be achieved without abolishing commodity production.

Was Stalin's new law applicable to all socialist countries? Whatever may be said of its applicability to the Soviet Union during his lifetime, it does not apply to the Yugoslav market economy based on workers' self-management or to the decentralized market economies of Eastern

Europe. Yugoslavia's dependence on the market has partly restored the anarchy of production. The role of centralized planning has been downgraded to the point that the bulk of economic decision making is in the hands of each enterprise. Far from an unbroken expansion of production, in Yugoslavia economic recessions continue to occur.

Stalin's law of motion fails to explain socialist accumulation. It ignores the role of exploitation, which is fundamental to socialist development. As in Marx's comparable law of capitalist development, the formulation of such a law must satisfy two basic conditions: it must show how production serves the interests of the economically dominant and exploiting class; and it must underline the so-called contradictions pointing toward the eventual dissolution of the dominant mode of production.

Marx's law of motion, presented in volume 1 of *Capital* as a law of capitalist accumulation, satisfies both of these conditions. First, it affirms that the production of surplus value "excludes every diminution in the degree of exploitation of labor . . . which could seriously imperil the continual reproduction, on an ever enlarging scale, of the capitalist relation." Second, it shows how capitalist accumulation runs up against several self-defeating factors: the tendency for the industrial reserve army of unemployed to increase in response to the amount of social wealth, the functioning capital, the size of the proletariat, and the productiveness of its labor; and the tendency for the rate of profit to fall in response to improved technology and increasingly expensive labor-saving devices. Ironically, the bourgeoisie is unfit to rule because its methods of exploitation are becoming less and less profitable. In the words of the *Communist Manifesto:* "It is unfit to rule because it is incompetent to assure an existence to its slave within his slavery, because it cannot help letting him sink into such a state that it has to feed him instead of being fed by him."

If the acknowledgment of bureaucratic exploitation is crucial to an understanding of socialist societies, then Stalin's law of motion suffers from two basic defects: it distorts the purpose of socialist production by claiming that production serves society as a whole independent of the interests of a new ruling class; and it ignores the fetters on economic growth that interfere with the "maximum satisfaction of the material and cultural requirements of society." Among the principal impediments to human welfare are the system of commodity production and the pyramid of bureaucratic salaries incompatible with the sharing of material incentives. Stalin's positive characterization of the new economic order and its law of motion is thus no contribution at all.

Neo-Stalinism and Beyond

Have Stalin's successors contributed anything of note? Despite their criticism of Stalin's errors and his so-called cult of personality, they reaffirmed his conception of socialism. The *Manual of Political Economy*, published by the Institute of Economics of the Soviet Academy of Sciences in January 1956 just prior to the Twentieth Congress of the CPSU, was promptly rewritten in response to the de-Stalinization campaign. Nothing significant was added. Not until the third edition, in July 1960, was Stalin's revision of Marxism carried somewhat further.

The *Manual* was the authoritative textbook on political economy proposed by Stalin in his *Economic Problems of Socialism in the USSR*. A preliminary draft already existed in February 1952. Unlike earlier Soviet manuals, it was the first to give more space to the socialist than to the capitalist mode of production. In summarizing the distinguishing features of the new economic system, the third edition follows closely Stalin's revision and addendum. Chapter 23 parrots his distinction between forms of socialist property and stresses production for use in conformity with scientific planning: "Socialism is, then, a regime based on social property in the means of production in its two forms (state-public and cooperative-collective), in which there is no exploitation of man by man, in which the material economy develops on the basis of a plan, having for its purpose the maximum satisfaction of the increasing demands of workers through the unbroken expansion of production on the basis of advanced technology."

The *Manual* reaffirmed Stalin's misguided interpretation of Marx's principle of distribution but gave it a new twist. Stalin had effectively repudiated that principle by interpreting the amount of work in monetary values, indirectly determined through the market mechanism instead of directly through an index of standard man-hours. Although nominally accepting Marx's principle, he had smuggled into it a qualitative factor. His successors went further by amending the principle itself. They spelled out the implications of Stalin's revision by openly basing distribution on the *quantity* and *quality* of work. In this amendment of Marx's principle, "quality" refers not only to higher and lower standards of craftsmanship but also to higher qualifications over and above the costs of specialized training. The greater one's qualifications, the greater one's pay; the possession of complex skills entitles one to a higher salary, regardless of one's performance. The category of "qualifications" includes such diverse factors as responsibility, seniority, and the social importance or ranking of each job. These are more important than craftsmanship in determining remuneration.

An outright revision of the Stalinist conception of socialism was of-

fered in the new "Third Program of the CPSU" adopted at the party's
Twenty-second Congress in 1961. Part 2, chapter 3, of the program affirms that the Soviet state, which had hitherto represented the dictatorship of the new working class in name if not in substance, "has become,
in the new contemporary period, a state of the entire people." It further
affirms that "the dictatorship of the working class will cease to be necessary before the state withers away." Stalin had held it to be necessary
until a majority of states adopted the socialist system, and until socialist encirclement replaced capitalist encirclement and war ceased to
threaten the socialist camp. These conditions were a long way from
being fulfilled in 1961, as they are today. So the revision of 1961 was a
major one.

The new period in the development of socialism was thought to be a
transition to a higher phase of communist society, but it marked the beginning of a full-scale assault on Marx's interpretation of the highest
stage of communism that went beyond Stalin's earlier revision of
Marx's concept of the first stage. The characterization of the Soviet
Union as a state of the whole people was in fact more accurate as a description of Soviet reality than Stalin's characterization of it as a dictatorship of the working class. Khrushchev did not scrap the workers'
state. It had already been scrapped: first, by the emergence of a petty-bureaucratic ruling stratum in the party as early as 1926 and its consolidation during the period of the First Five-Year Plan; second, by the bureaucratic political and social revolution that followed. These were the realities behind Stalin's Second Revolution during the early thirties.

Stalin's conception of the transition to communism gave precedence
to the transformation of property relations. In part 2 of his *Economic
Problems of Socialism in the USSR* he argued against the chief precur-
sor of Khrushchev's revisionism, the Soviet economist L. D. Yaroshenko, that new socialist relations of production constitute the chief
and decisive factor, "the one which in fact determines the further and
powerful development of the productive forces." Without it, production would be threatened by stagnation, as is the case today in the capitalist countries. But such property relations do not remain new forever;
eventually, according to Stalin, they too begin to obstruct production.
Furthermore, the effort to move forward to the higher stage of communist society should place the main emphasis not, as Yaroshenko would
have it, on the rational organization of the productive forces or on the
scientific planning of economic development but on the further transformation of property in the Soviet Union. Contrary to Yaroshenko,
"neither an abundance of products . . . nor the transition to the formula
'to each according to his needs' can be brought about if such economic

factors as collective-farm or group property, commodity circulation, etc., remain in force." Although collective ownership and commodity circulation are still useful in promoting socialist economic development, Stalin argued, they will hamper growth more as time elapses: "The task, therefore, is to eliminate these contradictions by gradually converting collective-farm property into public property, and by introducing—also gradually—products-exchange in place of commodity circulation."

A complete reversal of emphasis was offered in part 2, section 1, of the new 1961 program of the CPSU. As Khrushchev envisioned the transition in his *Report*, the fundamental task was to catch up with and surpass the technical level of the most advanced capitalist countries: "The main economic task of the Party and the Soviet people is to create *the material and technical basis of communism* [through] . . . complete electrification of the country . . . ; comprehensive mechanization of production operations and a growing degree of automation; widespread use of chemistry in the national economy . . . ; organic fusion of science and production, and rapid scientific and technical progress; a high cultural and technical level for the working people; and substantial superiority over the most developed capitalist countries in productivity of labor." These economic tasks were considered prerequisites for the solution of social tasks, including the transformation of forms of ownership. The raising of the Soviet Union to first place in world per-capita production, for example, was expected to "serve as a basis for the gradual transformation of socialist social relations into communist social relations," and automation and comprehensive mechanization were to "serve as a material basis for the gradual development of socialist labor into communist labor." Thus, Yaroshenko's views finally prevailed over Stalin's.

We have seen how Stalin's revision of the classical conception of socialism was further revised by his successors. Having the advantage of experiencing rather than merely anticipating a later development of the new order, these critics arrived at a comparatively sober judgment of it. But their interpretations were colored by ideological preconceptions. Marx and Lenin were mistaken mainly in their sketches of the future. Stalin and Khrushchev were mistaken about the present. Their efforts to justify the new social system interfered with an objective assessment of it. They falsely imputed to socialism a communist character. They wanted to believe they had constructed the first phase of communist society and were moving forward to Marx's higher phase.

Both Stalin and Khrushchev misrepresented the facts of Soviet society; there was to be no transition to a lower phase of communism during their lifetime or within the foreseeable future. By retaining Marx's theory of postcapitalist society when their practice belied it, they converted his theory into an apology for a new social formation that is basically opposed to communism.

8

Sources of Conflict in
Socialist Societies

In Marxist theory there are neither class nor intraclass antagonisms in postcapitalist society. In fact, we find both. The communist parties only partly overcame them. What then are the sources of conflict under socialism? Grounds for conflict remain between different factions and sectors of the bureaucratic class, between it and the petty bureaucrats, and between both of these and the new working class.

If we take the Soviet Union as our focus—as the principal center of world socialism—we see that the revolutionary elite grew tired of its proletarian status and transformed itself into a bureaucratic class. In the course of this tranformation it first had to settle matters with the working class, then with petty-bureaucratic elements opposed to its growing privileges, finally with a developing technobureaucratic stratum from within its own ranks. Because the workers' resistance was overcome fairly early, class conflicts developed mainly among different factions and sectors of the petty bureaucracy and then of the bureaucratic class. Originally, these centered on the political or class line of the revolution. Later, they focused on the most effective strategy for economic development consistent with the prevailing political line. This issue did not arise until after Stalin's death, nor did it come into prominence until Khrushchev was replaced and a new program of economic reforms was launched in Eastern Europe.

The Petty-Bureaucratic Opposition
During the early years of the Soviet regime until roughly 1934, most of the party's top officials gradually acquired the status of petty bureaucrats—bureaucrats were excluded from party membership by the *partmax* rule. This meant that intraparty conflicts centering on the struggle among Stalinists, Trotskyists, and Bukharinists during this period were led by different factions of the petty-bureaucratic class. The main differ-

ence between Stalin's faction and those of his principal rivals is that his faction represented the class interests of nonparty bureaucrats and of newly recruited, career-oriented, upward-aspiring members of the party's petty bureaucracy expecting to acquire the lion's share of the economic surplus. Thus, Stalin's victory over his rivals helped to transform the revolutionary elite into a new bureaucratic class.

In the struggle to determine the political direction of the Bolshevik Revolution Stalin represented a bureaucratic class in formation that identified its interests with the national interest. In the course of this struggle Stalin had to fight on two separate fronts; first, against the communist opposition represented by his party's left wing; then against concessions to the capitalist system favored by the party's right wing. Stalin first destroyed the communist opposition and then demolished the possibilities of a restoration of capitalism in the USSR. This struggle was carried on at all levels of the party, from the political bureau and central committee at the top down to the rank and file.

Stalin had to contend against two formidable opponents: Trotsky and Bukharin. Personified by Trotsky, the communist opposition was committed to orthodox Marxism and to what it believed were the fundamentals of Leninism. Trotskyism represented the "revolution in the revolution," calling belatedly for a political revolution against the Stalinist bureaucracy that had slammed the door on a communist development of Soviet society. The party's communist or left wing embodied the revolutionary thrust of the petty bureaucracy supported by elements of the working class. At the opposite pole, the party's social democratic wing—also led by petty bureaucrats—responded to surviving elements of the petty bourgeoisie and peasantry. To cater to their demands was tantamount to planting the acorns of small ownership from which giant capitalists grow. Nikolai Bukharin personified this "right deviation."

Although despairing that socialism could be constructed in the USSR without support from revolutions in Western Europe, Trotsky was still the main proponent of rapid industrialization, of the all-out expansion of industry at the expense of agriculture and the peasantry. This policy called for "primitive socialist accumulation"—the accumulation of capital for industrialization from the surplus product of peasant agriculture. The methods proposed were direct taxation and the setting of artificially high prices for the industrial goods exchanged for farm products. Led by Bukharin, the party's right wing attacked this policy for being economically unfeasible and for arousing the unwanted hostility of the peasants.

Bukharin argued that agriculture should be developed first, not industry. In "Notes of an Economist" (1927) he predicted that, if Trotsky's policies were applied, the peasants would retaliate by cutting back production for the official market, while selling products on the black market or consuming them directly. In any case, the vital alliance between workers and peasants would be broken. Bukharin recommended an alternative strategy for industrialization that would allow freedom for private agriculture and permit the big farmers to prosper without the imposition of burdensome taxes, that would rely on the gradual and voluntary introduction of farm cooperatives and not sacrifice agriculture to industrial production. For Russia to maximize the rate of economic growth, he concluded, industry must advance on the basis of a rapidly growing agriculture.

In the struggle between these two opposing tendencies for the leadership of the Bolshevik party, Stalin initially sided with Bukharin in an effort to defeat those whom he considered to be the principal internal enemy, namely, Trotsky and his allies. Only afterward did he turn his guns on the party's right wing.

In an address entitled "The Right Danger in the Communist Party" delivered on 19 October 1928, Stalin traced its origins to social democratic pressures both outside and inside the country. Outside the Soviet Union there were efforts to play down the urgency of class struggle, pressures to run independent candidates in the elections and to reach a compromise with the social democrats. Inside, there were pressures to "deny the need for an offensive against the capitalist elements in the rural districts." There were people in the party fearful of alienating the peasants and their bourgeois and petty-bourgeois allies, because Russia was still a small peasant society in which the majority of the population lived in the countryside.

As long as the roots of capitalism were not completely torn out, Stalin concluded that "there is a surer economic basis for capitalism than for communism." Where are those roots implanted? Precisely in the system of commodity production, in small peasant proprietorship that spontaneously engenders capitalism and the bourgeoisie on a mass scale. Whereas Trotskyism overestimated the strength of the revolution's enemies, the right danger underestimated it: "it does not see the danger of the restoration of capitalism; it does not understand the mechanism of the class struggle under the dictatorship of the proletariat; therefore it readily agrees to make concessions to capitalism, demanding a slowing down in the rate of development of our industry . . . , demanding that the question of collective farms and state farms be kept in the background, demanding that the monopoly of foreign trade be relaxed, etc."

A systematic inventory of the dangers represented by the right opposition was given by Stalin in a follow-up address in April 1929, "The Right Deviation in the Communist Party." The differences between Stalin's group and Bukharin's followers on internal policy were summarized under five principal headings. First, Bukharin was convinced that the capitalists and rich peasants would "*peacefully grow* into socialism . . . [notwithstanding] the irreconcilable antagonism of class interests between the exploiters and exploited." Second, Bukharin believed in the gradual disappearance of capitalist resistance to the policies of the Soviet government, although the class struggle was actually intensifying under the dictatorship of the proletariat. Third, he was wrong in his commitment to "*any kind* of alliance with the peasantry," because the only durable alliance is one directed against the rich peasants and capitalist elements in the cities. Fourth, he placed his confidence in the New Economic Policy, in free trade and competition with a minimum of state interference, as the most effective strategy for economic growth. And fifth, Bukharin thought that the lever for the reconstruction of agriculture was "not the speedy development of industry . . . but the development of individual peasant farming." In a biting remark Stalin conceded that Bukharin was a theoretician of no mean caliber, but "not all is well with his theorizing." Earlier, Stalin had campaigned against Trotskyism in an effort to purge the Third International of communist tendencies. Now he called for "purging the Communist Parties of Social Democratic traditions."

Trotskyism and Bukharinism represented the principal tendencies resisting the construction of the new bureaucratic social formation. This period extended from the start of the New Economic Policy in 1921 to the adoption of the Stalin Constitution in 1936. Although Trotsky was expelled from the party and deported to Alma Ata on the Russian-Chinese frontier as early as 1927, then forced into exile in 1929 and deprived of Soviet citizenship in 1932, the left opposition continued to operate as an effective underground within the USSR until the extensive purges that accompanied the Moscow Trials of 1936–38. The last to be tried in March 1938 were the leaders of the right opposition, including Bukharin, after which it too virtually disappeared from the Soviet scene. The Soviet Union then became a closed society dominated by the interests of the bureaucratic class. Within the central political bureaucracy the interests of other classes—petty bureaucracy, new working class, and new collective peasantry—struck a less responsive chord. The proponents of both capitalist restoration and communist subversion had been systematically eradicated.

Following the liberation of Eastern Europe in 1945, similar left and right trends appeared in other countries as they too began to face the problems of socialist construction. These trends appeared in response to internal pressures similar to those generated in the Soviet Union during an earlier period. They are not traceable to the dissemination of Trotskyist and Bukharinist propaganda, or are they derived from Trotskyist and Bukharinist cadres surviving from the days when the communist parties of every country contained a left and right petty-bureaucratic opposition modeled on those in the Soviet Union. Trotsky's legacy endured in the West and in the underdeveloped countries of the third world but completely lost its foothold in the socialist camp. Bukharin's legacy quickly dissolved into what remained of the left wings of the social democratic and socialist parties, also without any continuing influence in the socialist countries. Nonetheless, the similarities between these later left and right tendencies and their earlier counterparts in the Soviet Union are too striking to go unnoticed.

The Bukharinist trend was fed by the presence of strong petty-bourgeois and peasant elements under conditions of transition to a socialist society. Because these elements were never rooted out from the people's democracies of Eastern Europe, they continue to hold back the development of socialist relations in commerce and agriculture. In countries like Yugoslavia, where small trade is still economically important and the old peasantry dominates the rural areas, the forces of socialism must contend with an ideology representing the vestiges of petty-commodity production. Petty-bureaucratic sectors of the party are responsive to this ideology and to the corresponding social pressures. Thus, today's right-wing equivalent of Bukharinism in Eastern Europe supports market socialism and economic decentralization even though, as we shall see, these economic reforms represent a strengthening of the bureaucratic system, its technocratic future rather than its totalitarian past exemplified by Stalinism.

Unlike Bukharin's tendency, Trotskyism finds its sustenance in the working class. In Eastern Europe it too has a political equivalent opposed to bureaucratic domination and privilege. Although it was effectively eradicated by Stalin, the social forces that nourished it have found other independent forms of expression. A striking example of this is Jacek Kuron's and Karol Modzelewski's "Open Letter to the [Polish Workers'] Party" (1965). They attack the bureaucracy as a new ruling class, not as a ruling stratum as the Trotskyists contend, and favor the creation of a workers' democracy. In practice this means that workers' councils manage the factories, and councils of workers' delegates run the state. Wherever such councils have spontaneously sprung up, as in Poland and Hungary in 1956 and again in Czechoslovakia in 1968, there too we find petty-bureaucratic sectors allied to the workers in a struggle against the dominant political bureaucracy.

What the petty bureaucrats in Eastern Europe want are the debureaucratization and decentralization of both the state and the economy. What the workers want is self-management in industry and the democratization of all areas of social life. Both sets of reform measures are basic to Yugoslav theory and practice but they are interpreted differently by those in and out of power. Kuron and Modzelewski give them a revolutionary interpretation. First, they want a reduction in income disparities between highly qualified and ordinary workers. Second, they want the workers to make the key decisions at the level of the state as well as of the individual enterprise. It is not enough that managers are hired, fired, and controlled by workers' councils. Because the basic decisions are still made by government, the councils are dominated by the state bureaucracy even when those councils control their own experts.

This petty-bureaucratic and workers' tendency insists upon a number of reforms. Enterprises must be made independent of state authority; production must be decentralized. At the same time, the central authority must come under the control of workers' councils through the election of workers' delegates to a national assembly. Finally, the vestiges of small ownership in the countryside must be eliminated along with the system of petty commodity production. Although commodity production is not the enemy, it should be entirely socialist in character. These and other proposals are spelled out in "An Open Letter to the Party," a classic statement of both petty-bureaucratic *and* working-class demands.

The "left opposition" in Eastern Europe shares with Trotskyism the design for an antibureaucratic political revolution. To bring about this revolution Kuron and Modzelewski favor as a first step a popular front against the totalitarian state. Technocratic reform, they argue, would mean a radical, if not a revolutionary, change in production relations, "a conflict of social forces, a political struggle at the highest level, an acute political crisis and broader, if transient, political freedom." Once autonomy is granted to the individual enterprise, "the workers' teams would not have to combat the anonymous power of the state, but their own management." In Poland and Hungary in 1956, where the first antibureaucratic revolutions occurred, according to this analysis, the shift toward a decentralized system under technocratic control is said to have been a step toward "the collapse of bureaucratic rule."

These efforts were premature. They failed because the Soviet bureaucracy sensed a threat to its own existence. With few exceptions, the petty bureaucracy does not replace a central political bureaucracy in power; rather, a bureaucratic class is the successor to petty-bureaucratic rule. The excesses of a totalitarian political bureaucracy are likely to result not in a successful antibureaucratic revolution led by petty bureaucrats allied to the workers but in technocratic domination. *Although the seeds of future political revolutions may continue to sprout in socialist countries, the principal focus of antagonism has shifted from a struggle involving the petty bureaucracy to a struggle between the central political bureaucracy and the administrative and technical experts at the enterprise level.*

The Technobureaucratic Challenge
Underlying the issue of centralized planning versus the priority of market relationships in socialist countries is a political struggle for power between rival sectors of the bureaucracy. One is the central political bureaucracy whose members occupy leading positions in the party and government; it makes the key economic decisions. The other is the technobureaucracy of managerial, professional, and scientific workers at the enterprise level. These are two fractions of the bureaucratic class.

The champions of economic centralization say that a national plan is the essence of the new economic order and that to dismantle it amounts to a restoration of capitalism. The partisans of economic decentralization say that central planning is a bureaucratic-totalitarian distortion of socialism and that the monopoly of decision making by the state threatens to bring about either state capitalism or a system distinct from both capitalism and socialism. Each group accuses the other of being hostile to socialism, of betraying the fundamental principles of Marxism.

Is there any substance to these charges? In defense of centralized planning, Stalinists and neo-Stalinists point to the consequences of scrapping the plan: a reduction in the rate of capital accumulation; the restoration of the profit motive in production; the proliferation of waste in the form of high-priced luxury goods that do not reenter the cycle of production; goods designed to satisfy the high-level consumption of privileged strata under socialism; the anarchy of the marketplace and resulting sacrifice of long-run national priorities; and the return of the business cycle, crises of overproduction, and resulting unemployment. In defense of the market, their rivals emphasize the consequences of keeping the plan: production for its own sake without regard for demand; sacrifice of the workers' present needs in the interest of future generations; low levels of consumption; bottlenecks in production resulting from bureaucratic red tape, inadequate information, and noncompliance with directives; waste of scarce resources by emphasizing total output rather than cost-saving devices; misallocation of scarce resources when prices are not established through the market mechanism; and declining growth rates from a rough average of 10 percent annually throughout the 1950s to 5 percent and lower during the sixties. Marx anticipated a central plan under conditions of workers' democracy, not under bureaucratic domination. Both positions may be opposed to Marx's communism, but it does not follow that they are hostile to socialism.

At issue is a choice between alternative strategies of economic development. During the first stage of socialism there is no escaping either the feasibility or the urgency of central planning, at least for the underdeveloped countries that were the first to establish a new economic order. Nonetheless, the advantages of production according to a plan were comparatively short-lived. In the Soviet Union the "crisis of state socialism" began around 1960 when Soviet growth rates started to decline and the economy performed little better than that of the United States. The party bureaucracy felt threatened not only by falling growth rates and the prospect of negative growth, which set the Czech economy staggering backward in 1963, but also by the continued success of the decentralized Yugoslav model. Evidently, rapid growth could no longer be maintained, once the Soviet and East European economies had overcome their initially low level of production in key areas. At that point it was necessary to switch from extensive to intensive methods of development based on improved technologies and more efficient resource allocation. The goal was no longer quantity of production but labor efficiency or productivity. For that, it was necessary to rely increasingly on decision making at the enterprise level, and in the long run that meant an increased share of the economic surplus for the technocrats and a share in decision making at the top.

Kuron's and Modzelewski's "Open Letter to the Party" is an excellent source for viewing the political tensions generated by the subordinate role of technocrats under central planning. Although its discussion centers on Poland, in the USSR the situation of technocrats was substantially the same. Under the system of centralized planning, the technocrats had virtually no share in decision making but simply carried out political and economic directives. They supervised the exploitation of workers at the enterpise level because they were paid to do so, not because they were the principal beneficiaries. In some instances the political bureaucracy was willing to pay well, to bind the managers closer to itself and to the system. It began by bribing the technocrats; it ended by having to share power with them.

As the political bureaucracy became convicted of incompetence because of declining growth rates, the technocrats found their own influence increasing. They demanded higher levels of consumption for themselves. They demanded decentralized economic controls. With these they were able to determine their own level of payment independent of the central political bureaucracy. In short, they no longer worked mainly for others but worked for themselves. As Kuron and Modzelewski note: "Transforming the technocracy from simple executors of administrative orders and supervisors of hired labor into the 'de facto' powers that act at the enterprise level immediately raises its rank and significance in the state. . . . It must, therefore, be reckoned with when making economic decisions of a central nature."

The technocrats continued to carry out directives from above, but there were fewer directives than before and they began acting on their own initiative. For the first time management was given the right to make basic decisions about the factory. Kuron and Modzelewski stress that under the technocratic system production depends on the market and is limited by effective demand. Accordingly, the technocrats stand to gain from state policies aimed at increasing mass consumption, a condition of higher profits and bonuses for management, and in the long run a condition of inflated salaries as well. In this respect the technocrats have a vested interest in reducing the rate of capital accumulation and achieving an expanded growth rate by intensive means.

Under the decentralized market system, the enterprise cannot be evaluated, as in the centralized system, according to norms prescribed at the top. The criterion of performance is decentralized. An enterprise will have a high or low rating depending on its profitability and behavior on the market. It will rise or fall by its own merits and cannot count on the political bureaucracy always to bail it out in an emergency. Administrative prices give way to market prices. Interference from the center is limited to economic actions and controls related to the market mechanism: key investments, changes in interest rates, bank credits, and so forth.

Rapid industrialization in a backward country is initially achieved by a central political bureaucracy with the power to establish priorities and impose centralized planning. When the economic surplus is small, large doses of savings are required for substantial growth that are incompatible with a high level of personal consumption. Despite the privileges of the politbureaucracy, its hegemony is based on a solid foundation and is likely to survive as long as it contributes to building modern industry. The more effective the plan, however, the sooner is an underdeveloped country likely to reach the point of industrial saturation. According to Kuron and Modzelewski, the point of saturation in Poland was reached by the midfifties: "In 1956, the apparatus of industrial production was three times larger than in 1949, and in 1960, four times larger."

Once the stage of industrial saturation has been reached, the low level of consumption previously required for maximizing capital accumulation becomes an impediment to further growth. Because production of the means of production is wasteful if this productive potential is not put to use, a time must come when consumption becomes a top economic priority. Otherwise, this unused potential and waste of the economic surplus will lead to a slowing down of the economy. The crisis of state socialism begins when, with a growing investment, one gets a decreased instead of an increased growth rate.

Kuron and Modzelewski stress five key factors behind this slowdown. First, *the inflation barrier*: The rapid growth in employment under socialism results in a formidable expansion of nominal wages without a corresponding increase in the supply of consumer goods. This in turn leads to higher prices and a tendency for real wages to fall below the socially acceptable minimum, which further reinforces the braking effect of low consumption on economic growth. Second, *the raw materials barrier*: The rapid growth in the means of production requires increased consumption of raw materials and fuels leading to an acute shortage of both. Because material and fuel costs are much higher in this sector than in the production of consumer goods, the raw material base is more quickly exhausted. When the goal is volume of production rather than reduction of costs per unit of output, there is a squandering of raw materials and fuels necessary to continuing growth. Third, *the unutilized stock and plant barrier*: Production of unutilized reserves that cannot be marketed, whether because of poor quality or because of lack of effective demand, is a drain on the economic surplus that interferes with economic development. The nonutilization of reserves and productive capacity is also an unnecessary drain on the labor force and a symptom of the failure to adapt production to human needs. Fourth, *the technological barrier*: Once the stage of full employment is reached, further growth cannot occur except by intensive means and increased labor productivity. Investments tied up in the old technology have the effect of discouraging technological innovation, mechanization, and automation, and the availability of cheap labor operates as an incentive to the continued use of lower-cost but obsolete machinery. Fifth, *the export barrier*: Due to excessive raw material costs, poor craftsmanship, and low technical levels, goods for export tend to find no buyers at all or are sold at "a disadvantageous ratio of export production costs to the price of goods purchased abroad." Given the inability of manufacturing industry to export, a socialist country may end up either with an unfavorable foreign trade balance or without the necessary imports required for continued growth.

Because of these fetters on the productive forces that first manifested themselves after Stalin's death, the 1950s witnessed the beginning of a general crisis in the bureaucratic system. Among the symptoms of the international crisis were the general strike in East Germany and the demonstrations and street fighting in Berlin (June 1953), the series of strikes in Soviet labor camps (July 1953), the strikes and street demonstrations in Poznan, Poland (June 1956), and the first antibureaucratic revolution in Hungary (October 1956).

Once the foundations of industry had been built and full employment achieved, say Kuron and Modzelewski, the disparity between the expanded productive potential and the low level of social consumption became evident. Virtually the whole of society found itself in conflict with the central political bureaucracy: "The distinct class interests of the peasants forcibly deprived of their surpluses, of the workers receiving starvation wages, of the supervisors of hired labor relatively badly paid and deprived of the right to make decisions, necessitated increased consumption which was contrary to the class goal of production set by the bureaucracy." As the principal bulwark of the Stalinist system, totalitarian police surveillance and repression became the object of universal hatred and had to be dismantled. The Great Debate on decentralization launched in 1962 by Soviet economist Evsei Liberman, the September 1965 Kosygin Reform in the USSR, and the economic reforms in Eastern Europe that led to Soviet intervention in Czechoslovakia in 1968 were all responses to this crisis.

Liberman's famous proposals, known as the Kharkov incentive system, called for structural changes in the planning process at the enterprise level. All prices and outputs were to continue being centrally planned, but the individual firms would receive fewer directives from the central planning commission. Liberman recommended assigning only those targets pertaining to the firm's final *output mix*: volume of production, product destinations, and delivery dates. The *input mix* would be arrived at independently by each enterprise determining its own optimum combinations of investment in fixed plant, raw materials, and manpower. The planners would provide for each firm's needs through a centrally planned system of capital and manpower allocation. In the allocation of scarce resources to individual enterprises, priorities were to continue being determined by administrative decisions at the top, decisions relating to national security, industrialization, growth rates, and so on. Although the managers resented this continued dependence on the central authorities, they were left free to compete with each other in matters of efficiency and profitability. They were given authority to retain the firm's surplus profits and to utilize them as they saw fit, which included paying bonuses to themselves. For the first time, performance would be calculated on the basis of sales rather than output. This new marketing requirement put a premium on the production of more varied goods of higher quality than formerly.

One major objection to the Liberman Plan was that it left the allocation of scarce resources to the central planners. In a *Pravda* article, "Plan, Assignment, and Material Incentive" (21 September 1962), Soviet economist V. Nemchinov proposed that all intermediate goods should cease being allocated by the state and be turned over to the operation of market forces. According to this proposal, Soviet enterprises should be able to negotiate independent agreements with their suppliers because the complexity and inflexibility of the existing system of allocations from the center were interfering with freedom of input determination. Managers would be better served by allocation decentralization, to which the economic reformers later added price and output decentralization. The Kosygin Reform of 1965 did little more than implement the Liberman proposals. Thus, it stopped short of the more radical demands put forth by other reformers both inside and outside the Soviet Union.

The important consideration is not the different forms that economic decentralization took in the Soviet Union and the several countries of Eastern Europe but their common political denominator. The importance of technocracy was its claim to manage the economy in a way more compatible with national interests. The central plan, the chief economic agency of the political bureaucracy, had become a fetter on economic growth. In the frantic rush toward industrialization, central planning had become overambitious and taut. There was little room for miscalculation or human error without danger of exhausting the raw materials base. Unlike a capitalist economy in which the fundamental problem is to expand the market as a condition of absorbing current production, under the system of centralized planning socialist enterprises had their markets guaranteed; hence, they were preoccupied mainly with getting the necessary supplies. The decentralized system pursued to its ultimate conclusions would leave this task, as well as the determination of prices and outputs, to the managers. At the same time, the dismantling of the central plan was tantamount to transforming the political bureaucracy from a necessary economic agency into a dispensable one. The politbureaucracy had proved incapable of maintaining a high rate of economic growth; it had also become superfluous under the new system of production for mass consumption.

In capitalist societies power has become divorced from ownership in the large corporations with the anticipated result that managers and their fellow bureaucrats in government are gradually undermining the owners' political hegemony. Under socialism economic power has also tended to acquire a political foothold. Thus, one may anticipate that the new economic decision makers will continue to encroach upon the political authority of a central bureaucracy that has lost the initiative in economic matters. Unlike the class struggle between capitalists and managers, the antagonism between politbureaucrats and technobureaucrats arises between different sectors of the same class. It involves a struggle not between rival political and economic orders but between rival strategies for development under socialism. The conflict between centralists and decentralists in socialist countries is a family quarrel. Internal dissension may momentarily weaken the system, but social change is impossible without it.

The economic conflict over decentralization has given rise to a corresponding political struggle: between "conservatives" opposing decentralization and "liberals" advocating it. Considerable confusion has resulted from this choice of political terminology. Conservatives portray themselves as defenders of the socialist system. They accuse their liberal antagonists of aiming at a restoration of capitalism and of making common cause with liberals in the West. Liberals portray themselves as going beyond the status quo. They accuse conservatives of defending the vestiges of a state capitalist and bureaucratically deformed society. These self-portrayals are accurate. It is only the charges brought against each that are unfounded.

What precisely is the challenge of technocracy? Briefly, it is the contention that centralized economic planning is *not* essential to socialism. It is communism, not socialism, that has for its ultimate objective the abolition of the anarchy of production. If it happens that a return to the market mechanism is the most effective way of ensuring a continued high rate of economic growth, then so much the worse for central planning. Less than full employment may be a consequence of adopting the profit motive under socialism, but the resulting increase in efficiency can help raise productivity. It is a question of trade-offs in the interest of a new spurt forward. Unfortunately, workers are less secure under a market system; the revival of business cycles is tantamount to the reappearance of pockets of unemployment and a new mobility in the labor force. As always, the ultimate costs of economic progress are paid for by the underlying population. Nonetheless, to move forward to communism it is essential to break the back of the central political bureaucracy. And for this, the most effective strategy is an alliance of workers, petty bureaucrats, and technobureaucrats capable of overcoming existing fetters on the productive forces and raising the material level of civilization.

In conclusion, Communist practice is no longer monolithic but takes two principal forms: the centralizing tendency of the politbureaucracy and the decentralizing tendency of the technobureaucracy. What needs emphasizing is that both tendencies are anticommunist; both are critical in practice of Marxist theory. In fact, they show that Marx's working class is not the decisive agent shaping socialist revolutions. That agent is the bureaucratic class.

9

Competition among Socialist Systems

In Marxist theory national differences and antagonisms are already disappearing under capitalism, "owing to the development of the bourgeoisie, to freedom of commerce, to the world market, to uniformity in the mode of production and in the corresponding conditions of life." This overly sanguine judgment is followed in the *Communist Manifesto* with the forecast that competition among postcapitalist societies will be free of national antagonisms. "The supremacy of the proletariat will cause them to vanish still faster. . . . In proportion as the exploitation of one individual by another is overcome, the exploitation of one nation by another will also be put an end to. In proportion as the antagonism within the nation vanishes, the hostility of one nation to another will come to an end."

Oppressed by the lords of land and by the lords of capital, workers have had to resist not only economic exploitation but also the so-called blood tax levied in the course of national wars. The *Communist Manifesto* tells us that workingmen have no country until they rise to become the leading class of the nation. Only then, by workingmen constituting themselves into the national class, will wars and other antagonisms disappear. As Marx concludes his inaugural "Address of the Working Men's International Association": "If the emancipation of the working classes requires their fraternal concurrence, how are they to fulfill that great mission with a foreign policy in pursuit of criminal designs, playing upon national prejudices, and squandering in piratical wars the people's blood and treasure?"

Has current practice confirmed Marxist theory in these respects? On the contrary, postcapitalist societies exhibit the same national antagonisms, although in attenuated form, that we find under capitalism. Wars between socialist states are no longer unthinkable. The invasion of Hungary in 1956 and of Czechoslovakia in 1968 were not, technically speaking, wars; but these were followed by border warfare between China and the USSR in 1969 and by the full-scale war between socialist Vietnam and socialist Campuchea and by the Chinese punitive war against Vietnam in 1979.

What is the explanation of these intersocialist antagonisms? How do we account for the fact that the Soviet Union trampled on the independence of socialist countries in Eastern Europe, that Yugoslavia returned to a market economy and joined the bloc of unaligned nations in the third world, that the Chinese Communists see the Soviet Union as the principal enemy of the peoples of the world, that the Cubans tried to build communism and socialism simultaneously? In part, the answer lies in the different class compositions of their respective leaderships. Like the conflicts within socialist societies, the antagonisms among them need to be explained in terms of class struggles—the conflicts internal to each "writ large" as the class struggle is magnified and takes on national dimensions.

In Yugoslavia, China, and Cuba petty bureaucracies allied to the working class resisted the Soviet model of bureaucratic domination along with Soviet meddling in their internal affairs. The foreign policies of these mavericks reflected their domestic strategies, and their struggle against a bureaucratic class raised communist expectations even if it did not realize them. In each case the struggle against bureaucratic privilege forced them further to the left. What was the nature of their respective heresies, and how did they come to challenge Soviet orthodoxy?

The Yugoslav Model: Social Ownership and Workers' Self-Management

The significance of the Yugoslav model derives in part from the influence it has exerted on sectors of the established Communist parties in Poland, Hungary, and Czechoslovakia. Despite Soviet efforts to discredit it, Titoism fathered protest movements against bureaucracy, the centralized state, and the omnipresent party apparatus. Because Titoism represented the first successful revolt against Stalinist and Soviet domination of Eastern Europe, it became extremely contagious and reached epidemic proportions. Tito inspired the so-called nationalist deviations in Poland and Hungary in 1956 and encouraged Ota Šik's proposed "new model of socialism" in Czechoslovakia in 1968.

With the breakdown of Soviet-Yugoslav relations in 1948, Titoism was criticized by the Soviets as a rightist deviation in the tradition of Bukharin's "go slow" tactics in the Soviet Union. Its subsequent model of market socialism was also rejected. The Soviets claimed that state ownership *without* workers' self-management at the national level is a more advanced form of socialism than collective ownership *with* workers' self-management at the level of each enterprise.

Yugoslav socialism has evolved through two principal stages: the period from 1945 to 1949 that was modeled on the system of centralized planning in the Soviet Union; and the period of social ownership and workers' self-management that was inaugurated by the National Assembly on 26 June 1950 on the basis of a new law requiring the administration of state enterprises by workers' collectives. The transformation of Yugoslavia from a bureaucratic centralist into a decentralized system came in response to Tito's speech to the National Assembly calling for "Factories to the Workers!" In the official Yugoslav view the changes that ensued would have been undertaken independently of the Soviet-Yugoslav rupture of March 1948, but the frictions with the Soviet Union indicate that intersocialist rivalries were also coming into play.

Before the 1948 rift it was assumed that Yugoslavia would follow the Soviet example. What was unexpected was the speed with which Tito launched an all-out nationalization campaign in 1946, followed by a Five-Year Plan officially proclaimed in April 1947. Considering that the Soviet Union did not launch its industrialization campaign until 1926 and that its First Five-Year Plan did not go into effect until April 1929, more than a decade after the seizure of power, Tito skipped over several steps in Soviet economic and political development.

How can one account for Yugoslavia's uniqueness? It was the only country in Eastern Europe other than the Soviet Union that organized an effective resistance against the German occupation. Tito's partisans burgeoned from an initial 80,000 in 1941 to an estimated 800,000 by the end of 1944. It was the armed power of the Yugoslav Communists that allowed them to skip over the stage of so-called people's democracy.

The period of people's democracy lasted from 1945 to about 1948, during which the revolutionary vanguards in Eastern Europe collaborated with noncommunist parties in governments that escaped Communist domination. The only regime comparable to a people's democracy in Yugoslavia came in an agreement between Tito and the Yugoslav government-in-exile in Britain, providing for a provisional government with a three-man regency to act for King Peter until the future of the monarchy should be decided by plebiscite. The agreement, reached shortly after the liberation of Belgrade on 20 October 1944, led to the formation of a government with Tito as premier. But during the campaign to elect a Constituent Assembly, the Communists so harassed their opponents that the opposition parties ended by boycotting the elections. Because only the Communist-dominated Popular Front presented a list to the voters, when the new government first met in November 1945 the dictatorship of the party was already assured.

These exceptional conditions meant that the Yugoslav Communists were able to embark on a course of rapid industrialization, leading to socialism before any other East European country. Over 50 percent of Yugoslav industry had been nationalized even before the war was over. The Law on State Appropriations of Enemy Property and the Property of Absentee Persons was approved by the provisional government as early as November 1944. It was followed in August 1945 by the Basic Law on Agrarian Reform and Colonization, providing for the expropriation without compensation of more than 80 percent of the arable land, to be redistributed among landless peasants and veterans of the resistance. A limit of twenty-five to forty-five hectares was set for individual owners. In July 1946 the Basic Law on Cooperatives was enacted, paving the way toward collective farming and the organization of state tractor stations. And in December the first major nationalization law transformed all major industries, transportation, wholesale trade facilities, and banking institutions into state enterprises. The stage was set for the giant leap forward into industrialization. Yugoslavia's First Five-Year Plan was adopted in April 1947.

With the passage of a second nationalization law in April 1948, the whole of industry on the federal and republican levels had become nationalized. So had roughly 70 percent of local industry. At the same time the plan called for the rapid collectivization of the peasantry, setting a goal of 50 percent of the arable land to be plowed collectively by 1951. A forced collectivization campaign was launched in 1949 but was abandoned a year later because of peasant resistance, the Soviet economic blockade, and the launching of a new form of market socialism.

More than any other factor, the rift with the Soviet Union was responsible for Yugoslavia's continuing leftward course. Differences with the Soviet Union dated back to the early days of the resistance, when Stalin pressured Tito to unite his partisans with Mihajlović's Četniks in a subordinate role under Mihajlović's leadership. The Soviet Union had recognized the government-in-exile rather than Tito's own National Liberation Committee, which as early as 1943 had become a kind of de facto government at home. The Kremlin opposed any suggestion of Communist influence in the Yugoslav resistance, criticized the formation of shock military units called proletarian brigades, looked askance at the adoption of a partisan flag with a red star, refused to give military aid until after it had been provided by the West, and disapproved of the independent political organization of the partisans—first of the Anti-Fascist Council of National Liberation and then of the National Liberation Committee as its provisional government. Understandably, the Yugolslavs had been cautioned to "go slow" because of the Soviets' concern to preserve allied unity during the war. What was not so understandable was Stalin's pact with Churchill in Moscow in October 1944, which, over the heads of Tito's partisans, agreed to place Yugoslavia under the joint sphere of influence of the USSR and Great Britain after the war.

With Tito's public protest against the agreement in his speech at Ljubljana on 28 May 1945, there began veiled complaints against Soviet efforts to run roughshod over Yugoslav national interests. In his biography *Tito Speaks*, Vladimir Dedijer devotes an entire chapter to showing how the Soviets wanted to exploit the country economically. In all the negotiations with Yugoslavia concerning joint-stock companies for steel, iron, and nonferous metals, the Soviet line was the same: "the purpose was to prevent the industrialization of Yugoslavia, to found only such companies as would turn Yugoslavia into a raw-material base of the Soviet Union." During the negotiations in August 1946, for example, the chief of the Soviet delegation was reported as saying: "What do you need heavy industry for? In the Urals we have everything you need." If the Soviets had had their way, they would have secured a stranglehold over entire branches of Yugoslav industry and over the country's economy as a whole. The climax of the negotiations was reached with the Soviet proposal to found a Soviet-Yugoslav bank. This bank would have penetrated to the core of the Yugoslav economy: "Soviet organs were to take the Yugoslav central financing and credit body into their own hands. Through this bank they would control Yugoslavia's economy from one central point, and subordinate it to their requirements as they thought fit." The picture Dedijer painted was a dire one. Yet the Soviets pursued a similar policy with other socialist countries, which prompted the Polish and Hungarian revolts of 1956 and the Sino-Soviet split in 1963, likewise traceable to Soviet "big-power chauvinism."

A climate of tension developed between the two countries and reached a showdown in March 1948. Having postponed for a year the negotiations toward a renewal of its trade agreement with Yugoslavia, the Soviet government on 18 March abruptly withdrew all its military advisers, followed the next day by the withdrawal of all Soviet technical and civilian specialists. In response to Tito's letter asking for a clarification, Stalin replied on 27 March, listing among the principal causes of Soviet dissatisfaction: first, the Yugoslav Communists were responsible for circulating Trotskyist rumors concerning the degeneration of the Communist party of the Soviet Union; second, the Yugoslav CP was a militarist organization lacking internal democracy; and third, the Yugoslav CP with its People's Front were "being hoodwinked by the degenerate and opportunist theory of peaceful absorption of capitalist elements . . . borrowed from Bernstein . . . and Bukharin." For Tito these issues were a matter not of ideology but of independence. Stalin was furious with Tito's reply and after a further exchange of letters referred the question to the Cominform. Meeting in Bucharest in June, the Cominform formally excluded the Yugoslav CP from its ranks. .

To the other charges made by Moscow, the Cominform resolution of expulsion added a new one: the Tito regime had tried to cover up its mistakes by rushing through leftist measures, by adopting a new nationalization law and a new grain tax that were described as "adventurist," "demagogical," and "impracticable." The Yugoslav Communists were then invited to get rid of Tito and the people around him: "The interests of the very existence and development of the Yugoslav Communist Party demand that an end be put to this regime." The resolution also accused the Titoist leadership of a nationalist deviation that soon found other exponents throughout Eastern Europe in the form of "national communism."

By the beginning of 1949 a Soviet-imposed economic blockade was in effect. The damage done to the implementation of Yugoslavia's Five-Year Plan was staggering. Yugoslavia was dependent on the Soviet bloc for approximately 50 percent of its imports, without which its economy was in serious trouble. So the Yugoslavs were compelled to turn to the West for support. Even before the blockade they had expressed an interest in settling their economic differences with Washington. Three weeks after their expulsion from the Cominform an understanding was reached, followed in December by a trade agreement with Great Britain. In 1949 further economic ties were established with other Western nations, leading eventually to a rapprochement with the social democratic parties in those countries. By then the Yugoslav Communists had begun to rethink Marxism, charting a new course that departed from the Soviet model in domestic as well as foreign policy.

Yugoslavia's new course was assailed by the Soviet Union as simultaneously an "anarchosyndicalist" or "leftist" deviation and a "petty-bourgeois" or "right-wing" deviation aiming at the restoration of a capitalist market economy. It shared features of both, but the important and neglected point was in what areas of the economy each of these tendencies prevailed. On close inspection it was evident that the anarchosyndicalist current dominated industry, commerce, and banking in the form of urban collectives and workers' self-management. The petty-bourgeois tendency ruled the countryside where the policy of forced collectivization was abandoned in 1951 in favor of petty commodity production—the most effective means of developing agriculture in view of the mountainous terrain, the absence of kulaks, and the persistence of strong individualistic traits among the peasants. Which of these two courses was fundamental for the economy as a whole: the step forward toward social ownership and workers' self-management in industry, or the step backward toward precapitalist relations of production in agriculture? The outcome should never have been doubted, for the urban sector already dominated the economy and was bound to prevail over rural areas in the future.

Tito's new heresy was officially incorporated into the new program of the Communist League, or reorganized Communist party, adopted at its Seventh Congress in April 1958. Fundamental to the new Yugoslav model was its novel theory of the transition period between capitalism and socialism. Engels had foreseen in *Anti-Dühring* that, in order to develop further the productive forces and to soften class antagonisms, state intervention in the economy would end by modifying the capitalist system. Marx and Engels had foreseen that the expanded role of the state would also strengthen the economic and political power of the Bonapartist bureaucracy, making it a relatively independent force in society and an arbiter of the internal class struggle between bourgeoisie and proletariat. And they had foreseen the emergence of not only socialist tendencies but also socialist elements in the form of cooperatives within the womb of the old society. What they had not foreseen was that the capitalist system would become progressively more responsive to the pressures exerted by the working class toward improvements in social security and welfare. Tito's program, *Yugoslavia's Way: The Program of the League of Communists of Yugoslavia*, made up for this defect. Noting that there is no pure capitalism in contemporary society, chapter 1 proclaimed that "the specific forms of state capitalist relations may be either the last effort of capitalism to survive or the first step toward socialism," and that "the swelling-wave of state capitalist tendencies in the capitalist world is the best evidence that, inexorably and in a variety of ways, humanity is moving deep into the era of socialism."

Basic to the new program was a willingness to go beyond the letter of Marxism. We are told that in contemporary society there is no pure socialism, that Marx underestimated the elements of capitalism that would survive in the new order. Commodity production survives: socialist governments are compelled "to compromise with small-owner elements, even with the bourgeoisie, and to rely temporarily on various forms of state capitalist relations and methods." The more backward the country, the stronger tends to be the role of these factors and the related phenomenon of bureaucratism; in backward countries the state assumes the initiative in the economy and imposes itself as a force above society. Along with commodity production the state too survives. With the state we also find classes, class antagonisms, and exploitation: "in the socialist society of the transitional period the same social forces continue to operate which were specific to the last stages of capitalism." It is in this perspective that the Yugoslavs distinguish between the Soviet system and their own more advanced stage of socialism: an early stage defined exclusively by the abolition of bourgeois property or capital, and an advanced stage in which "the question of the gradual withering away of the state arises as the fundamental and decisive question of the socialist system." Only during this higher Yugoslav stage may we reasonably expect the democratization of society and the progressive abolition of bureaucratic domination, bureaucratic exploitation, and class antagonisms. But commodity production survives even during this higher stage.

The practical consequences of this new assessment of the transition period were developed in chapter 2, entitled "The Struggle for Socialism under New Conditions." Because the balance of social forces in the world was believed to have shifted substantially in favor of the working class, there was now the "possibility of a peaceful transition to socialism." That called for a strategy of working within the system, a strategy aimed at the extension of democracy through workers' participation in the ownership and control of industry. An effective strategy was also interpreted as requiring "united action and even the fusion and unification of workers' parties." In this perspective no single party could be said to have a monopoly of revolutionary thinking. Instead of opposing the social democratic parties in capitalist countries, the program relied on them and on their respective labor movements to advance socialist tendencies by evolutionary means. Although the program did not anticipate an automatic transition from capitalism to socialism and acknowledged the importance of a revolutionary vanguard, the focus of Yugoslav strategy was no longer on the privileged role of a Marxist-Leninist party or on the violent overthrow of a bourgeois government.

In foreign policy the program regarded the antagonism between the capitalist and socialist camps as no longer decisive in international relations. Because there is no pure capitalism and no pure socialism, the conflict between the two camps was not nearly so important as it had been imagined. The rationale for military blocs was rejected. These blocs were said to have retarded the overall development of the productive forces in both camps. They were held responsible for slowing down the move toward socialism in the West and for obstructing the transition to a higher form of socialism in the East. The existence of blocs, the program pointed out, "creates conditions enabling the reactionary forces in individual countries to suppress internal progress under the pretext of external danger." In view of the changed balance of social forces, these blocs had become superfluous. Because a new world war is no longer inevitable, there is no need for socialist countries to be continually preparing for one. Although the Warsaw Pact was a defensive response to the creation of NATO and the rearming of Germany, it ended by escalating the arms race instead of pushing toward general disarmament. Thus, the program called for the dismantling of both military blocs while opting for a policy of nonalignment: "Yugoslavia sees in the independent, non-bloc policies . . . a contribution to the broadest international cooperation and to the consolidation of peace in the world."

Socialist domestic policy, according to the program, did not have for its aim the creation of a new society on the basis of some blueprint worked out in advance. Its purpose was more modest: "to free the socialist factors which had already developed within the old society." To free these forces it is necessary to extend the scope of democracy in public life, so that "state administration begins to diminish in the direct management of the economy . . . and is more and more transferred to various social self-managing bodies, independent or interlinked in respective democratic organizations." This Yugoslav recipe for decentralizing governmental authority was in keeping with Lenin's conclusion in *State and Revolution* that the way to uproot bureaucratic privileges is to "enable everybody, without exception, to perform 'state functions.'" In this perspective the dictatorship of the proletariat depends on workers' self-management in both government and industry. The state and the bureaucracy must wither away, and so must the party. The party's relationship to the masses "must appear more and more as a relationship between equals."

The Yugoslav model gives precedence to direct social possession over indirect state ownership by the working class. Direct possession in the form of industrial collectives—"factories to the workers"—is considered a condition of workers' self-management. By putting the worker in a position to decide on the distribution of the surplus product, self-management allegedly nullifies bureaucratic salary differentials once capitalist exploitation is overcome. Only as direct possessors of the means of production can the workers supposedly overcome the commodity character of labor power. In principle, self-management transforms them into direct managers of production and distribution.

Although it is possible for disputes to arise between individual workers and management organs in the same enterprise, these are no longer regarded as class conflicts.

What is the reality behind this program? A distinguishing feature of the Yugoslav program is its democratic system of privilege by consensus. Workers' self-management does not preclude high salaries for professionally qualified workers; in fact, bureaucratic salaries are ostensibly justified by the operation of workers' democracy.

The socialist principle of distribution according to work is modified in Yugoslavia by the subjective will of the workers and by objective market tendencies. Industrial collectives with more advanced machinery perform better than those with obsolete means of production; they have more "profits" to redistribute among the workers. Collectives that stress their social responsibility generally earn less per capita than those that lay off their excess labor force. Democratic provisions for election instead of appointment, for popular initiative and immediate recall of representatives, are not sufficient guarantees against bureaucratic exploitation. Marx was right: the abolition of exploitation hinges on the abolition not only of the state as an oppressive institution but also of commodity production and the indirect tyranny of the market. Because commodity production survives under the system of workers' self-management, so does the measurement of work in acordance with market conditions. Even with workers' control, surplus value continues to be pocketed by managers and professionals whose expert services are quasicommodities administratively priced in response to market conditions.

Nonetheless, the Yugoslav model of a higher stage of socialism converges on Marx's model of the lower stage of communism. It exhibits several features of communism whose importance is minimized in the Soviet view: the erosion of state power and the establishment of workers' control. This is no mean accomplishment—it challenges both the authority and the salaries of the bureaucracy. Democracy may provide a screen for bureaucratic exploitation, but it also contains the mechanisms for overcoming bureaucratic privilege.

China's Great Leap Forward in Domestic and Foreign Policy

For years Maoism was notorious for its populist revision of Lenin's formula of the "revolutionary democratic dictatorship of the proletariat and peasantry." Mao had replaced it with his own strategy of a "people's democratic dictatorship" based on a broad alliance with the petty bourgeoisie and national bourgeoisie in what was called a "bloc of four classes." Its most extreme formulation is found in his essay *On New*

Democracy (1940), where he calls for a republic under the "joint dictatorship of all revolutionary classes." Although led by the working class in alliance with the peasantry, Mao's people's democratic dictatorship was responsive to the interests of the petty bourgeoisie and national bourgeoisie and also included representatives of these two classes in his ruling coalition.

Fundamental in formulating this populist component of Chinese Marxism is Mao's work *On the Correct Handling of Contradictions among the People* (1957). Criticized by Soviet Marxists for making too many concessions to petty-bourgeois and capitalist interests, it was also denounced for holding back the full-scale construction of socialism in China. Mao's justification for this go slow policy may be seen in his characterization of the leftist tendency in his own party in chapter 2 of the essay. Whereas the party's right wing mistakes the people's real enemies for friends, "[those] with a 'leftist' way of thinking so magnify contradictions between ourselves and the enemy that they . . . regard as counterrevolutionaries persons who really aren't."

In January 1956 Mao started his own liberalization campaign, "Let a Hundred Flowers Bloom, Let a Hundred Schools Contend"—the Chinese counterpart to the de-Stalinization campaign launched by Khrushchev at the Twentieth Congress of the CPSU. He did not suggest how liberalization might be implemented until February 1957 at the eleventh plenary session of the Supreme State Conference. It would be implemented by everyone criticizing without fear of repression what each considered wrong with China's domestic transition to socialism. No subject was taboo. Censorship was lifted, and the columns of the Communist press were opened to all and sundry. The result was an avalanche of social criticism until June 1957, when the period of open criticism was followed by one of self-criticism imposed on those malcontents who were denounced as rightists!

Mao hoped that criticism would help China along the road to socialism. Instead, it provided enemies of the regime with an opportunity to demand more freedoms and to encourage the same revisionist tendencies in China that had erupted in Poland and Hungary in 1956. The campaign failed; Mao was obliged to abandon it altogether. This failure taught him that Chinese intellectuals had not been won over to communist views and that more drastic steps were needed toward overcoming the legacy of the past and the roots of continued resistance to his domestic program. Mao's response to the failure of his new cultural policy was *to take a sharp turn to the left.*

With the Great Leap Forward (1958–60) an entirely new leftist strategy made its appearance in domestic matters. It was followed in April

1960 by a corresponding change in foreign policy directed at Soviet and Yugoslav revisionism. In June of that year, at the Third Congress of the Romanian Communist party, Khrushchev retorted by accusing Mao of being "an ultraleftist, an ultradogmatist, and indeed a left revisionist"! This attack was followed in August by the Soviet cancellation, without advance notice or consultation,of its technical assistance program. The Soviet political bureaucracy withdrew not only technical advisers but also blueprints for the half-completed factories and installations they left behind—which meant that the Chinese could not finish the projects themselves. Such were the pressures on the Chinese leadership to give up its criticism of Soviet revisionism.

Its response came in November at the meeting of communist and workers' parties in Moscow. The CPC's delegate, Teng Hsiao-ping, publicly denounced the Soviet bureaucracy for trying to impose its own line on other fraternal parties. Though conceding that the CPSU was still the "leading party," Teng did not believe that it was above criticism or that it had a right to decide all questions concerning ideology. How can each party retain its independence, how can there be equality between them, if whatever the Soviet party decides at its congresses is binding on all the rest? "In relations between parties, there is no reason to demand that the minority should submit to the majority, for between parties there are no superiors and inferiors: each party is independent."

What was the nature of Mao's heresy that had brought relations with the Soviet bureaucracy to this impasse? During the brief period of the Great Leap Forward, Mao called for the creation of new social relations of production in the countryside aimed at accomplishing the transition to communism during his lifetime. These were to take the form of communes or supercollectives and were to replace the recently established agricultural collectives based on the Soviet model. The people's communes set up in the countryside in 1958 were different from all existing forms of farm collectivization in three important respects: first, the merger of agricultural cooperatives in larger units for pooling resources and jointly controlling water, irrigation, and transportation; second, the merger of local industry, commerce, and education with agriculture for overcoming the traditional backwardness of rural life and the separation of town and country; third, the merger of farm cooperatives with state power as branches of the central government. This merger was for the purpose of legalizing the use of their combined resources and of fixing priorities in construction, electrification, and military defense. Unlike the situation in the Soviet Union where the collectives were separated from the state, there was no divorce between political and economic power in the people's commune. As the commune's economic contribution increased, so did its participation in government authority. This was interpreted as a first step in the withering away of the state as an institution beyond the control of the masses.

The specifically communist features of the commune are worth noting. Besides overcoming the gap between peasants and workers who now shared a common form of property, the commune also provided a number of free services. These included public dining rooms, nurseries, kindergartens, grain, and in some cases "free dishes," "free tailoring," "free barbering," and "free theater tickets." This system of distribution combined payment according to work with distribution according to need, thus bridging the gap between Marx's lower and higher stages of communism. Efforts were also made to eliminate the differences between mental and manual labor by upgrading the level of education and by teaching the peasants a variety of industrial skills. In his *Principles of Communism* (1848), Engels had anticipated that the "citizen's commune" would be the basic social unit in a full communist society. Mao's "people's commune," representing the majority of citizens under a single form of ownership, was the closest approximation to Engels's model that had yet been devised.

The communization of the countryside was the substance of Mao's new heresy. There was no need to wait, he said, for the mechanization of agriculture before advancing to higher forms of social property; the establishment of new property relations was possible in advance of the development of the forces of production. Both Lenin and Stalin had insisted upon agricultural mechanization before collectivization. Mao's *The Question of Agricultural Cooperatives* (1955) inverted the order: "In the field of agriculture, under the conditions prevailing in China . . . we must develop cooperativization first, and only thereafter can we utilize machinery." This was the key to Mao's first Great Leap Forward.

Mao's program was overly ambitious, but it was not a complete failure. At the beginning of 1958 roughly half a billion peasants were organized in approximately 750,000 cooperatives having an average membership of 160 families. By the end of the year they had merged into 25,000 communes with an average of several thousand families each. By the middle sixties, through a process of subdivision and adaptation to different local conditions, the communes doubled and then trebled to level off at roughly 75,000. Mao's Great Leap Forward suffered a setback, but it survived to become an integral part of China's new system of socialist agriculture and also put an end to the central bureaucracy's stranglehold on the countryside.

Relations with the Soviet political bureaucracy continued to deteriorate during this period. Finally, the differences were made public through an exchange of letters between the central committees of the CPSU and the CPC during the spring of 1963. On 14 June the Chinese responded to a Soviet letter of 30 March by putting forth a leftist interpretation of Marx's and Lenin's concept of the transition period: "the fundamental thesis of Marx and Lenin is that the dictatorship of the proletariat will inevitably continue for the entire historical period up to the abolition of all class differences and the entry into . . . the higher stage of communist society." Criticizing the New Program of the CPSU adopted at its Twenty-second Congress in 1961, the letter noted that the class struggle survives in all socialist countries without exception and that a "state of the whole people" is patently impossible, as long as collective ownership by part of the people survives alongside state ownership.

In July 1964 the editorial departments of *People's Daily* and *Red Flag* published an essay entitled "On Khrushchev's Phoney Communism," the ninth in a series of comments on a July 1963 open letter by the CPSU. This essay elaborates further the Chinese thesis concerning the political transition between capitalist and communist society. The section on socialist society and the dictatorship of the proletariat says that socialism "covers the important historical period of transition from class to classless society." A later section, attacking Khrushchev's thesis of a state of the whole people, affirms that the "dictatorship of the proletariat is the form of the state in the entire period of transition from capitalism to the higher stage of communism." Thus, the dictatorship of the proletariat *is* the form of the state under socialism. This dictatorship is necessary because the class struggle between the proletariat and bourgeoisie has yet to be resolved through a decisive victory: "[w]hether a socialist society will advance to communism or revert to capitalism depends upon the outcome of this protracted struggle." The dictatorship of the proletariat is not restricted, as it was for Lenin and for Marx before him, to the political transition between capitalism and the first stage of communist society; and socialism is not simply an equivalent, as it was in Lenin's usage, for the first stage of communism.

What Marx and Lenin had differentiated are conflated into a single historical period. Class antagonisms and exploitation are said to characterize socialism because they also characterize a dictatorship of the proletariat. Contrary to Khrushchev, this dictatorship is not dissolved during the transition to a higher phase of communism nor is it replaced by a "state of the whole people."

Despite the misreading of Marx's *Critique of the Gotha Programme* and Lenin's *State and Revolution*, there was an element of realism in this Chinese conception of socialism that went beyond Stalin's interpretation of the Marxist texts. For in addition to the dictatorship of the proletariat, only public ownership was deemed necessary for socialism: "In socialist society the dictatorship of the proletariat replaces bourgeois dictatorship, and the public ownership of the means of production replaces private ownership."

After the 1965 U.S. bombing attacks on North Vietnam close to the Chinese border, one group within the Chinese party wanted to send a delegation to the Twenty-third Congress of the CPSU to reactivate the Sino-Soviet military alliance. But Mao opposed such a rapprochement with the Soviet Union. Instead, he supported a strategy of people's self-defense—a strategy set forth in Lin Piao's essay, *Long Live the Victory of People's War*. What lay behind this decision?

By then the fundamental antagonism in the contemporary world had become identified by Mao with the struggle of third-world peoples against imperialism. This analysis involved a departure from earlier Chinese positions. During the fifties, the Chinese Communists had identified the main world antagonism with the struggle between the socialist and capitalist camps. In the letter of the CPC to the CPSU in June 1963 they shifted their attention to the third world where they claimed all the major antagonisms were "concentrated." By September 1965 they went even further: the fundamental antagonism was now identified with the struggle between U.S. imperialism and movements of national liberation.

The point of the Chinese polemics against the Soviet leadership from June 1963 until March 1966 was to pressure the Soviet Union to re-commit itself to the socialist road by abandoning its détente with the United States. In March 1966, when the Chinese CP sent its last letter to the CPSU refusing an invitation to attend its Twenty-third Congress, all direct relations between the two parties were terminated. Because the Soviet Union had placed the interests of its political bureaucracy above those of its third-world allies through a détente with the United States, this policy was denounced as an expression of "social imperialism"— socialist in words but imperialist in deeds. This assessment of the changed international role of the USSR gave rise to a new Chinese strategy based on a worldwide united front of oppressed peoples against both imperialism and "social imperialism." Although imperialism was still denounced as the main enemy, "social imperialism" was considered to be aiding and abetting it through the policy of détente. This was the point to which Sino-Soviet relations had degenerated by March 1966.

The "Sino-Soviet split" (1963–66) ended not with a thaw, as in the relations between the Soviet Union and Yugoslavia, but with the freezing of antagonisms between the two countries. There followed a further leftist development in domestic policy, a second big leap forward known as the Proletarian Cultural Revolution (1966–69). The communization policy earlier pursued in the countryside was extended to the cities. The Cultural Revolution finally came to a halt through a decision of the party's Ninth Congress in April 1969.

The new domestic strategy adopted during the Cultural Revolution dealt a blow to the central political bureaucracy and to the pro-Russian sector of the party led by Liu Shao-ch'i. In Mao's "Talks to Central Committee Leaders" (21 July 1966), which launched the Cultural Revolution, he called for a struggle against the ideology of the bourgeoisie that had wormed its way into official party circles. In effect, the Cultural Revolution was directed against the central political bureaucracy for allegedly taking the capitalist road. In August 1967 Liu was personally denounced for subordinating proletarian politics and the dictatorship of the proletariat to methods designed to modernize production and make each factory produce a profit. He was made a personal target for attempting to introduce material incentives as the decisive force in economic growth. Other charges included his efforts "to corrupt the masses by instilling bourgeois egoism, to divert people's attention from politics, to widen the income gap and create a privileged stratum." Instead of putting politics in command, he had relied on directors, engineers, and technicians to give orders. Thus, he established a "bourgeois dictatorship over the workers" by transforming administrative and professional workers into bureaucrats and into "new bourgeois elements" who rode roughshod over the masses. These new bourgeois elements were not capitalists in the traditional sense but economically privileged "bureaucrat capitalists" who shared in the exploitation of the workers. Trotsky had never gone so far; at most his critique of the Soviet leadership included a denunciation of the bureaucratic deformations of the workers' state, not the transformation of the bureaucracy into a bureaucratic bourgeoisie.

The Cultural Revolution had as its threefold objective the elimination of the stranglehold of the pro-Soviet revisionists on the party, the government, and the country. In Mao's view China was in danger of ceasing to be a socialist society. The so-called new revisionism represented more than a return to the capitalist road. In the Soviet Union, he believed, it had led to a restoration of capitalism. Thus, a year after the Cultural Revolution had run its course, an article entitled "Leninism or Social Imperialism?" in *People's Daily* (22 April 1970) quoted Mao on the transformation of the USSR into "a dictatorship of the big bourgeoisie, a dictatorship of the German fascist type." Here was another instance of Mao's leftism that made Trotsky's critique in *The*

Revolution Betrayed appear almost as a vindication of the Soviet bureaucracy.

This new assessment of the Soviet Union came in response to the Soviet invasion of Czechoslovakia in August 1968 and to the hostilities in March 1969 between Russian and Chinese troops on Chenpao Island in the Ussuri River—the boundary separating China's northeast provinces and the Soviet far east. In the first encounter on 3 March thirty-one Russians and an indeterminate number of Chinese soldiers were killed. In the second clash on 15 March the casualties on both sides numbered in the hundreds.

These acts of belligerence were sufficient evidence for Mao that the Soviet Union was no longer a socialist country. The Soviet Union had traveled down the capitalist road to become a new "bureaucrat capitalism." Czechoslovakia also was said to have abandoned socialism. Thus, Chinese support for Czechoslovakia was based mainly on China's struggle against Soviet imperialism. By 1969 Mao no longer considered the world to be divided into a socialist and an imperialist camp, because the socialist camp with a few exceptions had virtually ceased to exist for him.

The Soviet Union was included with the United States in the category of "superpowers" that dominate the rest of the world. The principal world antagonism was once again reinterpreted, this time as the struggle between the imperialist camp represented by the two superpowers and the oppressed and exploited peoples of the third world led by China. In this new perception of the correlation of social forces, the superpowers were seen as the enemies not only of the underdeveloped countries in Asia, Africa, and Latin America but also of the industrialized nations in Western and Eastern Europe constituting a buffer zone between them. Because this buffer zone was supposedly threatened mainly by the USSR, the Chinese hoped to establish a popular front of virtually all peoples against Soviet imperialism.

At the Ninth Congress of the CPC in April 1969, China incorporated its changed perception of the USSR into a series of formal resolutions. The principal social forces and corresponding world antagonisms were not only reformulated but also given a new ranking: "The contradiction between the oppressed nations on the one hand and imperialism and social imperialism on the other; the contradiction between the proletariat and bourgeoisie in the capitalist and revisionist countries; the contradiction between imperialist and social imperialist countries; and the contradiction between socialist countries on the one hand and imperialism and social imperialism on the other."

Since the 1965 publication of Lin Piao's essay, the Chinese have introduced several novel theses: the restoration of capitalism in the USSR, the liquidation of the socialist camp, and the equal status of imperialism and social imperialism as enemies of the popular forces in each country. These theses defined the new balance of power in the world. The popular front of small and middle-sized nations against imperialism was presented as the most effective strategy for neutralizing the two power blocs as each sought to retain hegemony in its zone of influence against potential breakaways. At the same time the weakening of imperialist domination was interpreted as a strike against the reactionary interests in the dependent countries and as support for the revolutionary forces.

The Ninth Congress was unable to reach an agreement over the increasingly unviable policy of having to confront two possible antagonists on two different fronts. China had to face U.S. troops converging on its southern border with Vietnam and Soviet troops to the north along the disputed frontier with the USSR. Despite this predicament a majority at the Ninth Congress supported Lin Piao, who favored a continuation of the earlier strategy directed equally against the two superpowers. They defeated the minority led by Chou En-lai, who pushed for a strategy of détente with the United States in the hope of making the USSR the principal enemy. With Mao's backing, Chou eventually got the upper hand but not until December 1970. Already arrangements were being made for President Nixon's visit to China in February 1972; it was against this background that the struggle on two fronts was finally abandoned. By then the United States had come to be regarded as an empire in decline and the Soviet Union as an empire on the make. The new strategy was designed to neutralize the United States and to mobilize the peoples of the second and third worlds against the main threat, the USSR. The new course placed Mao and Maoism to the left not only of Stalin and Stalinism but also of Trotsky and Trotskyism—formerly the principal heresy in the socialist world.

Cuba: The Parallel Construction
of Socialism and Communism

Unlike Mao, Fidel Castro did not initiate his armed struggle under Communist party auspices. But the development of Castroism moved from an early populist phase to a leftist application of Marxism-Leninism under the influence of Che Guevara. The most important difference between Fidel and Mao is that Fidel managed to extricate himself from the leftist tendency in international Marxism by converging in 1969 on its mainstream represented by the Soviet Union and Eastern Europe. It was only during his leftist or Guevarist phase that Fidel espoused the heresy that the Soviets scoffed at as "tropical communism."

In Cuba the turn toward socialism formally began with Fidel's May Day speech following the CIA-sponsored Bay of Pigs invasion in April 1961. In this speech he noted that the 1940 Cuban constitution had become outdated because of the socialization of major sectors of the economy. Instead of the old bourgeois constitution, a new socialist one was needed. Because the original populist-oriented 26 July Movement was ill prepared to administer the socialist reorganization of Cuba, Fidel made efforts to integrate it with the old communist or Popular Socialist party (PSP). Their merger with the Revolutionary Student Directorate gave rise to the Integrated Revolutionary Organizations (ORI), formally constituted in July. It was eventually to father a new political party, the United Party of the Socialist Revolution (PURS) in February 1963, later reorganized as the Communist party of Cuba in October 1965.

As in the case of Yugoslavia and China, the Cuban heresy arose following a conflict with the central political bureaucracy of the CPSU. During 1962 the Cuban leadership was twice confronted with the high-handed measures of a central political bureaucracy foreign to its own revolutionary traditions: first, the March political crisis in the relations between the Cuban government and the newly formed party being constructed along Soviet lines, the ORI under the "old" communist Aníbal Escalante; second, the October crisis involving the Cuban government and the Soviet bureaucracy over the unilateral withdrawal of Russian missiles from Cuba without so much as a consultation with Cuban leaders.

The rift between the Cuban government and the ORI arose because of Escalante's willful misinterpretation of Fidel's intentions for the new party. The ORI was supposed to rise above sectarian and factional differences, to unite instead of divide the principal revolutionary organizations in Cuba. Instead, the secretaries appointed by Escalante to head the party's six provincial committees were chosen exclusively from cadres of the former PSP members. He packed the local leaderships with his own comrades and was extending his tentacles into the highest levels of the central government. The Cubans refer to his machinations as their "Stalin period," which ended on 26 March 1962 with a vitriolic denunciation by Fidel on public television. This was followed by the purging of Escalante from all positions of responsibility within the ORI and by his exile to Eastern Europe.

As Fidel noted in his speech "Against Sectarianism," Escalante had created his own centralized political bureaucracy aimed ultimately at taking over the government. Escalante was accused of imposing a "yoke," a "straightjacket," on the party, while building a "nest of privileges" and a "system of patronage and favors" for his closest followers. Even worse, he was charged with "commandomania," a mania to establish the party's direct authority to intervene at all levels of government and administration. Thus, his error was believing that "the party nucleus commanded, that the nucleus could hire and fire administrators, that the nucleus itself governed."

The Soviet-Cuban rift over the missile crisis was the result not only of the unilateral withdrawal of Russian missiles but also of differences between Soviet and Cuban strategies for ending the crisis. Khrushchev's letter of capitulation to President Kennedy on 26 October asked in exchange from the U.S. government a promise not to invade Cuba—nothing more. That same day Fidel drew up his own conditions for a settlement: the United States must end the economic blockade, cease subversive activities inside Cuba, stop the "piratical" attacks by exile groups, end its violations of Cuba's air space, and give up its Guantánamo naval base. Further, the conditions of Khrushchev's capitulation included a provision for a United Nations' team to supervise withdrawal of the missiles, a stipulation Castro never accepted. The existence of a rift was confirmed by Fidel on 30 October in a speech relating his conversations with U Thant, secretary-general of the United Nations and the principal mediator during the crisis: "It is necessary to say that during the development of the crisis several differences arose between the Soviet and Cuban governments." He then warned that the proper occasion for airing any "well-founded reason for displeasure" with the Russians was not in public, where Cuba's enemies would try to take advantage of the discussion, but at official meetings with the Soviet government and the Communist party.

The break with socialist orthodoxy was initially launched not by Fidel but by Che Guevara as minister of industries—a position to which he had been appointed in February 1961. It first became publicized during the great economic debates of 1963–64 in which Che's economic views prevailed over those of other ministers and leaders of the party. Che's most influential antagonists were Alberto Mora, then minister of foreign commerce, and Marcelo Fernández, president of the National Bank. Various Soviet economists, along with Charles Bettelheim, the internationally known French economist and director of the Applied School of High Studies in Paris, also took issue with Che. That Guevara prevailed over his rivals meant in effect that Fidel was persuaded by his

theses. These were officially acknowledged as Cuban government policy in a speech by Fidel on 28 September 1966 celebrating the sixth an-
niversary of the Committees of Defense of the Revolution.

What was unorthodox in Che's theses? His concept of the revolutionary vanguard was abstracted from his strategy of guerrilla warfare and
adapted to the postinsurrectionary period. The same principle applies
before and after the seizure of power: "It is not necessary to wait for all
the conditions of revolution to be given; the revolutionary vanguard can
create them." During the struggle against Batista the revolutionary vanguard was equated with the so-called insurrectionary *foco* or center—an
armed nucleus for living and fighting together. After victory and by a
process of fusion with other revolutionary organizations, this vanguard
became the Marxist-Leninist party.

In "Socialist Planning: Its Significance," Che appealed to Lenin's essay "Our Revolution" for support. Replying to the old social democratic
thesis that the development of the productive forces in Russia had not
attained the level necessary for socialism, Lenin asked " 'why cannot
we begin by first achieving the prerequisites for that definite level of
culture in a revolutionary way, and *then*, with the aid of the workers'
and peasants' government and the Soviet system, proceed to overtake
the other nations?' " Specifically, Lenin asked "why could we not first
. . . expel the landowners and the Russian capitalists, and then start
moving toward socialism?" This coincided with Guevara's view that
"those in the vanguard . . . can prepare the way for bringing about the
triumphant socialist revolution, even though at a given level [of devel-
opment] the contradictions do not objectively exist between the growth
of the productive forces and relations of ownership that would make a
revolution unavoidable."

By taking advantage of exceptional historical circumstances, Che argued, the revolutionary vanguard can seize power and then skip stages.
In this perspective the vanguard is capable not only of anticipating the
drift of events but also of accelerating the march into the future. The
practical import of Che's argument was to repudiate the Soviet and East
European thesis that property relations could not be altered until after
the development of the technical and material base necessary to sustain
new social relations. Che claimed that both productive forces and new
forms of ownership could be developed simultaneously.

It was this thesis of the decisive role of the vanguard that led to Che's
peculiar heresy, whose classic statement was given in "Socialism and
Man in Cuba": "To build communism, a new man must be created simultaneously with the material base." But what is communism, and
what is the new man?

The transition period envisioned by Marx in the *Critique of the Gotha Programme*, Che claimed, had not materialized. Instead, there was a new phase unforeseen by Marx: "the first period in the building of socialism or in the transition to communism . . . takes place with elements of capitalism present and in the midst of violent class struggle." The contrast between Marx's forecast and the actual first stage of socialism was also underscored in Che's earlier essay, "On the Budgetary System of Financing." Marx anticipated the abolition of commodity production, the market mechanism, and money as a means of payment, but as Che points out, during the actual first stage of socialism these features of capitalism persist. Socialist countries continue to produce for profit, to charge interest to enterprises on loans from state banks, and to rely on capitalist methods of management. Material incentives survive that violate Marx's principle of distribution according to work; instead of work being measured directly by a yardstick of standard duration, intensity, and performance, it is measured by market forces. Why tolerate these survivals? Why wait, as the Soviet *Manual of Political Economy* advises, for the advent of a higher stage of communism to overcome them? Che invites a struggle against them now: because material incentives interfere with the development of communist consciousness, and because without that consciousness we cannot reach even the lowest stage of communist society.

Che conceded that capitalist methods of management would have to be retained for a certain time after the seizure of power. The Soviet view was that they would not only stimulate production over an entire historical epoch but also make a positive contribution to socialism. Che disputed this claim: "The tendency should be, in our opinion, to eliminate the old categories as vigorously as possible . . . the market, money, and consequently the motive force of material incentives." If not, socialism will be consolidated at the expense of holding back the transition to Marx's lowest stage of communism. Although the Soviet Union and Eastern Europe successfully established and consolidated the new socialist system, it is not enough merely to socialize and develop the forces of production, for without a change in human nature, in man's political and social consciousness, this experiment cannot go very far.

And what is the new man? He is the communist man as Marx understood him, not the actual man under socialism. The essence of the new man is voluntary labor, work performed for the sake of others rather than for material rewards. As Che noted in his speech, "A New Attitude toward Work": "Voluntary work is the factor that develops the consciousness of the workers more than any other, especially when those workers carry out their work in places that are not habitual for them as in cutting cane." It is then that voluntary work becomes a vehicle of union and comprehension between workers and peasants, between administrative and administered workers. Voluntary work paves the road toward a new stage of society "where classes will not exist and, therefore, where there will be no difference between a manual and an intellectual worker, between worker and peasant." What characterizes communist man is his willingness to give to society according to his abilities, in order that society may give to him according to his work. Contrary to Stalin's method of overcoming differences between intellectual and manual labor by raising the educational and technical qualifications of the workers, Che proposed making the leaders of industry and government examples of revolutionary commitment and sacrifice. By encouraging them to do voluntary work, the revolutionary government would achieve the leveling of society downward as well as upward.

In Che's classic discussion of this topic, "Socialism and Man in Cuba," he defined the new man as guided by strong feelings of love. The vanguard of the revolution cannot be content with small demonstrations of affection toward immediate neighbors: "revolutionary leaders must have a large dose of humanity, a large dose of a sense of justice and truth, to avoid falling into dogmatic extremes, into cold scholasticism, into isolation from the masses." They must struggle every day so that their love for the people may be transformed into concrete deeds capable of mobilizing and motivating the workers. The revolutionary is an ascetic who steels himself against the temptations to relax and seek a soft berth for himself. These features of the new man are indispensable not only to the highest stage of communist society, Che believed, but even to the lowest. By implication, there is no place for bureaucratic or petty-bureaucratic salaries in the new society.

Fidel made most of these ideas his own. In a speech on 3 October 1965, he defined communism as a society without exploiters or exploited. He did not claim that Cuba had already reached Marx's lowest stage, only that it had taken the communist road. Granted that the bulk of the means of production had already been socialized, socialism was still a far cry from communism.

The following year in his May Day speech, Fidel distinguished the traditional socialist principle of distribution from the communist, only to reject both of them. No formula can always be literally applied, he concluded, and "generally speaking, formulas in political and social matters are always bad." Socialist ideas require incessant development; yet some that are universally accepted diverge sharply from the essence of Marxism-Leninism. To what could Fidel have been referring, if not to the established but mechanical formulations of the Soviet manuals?

"On a certain occasion, with respect to the formation of the Central Committee, we said that . . . communism and socialism should be developed to some extent along parallel lines." It would be a grave error to try to build socialism up to a given point but to refrain from building communism until after that. Rather, "in the midst of striving to attain socialist goals, the development and creation of communist man should never be renounced or left to the distant future."

In his speech on 13 March 1968, Fidel argued that an underdeveloped country cannot tolerate waste. Bureaucratic salaries are a form of waste because they provide a quality of life that no one really needs. Material incentives imply a scale of privileges among workers that is patently incompatible with communism and is undesirable under socialism. But to do away with material incentives one must strike at their underlying cause, the use of money that permits people to enjoy goods without working for them. Disgracefully, Cuba cannot in the present situation do without this instrument of distribution, "but we ought to suppress at least unlimited access to it and all privileges related to it." Although money is still a useful instrument, it is a bitter and transitory one "toward whose abolition we should all work." That is what is implied by the communism of Karl Marx. Any other kind of communism is not worth the effort.

An underdeveloped country is compelled to make concessions to accumulation. For that reason alone, Fidel concluded, what is allocated toward material incentives would be better utilized in developing production directly. It is cheaper, not just fairer, to educate people to produce not for material gain but from love of country. The temptation to accept a higher salary is an imperialist trick, says Fidel, of which only a few can take advantage. An underdeveloped country cannot effectively compete on such terms. Thus, there is a need for moral incentives and a sense of patriotism to replace the material incentives of capitalist society.

In a speech on 26 July 1968 Fidel spelled out some of the practical details of his new heresy. A communist sector for students was being created side by side with the socialist sector by withdrawing certain products from the market: 200,000 scholarship holders were to receive room and board, clothing, medical care, recreation, and books free of charge. For some the highest stage of communism was already operative: "From each according to his abilities; to each according to his needs." A communist sector was also being developed, although on a more modest scale, for the population as a whole. Already, education was free for old and young; medical care was free; housing was free or virtually free for a majority of Cubans; sports events were free; and public transportation was in the process of becoming free. Later, water and electricity became free, although both subsequently reverted to the socialist sector when it became evident that they were being consumed in excessive amounts, that the people still lacked the political consciousness for conserving scarce resources.

By the parallel construction of communism and socialism Fidel understood at least two different processes: first, the parallel construction of de facto socialism *and* Marx's lower stage of communism; second, the additional construction of a sector of free goods corresponding to Marx's higher stage. In both cases he was going beyond Soviet guidelines. His attempt to cut corners was tantamount to skipping stages, to introducing a communist mode of distribution before the objective and subjective conditions for it had developed. We could not be sure of that in 1968, but a decade later it was evident. These projects are no longer mentioned in the Cuban press. During the 1970s they were discarded as premature.

Significance and Prospects of the
Principal Heresies

The principal heresies in the socialist camp—Yugoslav, Chinese, and Cuban—were responses not only to the different class compositions of their political vanguards but also to Soviet economic and political hegemony since World War II. To overcome their positions of inferiority, the less developed socialist countries tried to skip stages, to jump ahead of the Soviet Union in areas other than economic and military power where they were obviously at a disadvantage. The principal heresies were efforts to respond to Soviet superiority with what Mao called a "political atom bomb": the mobilization of the masses in support of new and more advanced forms of socialist ownership.

But these new model socialisms can no more be taken at face value than the older forms of socialism against which they revolted. To discover what they signified in practice, it is necessary to discover their principal beneficiaries. Each successfully challenged the Soviet polit-bureaucracy as well as its own central political bureaucracy. At the same time, the workers were unable to preserve their original gains. Only two alternatives remain: the principal heirs of the working class were either petty bureaucrats or technocrats. Let us see which in fact prevailed.

In chapter 4 we saw that the earning power of petty bureaucrats is confined within narrow limits. Other factors remaining equal, at a rate of exploitation of 100 percent, a petty bureaucrat must earn more than twice the minimum wage but no more than four times. Suppose x is the minimum wage. Then for an exploited wage earner to rise to the level of a petty bureaucrat he will have to recover his own surplus and share in the surplus of other workers; he will have to earn more than 2x. But if he earns more than 4x, he will derive the bulk of his income from the labor of others; he will become a full-fledged bureaucrat. Under these conditions, if the salary spread in a socialist country is roughly 4:1, then there are no bureaucrats. Suppose, however, that the spread increases to 12:1. There will be bureaucrats, but will they or the petty bureaucrats take home the bulk of the economic surplus?

Under these changed conditions, suppose that the average salary of petty bureaucrats is 3x and the average salary of bureaucrats is 8x. Then the average surplus appropriated from other workers will be 3x minus 2x for petty bureaucrats and 8x minus 2x for bureaucrats. Because the bureaucrats will be pocketing six times as much surplus as the petty bureaucrats, for petty bureaucrats to be the principal beneficiaries there would have to be more than six of them for every bureaucrat. Suppose there are less. Then the bureaucracy will be the principal beneficiary. Should there be as many as ten petty bureaucrats for every bureaucrat, then bureaucrats will be the principal beneficiaries only if the spread between the maximum salary and the minimum wage exceeds the ratio of 10:1. Because in 1970 the spread in East Germany was as high as 50:1, in the Soviet Union approximately 30:1, and between 15:1 and 12:1 in most of the other Soviet-bloc countries, it is a fair guess that in most, and possibly all, bureaucrats were the principal beneficiaries—if not the members of a central political bureaucracy, at least the members of a technobureaucracy or some combination of both. The politbureaucracy and technobureaucracy, we remind the reader, are both fractions of the bureaucratic class.

What is the spread in the countries harboring the major heresies? In Yugoslavia the critics of bureaucracy stress the alienating effects of wage and salary differentials rather than their magnitude. Initially, it was thought that the establishment of economic democracy and the right of workers to determine their own wages would have a leveling influence on distribution. Later, it was discovered that workers tend to vote according to the recommendations of management, much like stockholders in the United States. Presumably, the experts know what is best for everyone! When resistance mounts they flash their trump card: only by holding wages down today and investing the surplus in improved machinery or expanded operations can workers substantially raise them tomorrow. Higher profits, higher wages! That is the argument behind socialist accumulation under the Yugoslav system of workers' self-management. And it is also an argument for replacing the central political bureaucracy with the direct managers of collective enterprises.

Yet the pay spread in Yugoslavia is below that in the Soviet Union. One explanation is that the decentralization of the economy has encouraged industrial production in smaller units than those in a centrally planned system. The bureaucratic pyramid is less steep; there are fewer bureaucrats in proportion to petty bureaucrats, and there are fewer high-paid bureaucrats in relation to low-paid ones.

In *Socialismo de autogestión*, Abraham Guillén gives figures covering the wage spread at the automotive factory, Tomos, in the city of Koper, formerly Capri, in Slovenia. Although one of the largest factories in Yugoslavia, it employed only 3,000 workers in 1970. In old dinars the monthly wage of the forty lowest-paid unskilled workers was 6,000; for ordinary workers, 8,000; for highly skilled manual workers, 20,000; for technicians, 22,000; for engineers, 30,000; and for the director, 42,000. The spread was 7:1 and presumably was lower in light industry. Under these conditions the average bureaucratic salary could have been no more than twice the average for petty bureaucrats. With three or more petty bureaucrats for every bureaucrat, the bureaucrats could not have been the principal beneficiaries.

The Chinese Cultural Revolution seriously weakened the central government and party bureaucracy to the advantage of the petty bureaucracy. The Maoists rejected one-man management of production, replacing it with the leadership of the party committee in the enterprise. This reduced the technical managers from the role of bosses to that of hired specialists under the supervision of petty bureaucrats. But with the formal halt to the Cultural Revolution in 1969 and the 1976 purging of the so-called Gang of Four, the petty bureaucracy found itself on the defensive. In the new regime under Mao's successors, politics are no longer in sole command. Today the technobureaucracy is bringing technical and economic considerations to the fore.

Because of the impact of the Cultural Revolution one would expect the wage spread to have been even lower in China than in Yugoslavia. In an article in *Fortune* (August 1972) entitled "I Have Seen China—and They Work," Louis Kraar gives his figures for the Heavy Machine Tool Plant in Kwangchow, formerly Canton. Employing 5,000 workers in three shifts, this factory makes equipment for mines, petroleum refineries, chemical plants, and sugar mills. In 1971 new employees started at the U.S. equivalent of sixteen dollars per month; an experienced skilled worker with seniority received thirty-nine dollars; the vicechairman, sixty dollars. The spread was slightly less than 4:1, or roughly half that of a similar enterprise in Yugoslavia. A slightly steeper spread was reported by Joan Robinson in "For Use, Not for Profit," *Eastern Horizon* (1972). Although the general range for workers was from 30 yuan per month to 104 yuan, it was greater in the northeast where wages were highest. There the average monthly wage was 62 yuan, but technicians were presumably getting more. Only since the purging of the leaders of the Cultural Revolution in 1976 has the pay spread come to favor the technobureaucracy.

The Cuban Revolution under the influence of Che Guevara also went a long way toward leveling wages and salaries. During the 1960s the new wage and salary scale in Cuba was less steep than in Yugoslavia. A constitutional law of 1962 established a ceiling on salaries of 450 pesos monthly for all workers except government ministers and those who exceeded the limit under the old rates. In 1964 the new Law of Salaries froze wages and salaries for all workers under the old rates but permitted workers to shift to the new rates when they might so benefit. As late as 1970 the minimum wage was 60 pesos per month for agricultural workers, and 85 pesos for urban and industrial workers. With a few exceptions, the spread in urban areas was slightly less than 6:1, and the total spread was less than 8:1. Although in 1969 there were efforts to make further exceptions to the ceiling of 450 pesos, it is important to note that these figures, unlike those for China and Yugoslavia, cover the economy as a whole and not just the most advanced sectors.

In 1972, however, Cuba became a full-fledged member of the Soviet-dominated Council for Mutual Economic Aid (Comecon) and two years later was coordinating its Five-Year Plan with the highest-level planning agencies in the USSR. The acceptance of Soviet economic strategy was also evident at the First Party Congress in late 1975 when pre-Castro communists were to be seen in prominent positions. Fidel publicly reproved himself and the old leadership for not making use of the experience of other Soviet-bloc countries in the construction of socialism. Although the principal beneficiary of the Guevarist period had been the petty bureaucracy, sections of the bureaucracy stand to gain from this recent development.

On the basis of these and other data there is reason to believe that petty bureaucrats were the original beneficiaries of these heresies but that technobureaucrats displaced them during the seventies when the Chinese and Cuban heresies were effectively overcome. Only the Yugoslav heresy has survived because of its peculiar blend of petty bureaucratic *and* technobureaucratic ideologies. Socialist society is moving from a lower centralized and politbureaucratic stage toward a higher decentralized stage administered by technobureaucrats. In retrospect the heretical regimes that momentarily favored the petty-bureaucratic class were little more than historical aberrations.

As the Yugoslav, Chinese, and Cuban heresies played themselves out, as the technobureaucrats in each acquired a commanding role, these wayward children ceased to diverge radically from their Soviet parent. From opposite positions they now appear to be converging. In fact, both the Yugoslav and Cuban parties have made their peace with their Soviet counterpart. Only the Chinese party retains what are still hysterical elements of anti-Sovietism, despite its return to the Soviet model of economic growth and to a policy of modernization in the late seventies.

The erosion of the power of the central political bureaucracy in the Soviet Union has led to an increase in the decision-making powers and initiatives of the same managerial-scientific elites at the enterprise level that first acquired a leading position in the Yugoslav economy. The U.S. economic blockade and the resulting dependence of Cuba on the Soviet Union account for the restructuring of the Cuban economy along Soviet lines and for its increased emphasis on managerial initiatives. The softening of relations with the Soviet Union is a by-product of these tendencies. The class compositions of the leadership of the Soviet, Yugoslav, and Cuban parties have thus more in common today than formerly. The Soviet technobureaucracy makes more decisions than it did two decades ago. Both Yugoslavia and Cuba have seen an erosion in the position of petty bureaucrats resulting from the increased role of material incentives and the strengthening of managerial and technical elites.

In China the petty bureaucracy has also lost the controlling position it acquired during the Cultural Revolution, only there the result has been a hardening of the party's line toward the Soviet Union. Competition between the Soviet Union and China is now mainly national. It is a struggle within the socialist world between antagonistic state forms representing the same bureaucratic class. The backwardness of the Chinese economy, the economic chaos produced by the Cultural Revolution, and China's tremendous potential for economic growth have led to a reassessment of the importance of modernization. China is under greater pressure than either Yugoslavia or Cuba to break with the past. Until this pressure is lifted or overcome, the modernization tendency represented by the technobureaucracy may be expected to acquire full force. China will continue waging a cold war with the Soviets in the areas of domestic and foreign policy because, unlike Yugoslavia and

Cuba, it has the potential for becoming the second socialist superpower in this century.

In the seventies national antagonisms under socialism first began to approximate their equivalent under the capitalist system. China claimed to have its own nuclear capability with a real prospect of rivaling the Soviet Union as a world power. The Sino-Soviet split had developed into a big-power struggle, a contest no longer between antagonistic classes within socialist society but between antagonistic socialist states. For the past century military confrontations occurred mainly between capitalist powers. Under socialism matters were supposed to be different, but with the "hot war" between Vietnam and Campuchea and between China and Vietnam the new socialist order has ceased to be an exception to this historic rule. Because Sino-Soviet relations now resemble the antagonisms under capitalism, the Marxist theory that national antagonisms tend to disappear with the emergence of a new order is further from the mark today than ever before.

10

The Bureaucratization of Socialism

We have seen what happened to the original objectives of the socialist movement inspired by Marx and Engels. They were affirmed in name but abandoned in practice. When the German, French, and Belgian parties of the Second Socialist International voted war credits for their respective governments at the outbreak of World War I, Lenin shouted "betrayal." In "The European War and International Socialism," written in August-September 1914, he wrote: "Is it not treachery to social democracy when we see the German socialists' amazing change of front; the false phrases about a war of liberation against tsarism; forgetfulness of German imperialism. . . . Have the socialists of France and Belgium not shown the same kind of treachery?"

How was it possible for the leaders of the Second International to abandon their earlier professions of Marxism? In *The Collapse of the Second International*, chapter 7, Lenin pointed to their long-standing policy of "opportunism." He defined opportunism as a policy of sacrificing the fundamental interests of the proletariat to the temporary interests of an insignificant minority of the workers. "Opportunism was engendered in the course of decades by the special features of the development of capitalism, when the comparatively peaceful and cultured life of a stratum of privileged workers 'bourgeoisified' them, gave them crumbs from the table of their national capitalists and isolated them from the suffering, misery and revolutionary temper of the impoverished and ruined masses." It is the policy of gradual reforms through class collaboration instead of confrontation, a policy suited at most to the short-run interests of a privileged stratum: "an entire social stratum consisting of parliamentarians, journalists, labor officials, privileged office personnel and certain strata of the proletariat has sprung up and has been *amalgamated* with its own national bourgeoisie." Note that this privileged group includes a segment of the proletariat but is not reducible to it. The proletarian segment was identified by Lenin with a "labor aristocracy" of skilled manual workers—the social basis of opportunism in the labor movement. But it is only one component of a privileged group dominated by bureaucrats and petty bureaucrats—to use our terminology.

The parliamentarians of the socialist parties and the leaders of the big unions did not belong to this labor aristocracy. They had already graduated from the highest stratum of the proletariat into the ranks of the petty bureaucracy of labor. Some had even become labor bureaucrats. As Lenin presents the rationale for their policy of accommodation to the bourgeois both before and during World War I: "Legal mass organizations of the working class are perhaps the most important feature of the socialist parties in the epoch of the Second International. . . . The initiation of revolutionary actions would obviously have led to the dissolution of these legal organizations" (chapter 8). Thus, the proletariat's right to revolution was sold for a mess of pottage. Even before acquiring power, the bureaucrats and petty bureaucrats of the Second International were giving precedence to their own interests over those of the workers they represented.

This first crisis in Marxism, this first step in the bureaucratization of the socialist movement was followed by a second. In 1936 Trotsky published from exile a critique of the socialist bureaucracy in power. In *The Revolution Betrayed* he assailed the Soviet bureaucrats for betraying the revolutionary movement of the workers a second time. In his chapter on the degeneration of the Bolshevik party, he traces this "degeneration" to Stalin's efforts, following the death of Lenin in 1924, to free the party machine from control by rank and file members of the party. It was Stalin who put forth the thesis that the central committee is everything and the party nothing; it was he who encouraged the view that the chief merit of a Bolshevik is obedience. As a result, the proletarian vanguard found itself taking orders from a group of party officials. Party democracy went by the boards: "Democratic centralism gave place to bureaucratic centralism."

Trotsky's critique starts out from an earlier 1928 analysis of the Stalinist bureaucracy by Christian Rakovsky. Thinking communists, Rakovsky wrote to his friends from exile, are converted into docile machines; the bureaucratic apparatus replaces both the class and the party. "In the mind of Lenin and in all our minds, the task of the party leadership was to protect both the party and the working class from the corrupting action of privilege, place, and patronage on the part of those in power." Rakovsky denounces the party apparatus for having failed in this task. By 1928 a privileged stratum had emerged: "The social situation of the communist who has at his disposal an automobile, a good apartment, regular vacations, and receives the party maximum of salary, differs from the situation of the communist who works in the coal mines where he receives from fifty to sixty rubles a month." At that time party members were still limited to the wages of skilled manual workers, so Rakovsky is saying that the bureaucratic apparatus got around its self-imposed ceiling on incomes in the form of extramonetary privileges. Although this policy had not yet become a source of class differentiation, it was soon to become one.

What is Trotsky's explanation of what he called the "bureaucratization of the Soviet regime"? The historic conditions of the Soviet Thermidor, the triumph of the bureaucracy over the masses, he traced to three fundamental causes: first, the suppression and demoralization of the revolutionary vanguard of the proletariat; second, the weariness and disappointment of the masses who had become indifferent to what was happening at the summit; third, the erosion of workers' democracy and people's power, which gave way to generalized loyalty and deference to the ruling party. In short, the workers were subjectively unprepared for taking matters into their own hands. The masses, Trotsky concluded, could not or did not wish to exercise state power.

To this explanation in subjective terms Trotsky adds the objective conditions of socialist bureaucratization: "The basis of bureaucratic rule is the poverty of society in objects of consumption, with the resulting struggle of each against all." When there is not enough to go around of the basic necessities, he argues, the desperate struggle for them generates a policeman who arrogates to himself the power to distribute goods. Such is the origin of bureaucratic privilege: "Nobody who has wealth to distribute ever omits himself." Although the state of the Soviet economy in 1936 was still far from providing the basic necessities, "it is already adequate to give significant privileges to a minority." Unable as yet to satisfy the elementary needs of the population, the bureaucracy did not hesitate to satisfy its own claims to comfort.

Besides the political backwardness and economic poverty of the masses, Trotsky cites a third factor in "The USSR in War" (1939): a hostile imperialist environment that required an enormous share of the national income to be diverted from basic consumption to armaments. Together these conditions explain why the deposed bureaucracy of czarist times had again become incarnate in the figure—Trotsky's metaphor—of a monster with a club in its hand.

From Trotsky's description of the bureaucratization of the Soviet regime we see that there is an enormous difference between the practice of a communist party *in* and *out* of power. Before the seizure of power, the leading positions in the party were filled by old Bolsheviks who set a ceiling on their ambitions, supported inner party democracy, and encouraged workers' self-management. The party apparatus was dominated by revolutionary intellectuals constituting a stratum of the proletariat rather than of a petty-bureaucratic or bureaucratic class. That is because they did their jobs for workmen's wages.

Today such parties, where they are out of power, are miniatures of their Soviet counterpart. Their authoritarian and hierarchic structure is not enough to establish their bureaucratic character. On the contrary, like the Bolshevik party before October 1917 most of them have proletarian vanguards. Stories about "Soviet gold" and "aid from Moscow" are caricatures of the humble realities. The author, who was a member of the Communist party of the United States on two occasions, from 1943 to 1945 and again from 1977 to 1979, can testify that its leaders continue to pay themselves the minimum wage, that they live at the poverty level, that their spouses must work in order to survive, and that supplements to their wages are available only in the event of illness or injury to cover necessary medical bills.

The "betrayal" of the workers' interests occurs mainly after these parties acquire power. In this respect, communist parties differ from the older, established socialist parties, which have a long record of betraying the workers' interests even without a "dictatorship of the proletariat." These bureaucratized socialist parties have yet to make a serious revolutionary bid for power. Here lies the difference between the first and second crises in Marxism, between the first and second steps in the bureaucratization of socialism as a political movement.

Socialized Production versus Communist Appropriation

Because the conquest of power by a vanguard party constitutes a political rather than a social revolution, it may take up to a decade or more before the political revolution is followed by the introduction of a new mode of production. During this transitional period the "contradiction" or disparity between socialized production and capitalist appropriation continues, but alongside it a new "contradiction" appears between socialized production and communist appropriation for members of the ruling party. It takes time for the party to become bureaucratized—meanwhile, there is a lag between its former impotence out of office and its newly acquired power to appropriate the lion's share of the economic surplus. Two different wage and salary scales coexist at loggerheads: one representing the old scale of bureaucratic and petty bureaucratic salaries in the capitalist private sector; a second representing the new scale of compensation at workmen's wages in the socialist public sector with exceptions mainly in the case of foreign experts.

This disparity cannot last for long because the communist elites who are disadvantaged by it also have the authority to correct it. If the armed people had imposed controls on salaries, they might still be in power. In any case, this disparity between power and appropriation can be resolved in only two ways: first, by communizing production, which includes the socialization of expertise or the abolition of private property in specialized knowledge; second, by socializing appropriation in conformity with the principle of rewarding both the *quality* and the *quantity* of work. As we know, the second alternative has ultimately prevailed in every socialist country. Only for a brief period during the 1960s were the revolutionary elites in Cuba and China able to hold out or to reverse temporarily the tendency to replace a communist with a socialist mode of distribution for party members. Their efforts failed.

In the case of Cuba it is worth commenting on how this process of breaking through the party's self-imposed ceiling on salaries began. That ceiling imposed by Che Guevara in 1962 established a maximum salary of 450 pesos monthly for all new workers except for a handful of top government officials. This ceiling continued to be enforced until 1969 when efforts by prominent faculty members and heads of departments at the University of Havana succeeded in making a breakthrough. I was in Havana in December 1968, and I recall my astonishment at learning from the youthful head of the sociology department about the plans being laid to raise the rector's salary to 600 pesos. The new rector, she said, had given the kind of dynamic leadership the university required and should be rewarded commensurate to his services. Was the top salary not enough for that purpose? No, she replied, additional material incentives were needed to ensure continued leadership of the same kind. The increase in salary would be mainly a token of the faculty's esteem because there was nothing to spend it on; luxury goods were not yet available, although a decade later they became available. It occurred to me that raising the rector's salary might not be altogether disinterested. It could be the first step toward raising the salaries of senior faculty members and heads of departments from an average of 300 pesos up to the official ceiling.

What lay behind this change of perspective? The party leaders I interviewed in Cuba invariably complained of being "tired" and "overworked." Besides their professional responsibilities they had even more rigorous duties as party militants. Some complained of being worn thin by the interminable work of committees, political meetings, and rallies that required their leadership. Battle fatigue in the sierras had its counterpart in committee fatigue on the plains. The lack of leisure and privacy, combined with the need for continuing vigilance against conscious and unconscious enemies of the revolution, was taking its toll in subtle ways. Because they did more than their fair share of work, it was reasonable to expect that they would eventually demand some form of compensation. Having risked their lives in the sierras, they were now imperiling their health from excessive demands on their time. Why should nonparty professionals, they must have asked, be the only ones to enjoy material privileges? In the face of unequal salaries for equal work, one salary scale for party militants and another for "bribed" members of the former intelligentsia, is it a wonder that the revolutionary vanguard was becoming demoralized? This deteriorating morale of party militants during the late sixties goes a long way toward explaining the switch of emphasis from moral to material incentives during the seventies.

Added to this factor was the general political indifference of the Cuban masses. Because of widespread irresponsibility in the conservation of water and electricity, these utilities, which had become free services during the late sixties, reverted to the socialist sector during the seventies. Cuban workers have yet to take the initiative in controlling bureaucratic salaries. Until they do, the existing controls established by the party's elite can only be removed by the elite. Although the Committees of Defense of the Revolution show the initiative of the masses at their best, these organs of revolutionary vigilance are aimed at potential and actual counterrevolutionaries, not at ambitious elements inside the party. The armed people are far too generous and trusting of the revolution's elites; the strength of revolutionary solidarity and loyalty to the new regime has encouraged workers to rely on their leaders instead of taking matters into their own hands. It appears that the political consciousness required for the masses to become an independent political force can be learned not through exhortation but only through self-help. For that, the party must introduce a form of workers' self-management in industry along with workers' councils in government. Evidently, Cuba still has a long way to go before its workers become self-organized into a political movement capable of reversing current trends.

A decade after the Cultural Revolution we can see a similar process at work in the Chinese People's Republic. On 19 October 1979 a former graduate student of mine, Dr. Clifford DuRand, interviewed the heads of the Institute of Philosophy and of its department of dialectical materialism in Peking. The discussion centered on the deposed Gang of

Four's criticism that a new state bourgeoisie had emerged inside the Chinese CP, that the new bourgeoisie had power that constitutes a special kind of capital, and that its social basis lay in the continued and insufficiently restricted existence of what Marx called "bourgeois right." When DuRand suggested that there might be some truth to these claims, the Chinese philosophers replied that the privileged elements within the party were bureaucrats rather than bourgeois. These make up not an exploiting class, they argued, but a privileged stratum surviving from the old feudal and bourgeois societies. This is the prevailing view of bureaucracy in China today.

Dissatisfied with these answers, DuRand wrote an article for the *Guardian*, published during the second week of December 1979, that stresses the increasing economic inequalities in China and suggests that the bureaucrats are not simply a hangover from earlier social formations. In China's new experiment with workers' self-management, bonuses are being tied to profits with the consequence that managers get higher bonuses. In the past, only 10 percent of an enterprise's wages was allocated by the state for merit increases, and high-level professional and managerial cadres received lower bonuses than production workers. Party members now say this practice violates the socialist principle, "to each according to his work." DuRand quotes briefly from a 21 November interview with an official of the Shanghai Bureau of Industry: "high cadres have great responsibility and contribute more profits." Aside from the fetishism of expertise implicit in this remark, the implication is that they should be paid higher bonuses than manual workers.

In Shanghai this principle of higher bonuses for management is being applied as part of the new decentralized system of self-management based on the experience in Yugoslavia—which is now considered to be a socialist country. This is part of an overall plan to switch to a system of market socialism by 1990 that will put an end to the old system of centrally administered limits to wages and salaries. Thus, one official interviewed by DuRand reported that in Shanghai an average of 20 percent is currently being allocated for bonuses from earnings retained by those enterprises—mainly for the purpose of rewarding professional and administrative cadres.

The tendency toward strengthening the bureaucratic class in China is confirmed in an article on the "new capitalists" in *Time* (24 December 1979). There we learn that 1,500 former industrialists active in business before the Chinese Revolution were recently asked to become factory managers. The rehabilitation of former capitalists has resulted in the reemergence of 100 Chinese millionaires whose properties and bank accounts confiscated during the Cultural Revolution are being returned —with interest! One example: the former owner of a chemical and medicine factory was reimbursed the equivalent of $133,000 (U.S.) in back savings, $47,000 in back interest, and $26,000 in back salaries for himself and his wife for being deprived of their salaries as engineers. Although some of these rehabilitated managers obviously fit the article's description of "born-again capitalists," the vast majority are bureaucrats under the new Chinese system of workers' self-management.

The creeping bureaucratization of Chinese socialism since the Cultural Revolution augurs the emergence of Chinese technocrats as the principal decision makers in economic matters. This is the significance of the action by the party's central committee in February 1980 that posthumously rehabilitated Liu Shao-ch'i. During the Cultural Revolution Liu was assailed by Mao as the "Number One Enemy in the Party and the Government." Today he is exonerated as the "principal victim of the Cultural Revolution." The charges against him are said to have been totally false, resulting in the most sinister scandal in the party's history. Like China's present leaders, Liu favored rapid industrialization and modernization in opposition to Mao's efforts to "put politics first." Mao tried to curb the powers and privileges of the party bureaucracy, but the present leaders are encouraging them. Thus, the Cultural Revolution, which only five years ago was characterized as a great stride forward that will shine forever, is in 1980 denounced by the party as an appalling catastrophe suffered by the Chinese people.

The rehabilitation of Liu is a slap at Mao. The 1980 suppression of wall posters in Peking and the silencing of the critics of a new state bourgeoisie are also actions pointed at Mao. On at least one occasion Mao, like Trotsky, considered the possibility that a new bureaucratic or managerial class was emerging under socialism. In a 1964 directive on the socialist education movement he predicted: "If the managerial staff do not join the workers on the shop floor, work, study and live with them and modestly learn from them, then they will find themselves locked in acute class struggle with the working class" (*Peking Review*, 2 July 1976). And in the same directive he said: "The bureaucrat class on the one hand and the working class with the poor and lower-middle peasants on the other are two classes sharply antagonistic to each other." In his assessment of the bureaucracy as a class rather than a stratum, Mao's analysis of the bureaucratization of socialism went considerably further than Trotsky's analysis in *The Revolution Betrayed*.

Why did Mao's efforts fail? The usual Marxist response to questions of this kind is that the objective and subjective conditions of effective workers' power were lacking. As a result, Mao's efforts to communize

socialism were subtly undermined and then openly repudiated by
his successors.

The Cultural Revolution failed owing to the party's lack of professional cadres for managing the economy and carrying on the essential
services of the state. Production suffered a setback when politics were
placed in command. The cadres of the cp were insufficient to run things
without noncommunist experts who insisted on being "bribed" with
higher salaries. The failure to pay these salaries led to a deliberate with-
holding of their best efforts, to a withdrawal of efficiency, and to an
overall decline in industrial productivity. The party lost authority as a
consequence of the Cultural Revolution, because it was not delivering
the goods and the country was being mismanaged.

In recognition of its lack of specialized cadres, the party's new leadership is trying to incorporate more of the available expertise into its
ranks. But for that it has to pay a price in the form of petty-bureaucratic
and bureaucratic salaries. Besides this effort to improve its administrative and technical competence, the party is promoting experts to
leading positions within government and industry. In a paper read to the
Society for the Philosophical Study of Marxism on 28 December 1979,
"The Problem of a New Class in Socialist China," DuRand reports that
the party recently proposed a reform of its cadres system, "a major component of which is increasing the number of specialist cadres in leading
posts to 70 percent of the total." This reform can only serve to strength-
en and extend the authority of the bureaucratic class.

The insufficiency of trained cadres is an old problem. Lenin underscored its importance as early as January 1922 in "The Role and Functions of the Trade Unions under the New Economic Policy." There can
be no serious progress in the work of socialist construction, he wrote,
unless the Communist party, the Soviet government, and the trade
unions "guard as the apple of their eye every specialist who is working
conscientiously and knows and loves his work—even though the ideas
of communism are totally alien to him." We must achieve a situation,
continues Lenin, in which specialists "can enjoy better conditions of
life under socialism than they enjoyed under capitalism as regards material and legal status." A government department cannot be well
organized "which does not take systematic measures to provide for all
the needs of specialists, to reward the best of them." And not just in
passing as a temporary measure connected with the New Economic
Policy—for Lenin explicitly acknowledges that this privileged stratum
"will persist until we have reached the highest stage of communist
society."

The party's dependence on professional cadres is also examined by

Lenin in his political report to the Eleventh Party Congress in March 1922. The Communists have centralized political and economic power in their hands, he comments, but they still lack culture or expertise. "If we take Moscow with its 4,700 responsible Communists, and if we take that huge bureaucratic machine, that huge pile, we must ask: Who is directing whom?" Lenin doubts that Communists are doing the directing. Communist administrators are politically reliable, he says, but they lack administrative ability and are easily seduced by old bureaucratic ways. The Communists are only a drop in the ocean and cannot build socialism without the assistance of nonparty elements. By implication, the party must make concessions to this huge bureaucratic machine manned by noncommunists or give up trying to build socialism altogether. Owing to the party's lack of professional cadres, we may conclude, either socialism becomes bureaucratized or there will be no socialism.

The "betrayal" of the workers by the leaders of the Second and Third Internationals, the selling-out of the revolution, may now be understood as the prematureness of communism. Once ordinary workers squarely face the obstacles to establishing and then maintaining a dictatorship of their own, once they recognize that the conditions of a classless society are still a long way off, then they no longer have reason to criticize communist parties for "betraying the revolution." Claims of treason will have been put to rest along with the ultraleft sects nourishing them. Because a bureaucratic-type political and social revolution is a necessary stage to a communist or classless society—for the reasons we have given—the proletariat has an interest in supporting it. Despite the auxiliary role of workers under socialism, they have thus far benefited from a socialist transformation. At critical moments they have had the opportunity of leading the revolution, as in Russia during the first decade after October 1917 and in China during the early stages of its revolution. What the workers make of these opportunities depends on their own organization and initiative.

A strategy for establishing communism may become viable once the socialist system becomes consolidated, but it is hardly practical before that time—at least not in the developed socialist countries. In his own day, Marx supported the efforts to extend the capitalist system throughout Europe as a prior condition of the struggle for socialism. Today, and for the same reason, Marxists support the new socialist or bureaucratic order as a prior condition of the struggle for communism.

Communist Production versus Socialist Appropriation?
What are the prospects for the future? A Marxist analysis of the new

social formation would be incomplete without also examining the tendencies toward destabilization of the new order. Socialism too may be expected to generate internal "contradictions." Although Marx and Engels were mistaken about the polarization of classes under capitalism, there is a tendency toward polarization under the new social formation that may eventually bring about the classless communist society they anticipated. Even more important, there is a tendency toward workers' self-management that goes beyond technobureaucratic control of the production process. Workers' self-management contains the seeds of independent control and accounting by the workers themselves. Besides "creeping socialism" under capitalism, there is the phenomenon, barely visible as yet, of "creeping communism" under socialism. A new disparity is in sight between communist production and socialist appropriation. A communist society is not inevitable. It is enough for us that it is possible.

Part 1 of the *Communist Manifesto* opens with Marx's and Engels's classic statement of their polarization thesis. The epoch of the bourgeoisie is unique in having simplified class antagonisms: "Society as a whole is more and more splitting up into two great hostile camps, into two great classes directly facing each other: bourgeoisie and proletariat." The other classes perish or disappear in the face of modern industry: "The lower middle classes, the small manufacturers, the shopkeepers, the artisans, the peasants, all these fight against the bourgeoisie to save from extinction their existence as fractions of the middle class." In the past a middle class led the working majority in the class struggles that toppled the ruling minority, but in the modern world produced by capitalism there is no longer a middle class that can do the job.

This original polarization thesis has been refuted by the revolutions of the twentieth century. A new middle class arose that, after displacing the bourgeoisie from political and economic power, transformed itself into a new ruling class under socialism. Only in this new social formation has a real polarization of classes emerged. Of the four "great classes" we have considered, two either disappeared completely or were reduced to impotence: the landowning class and the bourgeoisie. That left only two great classes confronting each other: the managers and the managed.

Although a petty bureaucracy took the place of the petty bourgeoisie, it exhibits the same features of a dependent middle class tied to the interests of an economically dominant class. In Part 3 of the *Eighteenth Brumaire,* Marx calls the petty bourgeoisie a transition class in which the interests of two other classes are momentarily counterbalanced. It is a transitional class because it is a mixed class sharing some features with the class directly below it, others with the class immediately above it. In effect, the petty bourgeoisie is a stepping-stone from the proletariat into the bourgeoisie. A similar situation defines the petty bureaucrats in the revolutionary elite who, as we have seen, made their bid for power in both Cuba and China during the 1960s and then transformed themselves into full-fledged bureaucrats.

It is true that Marx and Engels believed the democratic petty bourgeoisie might succeed the bourgeoisie as the directly governing class; but they never imagined it might become the politically dominant or ruling class in place of the bourgeoisie. They anticipated that it would be structurally limited in its exercise of power by the prevailing capitalist mode of production. The petty bourgeoisie might govern, but it would never rule. Considering that the results of petty-bureaucratic power duing the sixties were undermined in both Cuba and China during the seventies, we may forecast the same fate for the petty bureaucracy.

What Marx and Engels said of the succession in positions of political power of fractions of the capitalist class and the petty bourgeoisie also applies to fractions of the bureaucratic class and the petty bureaucracy under socialism. To interpolate a passage from the concluding chapter of *Germany: Revolution and Counter-Revolution:* "History showed to the Communist Party how, after the [capitalists] had their turn at governing . . . , the first [bureaucrats] arose and seized the reins of government; how the social influence and rule of this [political] sector of the [bureaucracy] was superseded by the rising strength . . . of the [technocratic sector], and how at the present moment two more classes claim their turn at domination, the petty [bureaucratic] class and the industrial working class." On the premise that socialism is not the promised land of the proletariat but a stronghold of the bureaucratic mode of production, communism must be postponed until the bureaucratic and petty-bureaucratic classes have had their turn at governing and administering this new economic formation.

If there were only three factors of production, then one might expect communism to be the immediate historical successor to capitalism —the socialization of capital would be sufficient. But given the existence of a fourth factor, it is not enough to nationalize or collectivize the principal means of production in order to establish a classless society; it is also necessary to socialize bureaucratic expertise as the personification of science and organization. With private property abolished only in the physical forces of production, we have merely socialism. Communism is a separate mode of production rather than, as Marxists have traditionally believed, a higher or more advanced phase of socialist society.

Because the economic hegemony of the bureaucratic class cannot last forever, the new tendency toward polarization opens the way to eventual confrontation. Although the new working class in the socialist countries lacks a political party of its own, although the CP's have been effectively taken over by bureaucratic and petty-bureaucratic elements, one may anticipate the day when a new type of vanguard challenges the political hegemony of the old. Today, the working class under socialism continues to "fight the enemies of its enemy" in mobilizations for peace against the threat of a third world war and in resistance to anti-Sovietism and a hostile international bourgeoisie. But this state of affairs promises to change. As soon as socialism becomes the dominant social formation on an international scale, the workers will have overcome the enemy of their enemy and will have only one major enemy to contend with—the bureaucratic class. At that point the politics of confrontation will tend to replace the present politics of solidarity and class collaboration.

In addition to this political factor, there is the economic factor of "creeping communism" under the influence of the Yugoslav model of workers' self-management. If the workers in Yugoslavia can participate in the management of their own enterprises, why cannot the workers in other socialist countries? This question has subversive implications. It suggests that the workers who ask it already have the technical experience required to manage their own enterprises.

The scientific and technical revolution of the twentieth century requires a general upgrading in the skills of ordinary workers. This upgrading of technical requirements has had and is having important repercussions on the organization of work relations. Knowing more about the techniques of production, the workers are better qualified to manage their enterprises through workers' councils. In time, workers' self-management may cease being an auxiliary of professional management and become a means of ensuring workers' initiative and control. Lenin's two conditions of industrial democracy sketched in *State and Revolution*—accounting and control—may eventually become a reality. For this to happen the workers will need an all-around comprehension of production and distribution in addition to improved technical skills. In the Yugoslav textile factory in Zrenjanin that I visited in 1967, the members of the workers' council noticeably lacked this understanding. They could not explain the "point system" they had voted for in order to ensure an equitable division of their common earnings. But they were distressed by their ignorance and eager to overcome it.

The tendency to upgrade the labor force goes hand in hand with a tendency to devalue expertise. The abundance of professional cadres reduces the possibility that those in management may withdraw their services in an effort to extort higher salaries, for there will be others available who can immediately fill their shoes. From a scarcity of trained cadres during the early years of the transition to socialism, the socialist countries are approaching the point of breaking the monopoly of expertise by the bureaucratic class. Today many petty bureaucrats share this expertise without also sharing its benefits. Extortionate salaries are no longer necessary to bribe experts to do their jobs. A tendency is already visible in the economically advanced socialist countries toward establishing an informal ceiling on salaries while simultaneously upgrading the material incentives of production-line workers. In the German Democratic Republic and Czechoslovakia increased productivity is more likely to be achieved by democratizing material incentives, by improving the skills and wages of manual workers, than by a policy of coddling managerial cadres. The gap between intellectual and manual workers may be progressively reduced as a result of the devaluation of expertise at one pole and the upgrading of manual skills at the other. In the long run these two tendencies together may produce the euthanasia of the salariat.

In addition to these objective conditions, creeping communism is supported by subjective factors. The process of overcoming the gap between intellectual and manual workers should suffice to erode the present socialist mode of appropriation based on personal property in science. Should the new working class also become organized politically into a party of its own, this process of erosion may be accelerated by a political confrontation with the bureaucratic class.

Together these objective and subjective conditions may generate a new "contradiction" or disparity peculiar to socialist societies: the contradiction between communized production and socialist appropriation. By "communized production" I mean workers' self-management in the literal sense of production managed by the direct producers. As in the case of the earlier contradiction between socialized production and capitalist appropriation, this new contradiction can be resolved in the long run only by a corresponding change in the mode of distribution.

For Marx and Engels the objective conditions that explain the eventual breakup of any given social formation include the development of the productivity of human labor and the obstructing role of property relations and material privileges operating as fetters on the productive forces. To cite the relevant passages from Marx's preface to *A Contribution to the Critique of Political Economy:* "At a certain stage in their development the material productive forces of society come in conflict with the existing relations of production . . . with the property relations within which they have been at work. From forms of development of the productive forces these relations turn into their fetters." We know what happens after that. Then comes the social revolution.

The developing productivity of human labor under socialism is sowing the seeds of the eventual dissolution of the socialist mode of production. Consider what Engels had to say concerning the developing productivity of labor under capitalism. In *Anti-Dühring* 2.4, he says that all historical antagonisms between exploiting and exploited, oppressing and oppressed classes have their explanation in the same relatively undeveloped state of the productive forces. "So long as the really working people were so much occupied with their necessary labor that they had no time for looking after the common affairs of society—*the direction of labor,* affairs of state, legal matters, art, science, etc.—so long was it necessary that there should constantly exist a special class, freed from actual labor, to manage these affairs" (italics mine). Without workers' self-management, Engels is saying, there can be no communism. But precisely capitalism makes workers' self-management possible: "the immense increase in the productive powers of modern industry has made it possible to distribute labor among all members of society without exception, and thereby to limit the labor-time of each individual member to such an extent that all have enough free time left to take part in the general—both theoretical and practical—affairs of society." We know now that Engels's judgment was premature under capitalism. But is it premature under socialism?

The emergence of the bureaucracy as a new ruling class was inevitable for the reason Lenin gives: the vanguard party's own lack of specialized cadres. It is only now, to update Engels's view, that every ruling and exploiting class is becoming superfluous and a hindrance to social development. With the proliferation of expertise and the technical upgrading of ordinary workers, with the abundance of specialized cadres in developed socialist societies, eventually there may be enough qualified labor to make it "free." Salaries may cease to be necessary. Where there is more than enough expertise to go around, it is enough to pay the experts a living wage to get them to perform.

To pay them more is "dysfunctional," sheer waste, an unnecessary luxury, a fetter on the optimum development of the productive forces. More wealth will be produced if the funds for surplus consumption are directed to reentering the cycle of production. Man does not live by bread alone, but neither does he always have to live under conditions in which one man's luxury is another man's toil. Other things being equal, communism is more efficient and productive of wealth than socialism. In the competition among social systems, that system eventually prevails that curtails waste and develops the forces of production to the utmost.

Bibliographical Guide

Books and Pamphlets

Adler, Solomon. *The Chinese Economy.* New York: Monthly Review, 1957.

Alasco, Johannes. *Intellectual Capitalism.* New York: World University Press, 1950.

Aron, Raymond, et al. *World Technology and Human Destiny.* Ann Arbor: University of Michigan Press, 1963.

Avrich, Paul, *Kronstadt 1921.* Princeton: Princeton University Press, 1970.

Bahro, Rudolf. *The Alternative in Eastern Europe.* Translated by D. Fernbach. London: New Left Books, 1978.

Bambirra, Vania. *La revolución cubana: Una reinterpretación.* 2nd ed. Mexico D.F.: Nuestro Tiempo, 1974.

Bazelon, David. *The Paper Economy.* New York: Vintage, 1963.

———. *Power in America: The Politics of the New Class.* New York: New American Library, 1967.

Bendix, Reinhard. *Work and Authority in Industry.* New York: Harper and Row, 1963.

Bergson, Abram. *The Economics of Soviet Planning.* New Haven: Yale University Press, 1964.

Berle, Adolf. *Power without Property.* New York: Harcourt, Brace and World, 1959.

Berle, Adolf, and Gardiner C. Means. *The Modern Corporation and Private Property.* New York: Macmillan, 1933.

Bernardo, Robert M. *The Theory of Moral Incentives in Cuba.* Tuscaloosa: University of Alabama Press, 1971.

Bettelheim, Charles. *Les luttes de classes en URSS.* Vol. 1 (1917–23), vol. 2 (1923–30). Paris: Seuil/Maspero, 1974–77.

———. *La transition vers l'economie socialiste.* Paris: Maspero, 1968.

Bettelheim, Charles, et al. *La construction du socialisme en Chine.* Paris: Maspero, 1965.

Bilandzić, Dušan. *Management of Yugoslav Economy (1945–1966).* Belgrade, 1967.

Boffato, Carlo, ed. *Socialismo e Mercato in Jugoslavia.* Turin: Einaudi, 1968.

Bonachea, Rolando E., and Nelson P. Valdés, eds. *Che: Selected Works of Ernesto Guevara.* Cambridge: The M. I. T. Press, 1969.

———. eds. *Cuba in Revolution.* Garden City, N.Y.: Doubleday, 1972.

Boorstein, Edward. *The Economic Transformation of Cuba.* New York: Monthly Review, 1968.

Bottomore, T. B. *Classes in Modern Society.* New York: Pantheon, 1966.

———. *Elites and Society.* New York: Basic Books, 1964.

Bruz, Wladzimierz. *The Market in a Socialist Economy.* London: Routledge and Kegan Paul, 1972.

Bukharin, Nicolai. *Building up Socialism.* London, 1926.

———. *Historical Materialism: A System of Sociology.* New York: International Publishers, 1925.

Bukharin, Nicolai, and E. Preobrazhensky. *The ABC of Communism.* Translated by Eden and Cedar Paul. Ann Arbor: University of Michigan Press, 1966.

Burnham, James. *The Machiavellians: Defenders of Freedom.* New York: John Day, 1943.

———. *The Managerial Revolution.* New York: John Day, 1941.

Carr, E. H. *The Bolshevik Revolution, 1917–1923.* 3 vols. London: Penguin, 1966.

———. *Socialism in One Country.* Vol. 1. London: Macmillan, 1964.

Carr, E. H., and R. W. Davies. *Foundations of a Planned Economy, 1926–1929.* London: Macmillan, 1969.

Carrillo, Santiago. *Eurocomunismo y estado.* Barcelona: Crítica, 1977.

Castoriadis, Cornelius. *La Société bureaucratique 1.* Paris: Union Générale d'Éditions, 1973.

Castro, Fidel. *Discursos, 1965–1968.* Havana: Instituto del Libro, 1968.

———. *La revolución cubana, 1953–1962.* Edited by Adolfo Sánchez Rebolledo. Mexico D.F.: Era, 1972.

Chase, Stuart. *Technocracy, an Interpretation.* New York: John Day, 1933.

Claudín, Fernando. *The Communist Movement: From Comintern to Cominform.* 2 vols. New York: Monthly Review, 1974–75.

———. *Eurocomunismo y socialismo.* Madrid: Siglo XXI, 1977.

Cliff, Tony. *Lenin.* 2 vols. London: Pluto, 1975–76.

———. *Russia: A Marxist Analysis.* London: International Socialism, 1964.

Cohen, Arthur A. *The Communism of Mao Tse-tung.* Chicago: University of Chicago Press, 1964.

Cohen, Stephen F. *Bukharin and the Bolshevik Revolution.* New York: Vintage, 1975.

Dahrendorf, Rolf. *Class and Class Conflict in Industrial Society.* Stanford: Stanford University Press, 1959.

Dedijer, Vladimir. *Tito Speaks.* London: Weidenfeld and Nicolson, 1953.

Denno, T. *The Communist Millenium: The Soviet View.* The Hague: Nijhoff, 1964.

Deutscher, Isaac. *Ironies of History: Essays on Contemporary Communism.* London: Oxford University Press, 1966.

———. *The Prophet Armed: Trotsky, 1879–1921.* New York: Oxford University Press, 1965.

————. *The Prophet Unarmed: Trotsky, 1921–1929*. New York: Oxford University Press, 1965.

————. *The Prophet Outcaste: Trotsky, 1929–1940*. New York: Oxford University Press, 1965.

————. *Soviet Trade Unions*. London: Oxford University Press, 1950.

————. *Stalin: A Political Biography*. New York: Oxford University Press, 1967.

The Differences between Comrade Togliatti and Us. Peking: Foreign Languages Press, 1963.

Djilas, Milovan. *The New Class*. New York: Praeger, 1957.

Dobb, Maurice. *Economic Theory and Socialism*. New York: International Publishers, 1955.

Draper, Hal. *Karl Marx's Theory of Revolution: State and Bureaucracy*. 2 vols. New York: Monthly Review, 1977.

Draper, Theodore. *Castroism: Theory and Practice*. New York: Praeger, 1965.

Dubček, Alexander. *Il nuovo corso in Cecoslovacchia*. Translated by Lorenzo del Giudice. Rome: Riuniti, 1968.

Dunayevskaya, Raya. *Marxism and Freedom*. New York: Bookman, 1958.

Durkheim, Emile. *Socialism and Saint-Simon*. Edited by Alvin Gouldner and translated by C. Sattler. Yellow Springs: Antioch Press, 1958.

Elsner, Harry. *The Technocrats: Prophets of Automation*. Syracuse: Syracuse University Press, 1967.

Engels, Friedrich. *Anti-Dühring*. New York: International Publishers, 1972.

————. *Principles of Communism*. Translated by Paul Sweezy. New York: Monthly Review, 1952.

————. *Socialism: Utopian and Scientific*. In *Marx-Engels Selected Works*, vol. 2. Moscow: Foreign Languages Publishing House, 1962.

Erlich, Alexander. *The Soviet Industrialization Debate, 1924–1928*. Cambridge: Harvard University Press, 1967.

Fan, K.H., ed. *The Chinese Cultural Revolution: Selected Documents*. New York: Monthly Review, 1968.

Fan, K. H., and K. T. Fan, eds. *From the Other Side of the River: A Self-Portrait of China Today*. Garden City, N.Y.: Anchor, 1975.

Felker, Jere L. *Soviet Economic Controversies*. Cambridge: The M. I. T. Press, 1966.

Feoktistov, V. F., ed. *Maoism Unmasked*. Moscow: Progress Publishers, 1972.

Galbraith, John K. *The New Industrial State*. Boston: Houghton Mifflin, 1967.

Gandy, Ross. *Marx and History*. Austin: University of Texas Press, 1979.

Glucksman, André. *Hacia la subversión del trabajo intelectual*. Translated by O. Barahona and O. Doyhamboure. Mexico D.F.: Era, 1976.

Gottheil, Fred M. *Marx's Economic Predictions*. Evanston: Northwestern University Press, 1966.

Gould, Jay. *The Technical Elite*. New York: Augustus M. Kelley, 1966.

Gouldner, Alvin. *The Future of Intellectuals and the Rise of the New Class*. New York: Seabury, 1979.

Granick, David. *The Red Executive*. Garden City, N.Y.: Doubleday, 1961.

Guillén, Abraham. *Socialismo de autogestión*. Montevideo, 1972.

Hacker, Andrew, ed. *The Corporation Take-Over*. Garden City, N.Y.: Double-day, 1965.

Halperin, Ernst. *The Triumphant Heretic: Tito's Struggle against Stalin*. Translated by Ilsa Barea. London: Heinemann, 1958.

Hangen, Welles. *The Muted Revolution: East Germany's Challenge to Russia and the West*. New York: Knopf, 1966.

Harnecker, Marta. *Los conceptos elementales del materialismo histórico*. 5th ed. Mexico D.F.: Siglo XXI, 1970.

Hegedus, Andras. *Socialism and Bureaucracy*. New York: St. Martin's Press, 1976.

Hilferding, Rudolf. *Böhm-Bawerk's Criticism of Marx*. Edited by Paul Sweezy. New York: Augustus M. Kelley, 1949.

History of the Communist Party of the Soviet Union. Edited by Andrew Rothstein and Clemens Dutt. Moscow: Foreign Languages Publishing House, 1963.

History of the Communist Party of the Soviet Union (Short Course). New York: International Publishers, 1939.

Hodges, Donald C. *The Latin American Revolution*. New York: William Morrow, 1974.

———. *The Legacy of Che Guevara: A Documentary Study*. London: Thames and Hudson, 1977.

———, ed. *Philosophy of the Urban Guerrilla: The Revolutionary Writings of Abraham Guillén*. Translated by Donald C. Hodges. New York: William Morrow, 1973.

———. *Socialist Humanism: The Outcome of Classical European Morality*. St. Louis: Warren Green, 1974.

Hoffman, George W., and Fred Warner Neal. *Yugoslavia and the New Communism*. New York: Twentieth Century Fund, 1962.

Horowitz, David, ed. *Marx and Modern Economics*. New York: Monthly Review, 1968.

Horvat, Branko. *Towards a Theory of Planned Economy*. Belgrade: Yugoslav Institute of Economic Research, 1964.

Howard, Dick. *The Marxian Legacy*. London: Macmillan, 1977.

Hudson, G. F. *Fifty Years of Communism: Theory and Practice, 1917–1967*. Baltimore: Penguin, 1968.

Jackson, Bruce D. *Castro, the Kremlin, and Communism in Latin America*. Baltimore: Johns Hopkins University Press, 1969.

James, Daniel. *Che Guevara*. New York: Stein and Day, 1969.

Karol, K. S. *China: The Other Communism*. Translated by Tom Baistow. New York: Hill and Wang, 1967.

———. *Guerrillas in Power: The Course of the Cuban Revolution*. Translated by Arnold Pomerans. New York: Hill and Wang, 1970.

Kenner, Martin, and James Petras, eds. *Fidel Castro Speaks*. New York: Grove, 1969.

Khrushchev, Nikita. *For Victory in the Peaceful Competition with Capitalism*. Moscow: Foreign Languages Publishing House, 1959.

Konrád, George, and Ivan Szelényi. *The Intellectuals on the Road to Class Power.* Translated by A. Arato and R. E. Allen. New York: Harcourt, Brace, Jovanovich, 1979.

Kuusinen, O. V., et al. *Fundamentals of Marxism-Leninism.* Moscow: Foreign Languages Publishing House, 1963.

Lange, Oscar, et al. *Problemas de la economía política del socialismo.* Havana: Publicaciones Económicas, 1966.

La via cecoslovacca al socialismo. Rome: Riuniti, 1968.

Lenin, V. I. *The Collapse of the Second International.* In V. I. Lenin's *Collected Works,* vol. 21. Moscow: Progress Publishers, 1964.

———. *The State and Revolution.* In V. I. Lenin's *Selected Works,* vol. 2. New York: International Publishers, 1967.

———. *Two Tactics of Social-Democracy in the Democratic Revolution.* In V. I. Lenin's *Selected Works,* vol. 1. New York: International Publishers, 1967.

Lewis, John Wilson, ed. *Major Doctrines of Communist China.* New York: Norton, 1964.

Lin Piao. *Long Live the Victory of People's War!* Peking: Foreign Languages Press, 1965.

Lockwood, Lee. *Castro's Cuba, Cuba's Fidel.* New York: Macmillan, 1967.

Lorenz, Richard. *Sozialgeschichte der Sowjetunion, 1917–1945.* Vol. 1. Frankfurt: Suhrkamp, 1976.

Lowy, Michael. *El pensamiento del Che Guevara.* Translated by Aurelio Garzón del Camino. Mexico D.F.: Siglo XXI, 1971.

Machajski, Waclaw (pseudonym: A. Volski). *Umstvennii Rabochii* (The Intellectual Worker). 3 vols. Geneva, 1905.

Mallet, Serge. *La nouvelle classe ouvrière.* Paris: Éditions du Seuil, 1963.

Mandel, Ernest, and Fernand Charlier. *L'URSS e uno stato capitalista?* Translated by Sirio di Giuliomaria and Giorgio Meucci. Rome: Samoná e Savelli, 1971.

Manual de economía política. Edited by the Economics Institute of the Soviet Academy of Sciences. Mexico D.F.: Grijalbo, 1966.

Mao Tse-tung. *On the Correct Handling of Contradictions among the People.* Peking: Foreign Languages Press, 1960.

———. *A Critique of Soviet Economics.* Translated by M. Roberts. New York: Monthly Review, 1977.

———. *On New Democracy.* In *Selected Works of Mao Tse-tung,* vol. 2. Oxford: Pergamon Press, 1965.

———. *The Question of Agricultural Cooperatives.* Peking: Foreign Languages Press, 1956.

———. *Selected Works.* 4 vols. Peking: Foreign Languages Press, 1965.

Marcuse, Herbert. *Soviet Marxism.* New York: Columbia University Press, 1958.

Marshall, Alfred. *Principles of Economics.* 8th ed. London: Macmillan, 1927.

Martinet, Giles. *Les cinq communismes.* Paris: Éditions du Seuil, 1971.

Martínez, Fernando, and Hugo Azcuy, et al. *Lecturas de filosofía.* 2 vols. Havana: Instituto del Libro, 1968.

Marx, Karl. *Capital*. Edited by Friedrich Engels. 3 vols. Moscow: Foreign Languages Publishing House, 1961–62.

———. *The Civil War in France*. In *Marx-Engels Selected Works*, vol. 1. Moscow: Foreign Languages Publishing House, 1962.

———. *A Contribution to the Critique of Political Economy*. Translated by N. I. Stone. Chicago: Charles Kerr, 1904.

———. *Critique of the Gotha Programme*. In *Marx-Engels Selected Works*, vol. 1. Moscow: Foreign Languages Publishing House, 1962.

———. *Economic and Philosophical Manuscripts of 1844*. In *Karl Marx: Early Writings*, edited and translated by T. B. Bottomore. New York: McGraw-Hill, 1964.

———. *The Eighteenth Brumaire of Louis Bonaparte*. In *Marx-Engels Selected Works*, vol. 1. Moscow: Foreign Languages Publishing House, 1962.

———. *The Poverty of Philosophy*. In *Marx-Engels Collected Works*, vol. 6. New York: International Publishers, 1976.

———. *Theories of Surplus Value*. Edited by S. Ryazanskaya. 3 vols. Moscow: Progress Publishers, 1968–71.

———. *Wage-Labor and Capital*. In *Marx-Engels Selected Works*, vol. 1. Moscow: Foreign Languages Publishing House, 1962.

Marx, Karl, and Friedrich Engels. *Germany: Revolution and Counter-Revolution*. In *Karl Marx: Selected Works*, vol. 2. New York: International Publishers, n.d.

———. *Manifesto of the Communist Party*. In *Karl Marx: Selected Works*, vol. 1. New York, International Publishers, n.d.

Matthews, Herbert L. *Fidel Castro*. New York: Simon and Schuster, 1969.

Meek, Ronald. *Studies in the Labour Theory of Value*. New York: International Publishers, 1956.

Melotti, Umberto. *Marx and the Third World*. Translated by Pat Ransford. Atlantic Highlands, N.J.: Humanities Press, 1977.

Meyer, Alfred. *Leninism*. New York: Praeger, 1957.

———. *Marxism: The Unity of Theory and Practice*. Cambridge: Harvard University Press, 1964.

Mills, C. Wright, ed. *The Marxists*. New York: Dell, 1962.

More on the Differences between Comrade Togliatti and Us. Peking: Foreign Languages Press, 1963.

Morray, J. P. *The Second Revolution in Cuba*. New York: Monthly Review, 1962.

Mrachkovskaya, I. M. *From Revisionism to Betrayal: A Criticism of Ota Šik's Economic Views*. Translated by Don Danemanis. Moscow: Progress Publishers, 1972.

Nagy, Imre. *On Communism: In Defense of the New Course*. New York: Praeger, 1957.

Nicolaus, Martin. *Restoration of Capitalism in the USSR*. Chicago: Liberator, 1975.

Nomad, Max. *Aspects of Revolt*. New York: Bookman, 1959.

———. *Rebels and Renegades*. New York: Macmillan, 1932.

Nove, Alec. *The Soviet Economy*. Revised ed. New York: Praeger, 1966.

O'Connor, James. *The Origins of Socialism in Cuba*. Ithaca: Cornell University Press, 1970.

Ossowski, Stanislau. *Class Structure in the Social Consciousness*. Translated by Sheila Patterson. Glencoe, Ill.: Free Press, 1963.

Page, Benjamin B. *The Czechoslovak Reform Movement, 1963–1968: A Study in the Theory of Socialism*. Amsterdam: Grüner, 1973.

Paillet, Marc. *Marx contre Marx: La société technobureaucratique*. Paris: De-noël, 1971.

Parry, Albert. *The New Class Divided*. New York: Macmillan, 1966.

Pelikan, Jiri. *Socialist Opposition in Eastern Europe*. Translated by Marian Sling and V. and R. Tosek. New York: St. Martin's Press, 1976.

The Polemic on the General Line of the International Communist Movement. Peking: Foreign Languages Press, 1965.

Poulantzas, Nicos. *Pouvoir politique et classes sociales de l'état capitaliste*. Paris: Maspero, 1968.

Preobrazhensky, E. *The New Economics*. Translated by Brian Pearce. London: Oxford University Press, 1965.

Rizzi, Bruno. *La bureaucratisation du monde*. Paris, 1939.

———. *In margine al collettivismo burocratico*. In Bruno Rizzi's *Il collettivismo burocratico*. Imola: Galeati, 1967.

Rostow, W. W. *The Stages of Economic Growth*. London: Cambridge University Press, 1960.

Rubin, I. I. *Essays on Marx's Theory of Value*. Translated by Miloš Samardzya and Fredy Perlman. Detroit: Black and Red, 1972.

Schram, Stuart R. *The Political Thought of Mao Tse-tung*. New York: Praeger, 1965.

Schumpeter, Joseph. *Capitalism, Socialism, and Democracy*. 3rd ed. New York: Harper, 1947.

Schurmann, Franz, and Orville Schell, David Milton, et al. *The China Reader*. 5 vols. New York: Vintage, 1967–74.

Shachtman, Max. *The Struggle for the New Course*. New York: New International, 1943.

Shaffer, Harry G., ed. *The Soviet Economy: A Collection of Western and Soviet Views*. New York: Appleton-Century-Crofts, 1963.

———, ed. *The Soviet System in Theory and Practice: Selected Western and Soviet Views*. New York: Appleton-Century-Crofts, 1965.

Sharpe, Myron, ed. *Planning, Profit, and Incentives in the USSR*. 2 vols. White Plains, N.Y.: International Arts and Sciences, 1966.

Sherman, Howard J. *The Soviet Economy*. Boston: Little, Brown, 1969.

Šik, Ota. *Plan and Market under Socialism*. Translated by Eleanor Wheeler. White Plains, N.Y.: International Arts and Sciences, 1967.

Sladowsky, M. I., et al. *Leninism and Modern China's Problems*. Translated by David Skvirsky. Moscow: Progress Publishers, 1972.

Smith, Adam. *The Wealth of Nations*. New York: Modern Library, 1937.

Smith, Jack A. *Unite the Many, Defeat the Few: China's Revolutionary Line in Foreign Affairs.* New York: Guardian, 1973.

Stalin, Joseph. *Dialectical and Historical Materialism.* In Joseph Stalin's *Leninism: Selected Writings.* New York: International Publishers, 1942.

———. *Economic Problems of Socialism in the USSR.* Moscow: Foreign Languages Publishing House, 1952.

———. *The Foundations of Leninism.* New York: International Publishers, 1936.

———. *Leninism: Selected Writings.* New York: International Publishers, 1942.

———. *The October Revolution and the Tactics of the Russian Communists.* In *Leninism: Selected Writings.* New York: International Publishers, 1942.

———. *Problems of Leninism.* New York: International Publishers, 1935.

Stojanović, Peter. *Industry: Worker Management in Practice.* Translated by Kordia Kveder and Nina Udovički. Belgrade: Export Press, 1966.

Stojanović, Radmila, ed. *Yugoslav Economists on Problems of a Socialist Economy.* Translated by Marko Pavičić. New York: International Arts and Sciences, 1964.

Stojanović, Svetozar. *Between Ideals and Reality: A Critique of Socialism and its Future.* Translated by Gerson G. Sher. New York: Oxford University Press, 1973.

Suárez, Andrés. *Cuba: Castroism and Communism, 1959–1966.* Translated by Joel Carmichael and Ernst Halperin. Cambridge: The M. I. T. Press, 1967.

Sweezy, Paul. *The Present as History.* New York: Monthly Review, 1962.

———. *The Theory of Capitalist Development.* New York: Monthly Review, 1956.

Triska, Jan F. *Soviet Communism: Programs and Rules.* San Francisco: Chandler, 1962.

Trotsky, Leon. *The Death Agony of Capitalism and the Tasks of the Fourth International: The Transitional Program.* New York: Pioneer, 1964.

———. *The History of the Russian Revolution.* 3 vols. Translated by Max Eastman. New York: Simon and Schuster, 1932–34.

———. *The Permanent Revolution,* and *Results and Prospects.* Translated by John Wright and Brian Pearce. New York: Pioneer, 1965.

———. *The Revolution Betrayed.* Translated by Max Eastman. New York: Merit, 1965.

———. *The Stalin School of Falsification.* Translated by John G. Wright. 2nd ed. New York: Pioneer, 1962.

———. *The Third International after Lenin.* Translated by John G. Wright. 2nd ed. New York: Pioneer, 1957.

Tucker, Robert C. *Stalin as Revolutionary, 1879–1929.* New York: Norton, 1973.

Varga, Eugen. *El testamento de Eugen Varga.* Translated by Claudia Schilling. Montevideo: Marcha 1970.

Veblen, Thorstein. *The Engineers and the Price System.* New York: Viking, 1921.

Wittfogel, Karl A. *Oriental Despotism*. New Haven: Yale University Press, 1957.
Yugoslavia's Way: The Program of the League of Communists of Yugoslavia. Translated by Stoyan Pribechevich. New York: All Nations Press, 1958.
Zeitlin, Maurice. *Revolutionary Politics and the Cuban Working Class.* Princeton: Princeton University Press, 1967.

Journal Articles, Essays, Speeches
Bakunin, Michael. "The International and Karl Marx." In *Bakunin on Anarchy,* edited and translated by Sam Dolgoff. New York: Knopf, 1972.
————. "Statism and Anarchy." In *Bakunin on Anarchy,* edited and translated by Sam Dolgoff. New York: Knopf, 1972.
Bettelheim, Charles. "Dictatorship of the Proletariat, Social Class, and Proletarian Ideology." *Monthly Review,* November 1971.
————. "More on the Society of Transition." *Monthly Review,* December 1970.
————. "On the Transition between Capitalism and Socialism." *Monthly Review,* March 1969.
Boehme, Hans. "East German Price Formation under the New Economic System." *Soviet Studies* 19, no. 3 (January 1968).
"Build the Party in the Course of Struggle." Editorial. *Peking Review,* 2 July 1976.
Carlo, Antonio. "La natura socio-economica dell'URSS." *Giovane Critica,* Spring 1971.
Castoriadis, Cornelius. "An Interview with C. Castoriadis." *Telos,* Spring 1975.
————. "Les rapports de production en Russie." First published in *Socialisme ou Barbarie,* no. 2 (May 1949). Reprinted in his *La société bureaucratique 1.* Paris: Union Générale d'Éditions, 1973.
————. "Socialisme ou Barbarie." First published in *Socialisme ou Barbarie,* no. 1 (March 1949). Reprinted in his *La société bureaucratique 1.* Paris: Union Générale d'Éditions, 1973.
————. "The Social Regime in Russia." *Telos,* Winter 1978–79.
Castro, Fidel. "Creating wealth with political awareness, not creating political awareness with money or wealth" (26 July 1968). In *Fidel Castro Speaks,* edited by M. Kenner and J. Petras. New York: Grove, 1969.
————. "We did not make a revolution to establish the right to trade" (13 March 1968). In *Fidel Castro Speaks,* edited by M. Kenner and J. Petras. New York: Grove, 1969.
————. "Communism cannot be built in one country in the midst of an underdeveloped world" (May Day 1966). In *Fidel Castro Speaks,* edited by M. Kenner and J. Petras. New York: Grove, 1969.
————. "Discurso pronunciado por el Comandante Fidel Castro" (3 October 1965). In Fidel Castro, *Discursos, 1965–1968.* Havana: Instituto del Libro, 1968.
————. "Discurso pronunciado por el Comandante Fidel Castro" (30 October 1962). In Fidel Castro, *La revolución cubana, 1953–1962.* Edited by Adolfo Sánchez Rebolledo. Mexico D.F.: Era, 1972.

———. "Discurso pronunciado por el Comandante Fidel Castro" (26 March 1962). In Fidel Castro, *La revolución cubana, 1953–1962*. Edited by Adolfo Sánchez Rebolledo. Mexico D.F.: Era, 1972.

———. "Discurso pronunciado por el Comandante Fidel Castro" (May Day 1961). In Fidel Castro, *La revolución cubana, 1953–1962*. Edited by Adolfo Sánchez Rebolledo. Mexico D.F.: Era, 1972.

Dragičević, Adolf. "Self-Management and the Market Economy." *Socialist Thought and Practice*, no. 3 (April–June 1968).

DuRand, Cliff. "The Problem of a New Class in Socialist China." Presented to the Society for the Philosophical Study of Marxism at a symposium entitled "Marxism in China Today" (28 December 1979).

Engels, Friedrich. "On Authority." In *Marx-Engels Selected Works*, vol. 1. Moscow: Foreign Languages Publishing House, 1962.

———. "Karl Marx." In *Karl Marx: Selected Works*, vol. 1. New York: International Publishers, n.d.

Gómez, Jorge, and Angel Hernández. "Acerca del período de transición." In *Lecturas de filosofía*, vol. 2. Edited by Fernando Martínez and Hugo Azcuy, et al. Havana: Instituto del Libro, 1968.

"The Great Proletarian Cultural Revolution and the Reversal of Workers' Power in China." *Progressive Labor* 8, no. 3 (November 1971).

Guevara, Ernesto (Che). "Una nueva actitud hacia el trabajo" (15 August 1964). *Obras, 1957–1967*, vol. 2. Havana: Casa de las Américas, 1970.

———. "La planificación socialista: su significado" (April 1965). *Obras, 1957–1967*, vol. 2. Havana: Casa de las Américas, 1970.

———. "Sobre el sistema presupuestario de financiamiento" (February 1964). *Obras, 1957–1967*, vol. 2. Havana: Casa de las Américas, 1970.

———. "El socialismo y el hombre en Cuba" (March 1965). *Obras, 1957–1967*, vol. 2. Havana: Casa de las Américas, 1970.

Hinton, William. "China's World View." *Guardian*, 5 May 1976.

Hodges, Donald C. "The Anatomy of Exploitation." *Science and Society*, Summer 1960.

———. "Class, Stratum, and Intelligentsia." *Science and Society*, Winter 1963.

———. "Classical Economics and Marx's Theory of Social Class." *Indian Journal of Social Research* 2, no. 2 (July 1961).

———. "La controverse sur la reduction du travail." *Economie et Politique*, no. 78 (January 1961).

———. "Elements of a Theory of Salary." *All-Indian Congress Economic Review*, March 1963.

———. "Fifty Years of Socialist Power: Achievements and Prospects." *Minority of One* 9, no. 10 (October 1967).

———. "The Human Costs of Industry." *Indian Sociological Bulletin* 3, no. 2 (May 1966).

———. "The 'Intermediate Classes' in Marxian Theory." *Social Research* 28, no. 1 (April 1961).

———. "Ironies of Communism, Left, Right, and Center." *Minority of One* 9, nos. 4 and 5 (April and May 1967).

200   The Bureaucratization of Socialism

———. "The Ministry of Labor in a Socialist State." *Cohesion*, January 1971.
———. "The New Class in Marxian Sociology." *Indian Journal of Social Research* 4, no. 1 (April 1963).
———. "New Working Class Theories." *Radical America* 5, no. 1 (January–February 1971).
———. "Philosophy in the Cuban Revolution." In *Marxism, Revolution, and Peace*, edited by H. L. Parsons and J. Somerville. Amsterdam: Grüner, 1977.
———. "Rekonstrukcija Sirovog Komunizma" (The Reconstruction of Raw Communism). *Praxis*, nos. 4–6 (July–December 1966).
———. "The Relevance of *Capital* to Studies of Bureaucracy." *Telos*, Fall 1970.
———. "Significance of the Economic Reforms in Eastern Europe." *Cohesion*, July–December 1971.
———. "The Sino-Soviet Split in Philosophy." *Monthly Review*, June 1967.
———. "Sources of Conflict within Socialist Societies." *Indian Journal of Social Research* 5, no. 1 (April 1964).
———. "Technokratiski Put U Socijalizam" (The Technocratic Basis of Socialism). Translated by Ivan Babić. *Politicka Misao*, no. 4 (Fall 1967).
———. "Sur le theorie marxiste des classes." *Economie et Politique*, no. 83 (June 1961).
———. "Yugoslav Marxism and Methods of Social Accounting." In *The Florida State University Slavic Papers* 2, 1968.
———. "Yugoslav Philosophers in the Struggle against Bureaucracy." In *The Florida State University Slavic Papers* 1, 1967.
Howard, Dick. "Introduction to Castoriadis." *Telos*, Spring 1975.
"Is Yugoslavia a Socialist Country?" In *The Polemic on the General Line of the International Communist Movement*. Peking: Foreign Languages Press, 1965.
Kardelj, Edward. "The Practice of Socialist Democracy in Yugoslavia." In *The Marxists*, edited by C. Wright Mills. New York: Dell, 1962.
———. "What Is the 'Authentic' Revolutionary Nature of the Working Class?" *Socialist Thought and Practice*, no. 30 (April–June 1968).
———. "The Working Class, Bureaucracy, and the League of Communists." *Socialist Thought and Practice*, no. 29 (January–March, 1968).
Kraar, Louis. "I have Seen China—And They Work." *Fortune*, August 1972. Reprinted in *The China Reader*, vol. 4. Edited by F. Schurmann, O. Schell, et al. New York: Vintage, 1974.
Lange, Oscar. "The Political Economy of Socialism." *Science and Society*, Winter 1959.
Lenin, V. I. "Our Revolution." In *Collected Works of V. I. Lenin*, vol. 33. New York: International Publishers, 1929.
———. "The Role and Functions of the Trade Unions under the New Economic Policy." In *V. I. Lenin's Collected Works*, vol. 33. Moscow: Progress Publishers, 1966.
"Leninism or Social Imperialism?" First published in *People's Daily*, 22 April 1970. Reprinted in *Peking Review*, 24 April 1970.

Machajski, Waclaw. "On the Expropriation of the Capitalists." In *The Making of Society*, edited by V. F. Calverton. New York: Modern Library, 1937.

Mandel, Ernest. "The Law of Value in Relation to Self-Management and Investment in the Economy of Workers' States." *World Outlook*, n.d.

Mao Tse-tung. "On the People's Democratic Dictatorship" (30 June 1949). In *Selected Works of Mao Tse-tung*, vol. 4. Oxford: Pergamon, 1967.

———. "Talks to Central Committee Leaders" (21 July 1966). In *The Chinese Cultural Revolution*, edited by K. H. Fan. New York: Monthly Review, 1968.

Marx, Karl. "Speech on the Question of Free Trade" (9 January 1848). In *Marx-Engels Collected Works*, vol. 6. New York: International Publishers, 1976.

Nomad, Max. "The Saga of Waclaw Machajski." In *Aspects of Revolt*. New York: Bookman, 1959.

"On Khrushchev's Phoney Communism." In *The Polemic on the General Line of the International Communist Movement*. Peking: Foreign Languages Press, 1965.

Petrović, Gajo. "Marxism versus Stalinism." In Gajo Petrović's *Marx in the Mid-Twentieth Century*. Garden City, N.Y.: Doubleday, 1967.

Robinson, Joan. "For Use, not for Profit." *Eastern Horizon* 9, no. 4 (1972). Reprinted in *The China Reader*, vol. 4. Edited by F. Schurmann, O. Schell, et al. New York: Vintage, 1974.

Stalin, Joseph. "New Conditions, New Tasks in Economic Construction." In Joseph Stalin, *Leninism: Selected Writings*. New York: International Publishers, 1942.

———. "The Right Danger in the Communist Party of the Soviet Union." In *Leninism: Selected Writings*. New York: International Publishers, 1942.

———. "The Right Deviation in the Communist Party of the Soviet Union." In *Leninism: Selected Writings*. New York: International Publishers, 1942.

———. "The Tasks of Business Executives." In *Leninism: Selected Writings*. New York: International Publishers, 1942.

Stojanović, Svetozar. "From Post-Revolutionary Dictatorship to Socialist Democracy." *Praxis*, no. 4 (1973).

Supek, Rudi. "Some Contradictions and Insufficiencies of Yugoslav Self-Managing Socialism." *Praxis*, nos. 3 and 4 (1971).

Svitak, Ivan. "The Gordian Knot: Intellectuals and Workers in Czechoslovak Democratization." *New Politics* 7, no. 2 (March 1969).

———. "Illusions of Czech Socialist Democracy." *Telos*, Winter 1974–75.

Sweezy, Paul. "Bettelheim on Revolution from Above: The USSR in the 1920s." *Monthly Review*, October 1977.

———. "The Invasion of Czechoslovakia—Czechoslovakia, Capitalism, and Socialism." *Monthly Review*, October 1968.

———. "Lessons of Soviet Experience" (with Leo Huberman). *Monthly Review*, November 1967.

———. "The Nature of Soviet Society." *Monthly Review*, November 1974.

———. "The Nature of Soviet Society—Part II." *Monthly Review*, January 1975.

————. "Peaceful Transition from Socialism to Capitalism?" *Monthly Review*, March 1964.

————. "Reply" (to Bettelheim's "More on the Society of Transition"). *Monthly Review*, December 1970.

————. "Reply" (to Bettelheim's "On the Transition between Capitalism and Socialism"). *Monthly Review*, March 1969.

————. "Toward a Program of Studies of the Transition to Socialism." *Monthly Review*, February 1972.

Szelényi, Ivan. "The Position of the Intelligentsia in the Class Structure of State Socialist Societies." *Critique*, nos. 10–11 (Winter–Spring 1978–79).

Tao Chu. "A Discussion of the Problems of Economic Laws during the Transitional Period." *Chinese Economic Studies* 1, no. 1 (Fall 1967).

Trotsky, Leon. "The USSR in War." *In Defense of Marxism.* New York: Pioneer, n.d.

Ts'ai Chien-hua. "Refuting the Production Price Theory of Comrade Yang Chien-pai and Others." *Chinese Economic Studies* 1, no. 1 (Fall 1967).

Wittfogel, Karl A. "The Marxist View of Russian Society and Revolution." *World Politics* 12, no. 4 (July 1960).

Letters, Reports, Newspaper Articles

Brezhnev, Leonid. *Report of the Central Committee to the Twenty-fourth Congress of the CPSU, March 30, 1971.* Moscow: Novosti, 1971.

Bukharin, Nicolai. "Zametki ekonomista" (Notes of an Economist). *Pravda*, 30 September 1928.

Central Committee of the Chinese Communist Party. "Proposal Concerning the General Line of the International Communist Movement." (Reply to the letter by the Central Committee of the Communist Party of the Soviet Union, dated 30 March 1963.) Reprinted in *The China Reader*, vol. 3. Edited by F. Schurmann, O. Schell, et al. New York: Vintage, 1967.

DuRand, Cliff. "China: Workers' Self-Management." *Guardian*, 12 December 1979.

————. Report on an interview with officials of the Institute of Philosophy in Peking (19 October 1979)—unpublished.

Engels, Friedrich, "Engels an Marx in London," 6 June 1853. In *Marx-Engels Werke*, vol. 28. Berlin: Dietz Verlag, 1963–68.

————. "The Turkish Question." First published in the *New York Daily Tribune* 19 August 1853. In *Marx-Engels Collected Works*, vol. 12. New York: International Publishers, 1979.

Khrushchev, Nikita. *Report on the Program of the Communist Party of the Soviet Union, October 17, 1961.* New York: Crosscurrents, 1961.

Kuron, Jacek and Karol Modzelewski. "An Open Letter to the Party." *New Politics* 5, nos. 2 and 3 (Spring and Summer 1966).

Lenin, V. I. "Carta del 24 de diciembre de 1922." (Letter containing his last will and testament.) Appended to *El testamento de Eugen Varga*. Translated by Claudia Schilling. Montevideo: Marcha, 1970.

————. "Letters on Tactics" (April 1917). In *Collected Works of V. I. Lenin*, vol. 20, book 1. New York: International Publishers, 1929.

Marx, Karl. "Address and Provisional Rules of the Working Men's International Association." In *Karl Marx: Selected Works*, vol. 2. New York: International Publishers, n.d.

————. "The British Rule in India." First published in the *New York Daily Tribune*, 25 June 1853. In *Marx-Engels Collected Works*, vol. 12. New York: International Publishers, 1979.

————. "Letter to Ludwig Kugelmann, 12 April 1871." In *Marx-Engels Selected Correspondence*. Moscow: Foreign Languages Publishing House, n.d.

————. "Letter to J. D. Weydemeyer, 5 March 1852." In *Marx-Engels Selected Correspondence*. Moscow: Foreign Languages Publishing House, n.d.

————. "Marx to P. V. Annenkov, *December 28, 1846.*" In *Karl Marx: Selected Works*, vol. 1. New York: International Publishers, n.d.

————. "Marx an Friedrich Bolte in New York," 23 November 1871. In *Marx-Engels Werke*, vol. 33. Berlin: Dietz Verlag, 1963–68.

————. "Marx an Engels in Manchester," 2 June 1853. In *Marx-Engels Werke*, vol. 28. Berlin: Dietz Verlag, 1963–68.

————. "The War Question. —Doings of Parliament. —India." First published in the *New York Daily Tribune*, 5 August 1853. In *Marx-Engels Collected Works*, vol. 12. New York: International Publishers, 1979.

Nemchinov, V. "Plan, Assignment, and Material Incentive." First published in *Pravda*, 21 September 1962. Reprinted under the title "The Plan Target and Material Incentive" in *Planning, Profit, and Incentives in the USSR*, vol. 1. Edited by Myron Sharpe. White Plains, N.Y.: International Arts and Sciences, 1966.

Practice and Theory of Socialist Development in Yugoslavia: Eighth Congress of the League of Communists of Yugoslavia. Belgrade: Medunarodna Politika, 1965.

"Pronostican economistas chinos que en 1990 su país será una colmena de empresas al estilo capitalista." In the Mexican daily *Unomásuno*, 1 March 1980.

"Pronostican economistas chinos que en 1990 su país será una colmena de empresas al estilo capitalista." In the Mexican daily *Unomásuno*, 12 March 1980.

Rakovsky, Christian. "A brief inquiry into the Soviet bureaucracy." Cited by Leon Trotsky in *The Revolution Betrayed*, chapter 5. New York: Pioneer, 1945.

"Rehabilitó el PC de China a Liu Shao-ch'i." In the Mexican daily *Unomásuno*, 1 March 1980.

Stalin, Joseph. "On the Draft Constitution of the USSR." In *Leninism: Selected Writings*. New York: International Publishers, 1942.

————. "Report on the Work of the Central Committee to the Eighteenth Congress of the Communist Party of the Soviet Union." In *Leninism: Selected Writings*. New York: International Publishers, 1942.

Index